THE IDEA OF THE DIGITAL UNIVERSITY

Ancient Traditions, Disruptive Technologies
and the Battle for
the Soul of Higher Education

THE IDEA OF THE DIGITAL UNIVERSITY

Ancient Traditions, Disruptive Technologies and the Battle for the Soul of Higher Education

FRANK BRYCE MCCLUSKEY
MELANIE LYNN WINTER

Westphalia Press
An imprint of the Policy Studies Organization

The Idea of the Digital University:
Ancient Traditions, Disruptive Technologies

All Rights Reserved © 2012 by Policy Studies Organization

Westphalia Press

An imprint of Policy Studies Organization

For information:
Westphalia Press
5127 New Hampshire Ave., N.W.
Washington, D.C. 20036
dgutierrezs@ipsonet.org

ISBN-13: 978-1935907985

ISBN-10: 1935907980

To the countless men and women in America's colleges and universities who labored in the fields of digital technology to bring learning into the new millennium. You know who you are and we salute you. It has not been easy.

CONTENTS

ACKNOWLEDGMENTS

This book has been years in the making. While the thoughts, conclusions and any errors in this book reflect only the authors' point of view, we wish to thank the following individuals for conversations, ideas, presentations or contributions to our thinking on these complex matters: Dr. Katy Marre of the University of Dayton, Dr. Denise Dezolt of Walden University, Dr. William Maker of Clemson University, Ms. Ellen Wagner and Ms. Cali Morrison of WCET, Dr. Lucie Lapovsky, Dr. Boria Sax, Dr. Joshua Berrett, Dr. Joel Feimer, Dr. Howard Canaan and Mr. Alfred Romeo of Mercy College, Dr. Calvin Allen of Shenandoah University, Dr. Fred Stielow of the American Library Association. Dr. Jim Reilly of NASA, Dr. Judith Eaton of the Council on Higher Education Accreditation, Dr. Milton Greenberg of the American University, Dr. Tony Picciano of The City University of New York, Mr. Josh Jarrett of the Bill and Melinda Gates Foundation, Mr. Vernon Smith of Rio Salado Community College, Dr. Karan Swan of the University of Illinois, Mr. Gary Miller of Penn State University, Mr. Seth Marc Kaymen of the American Association of Colleges and Universities, Dr. Lori Kupczynski of Texas A&M University, Dr. John Briggs and Dr. James Munz of Western Connecticut State University, Dr. Meg Benke of the Sloan Foundation, Dr. Tom Pfundstein of the Finishing Trades Institute, Mr. Brandon McCluskey of Pace University, Mr. Michael Goldstein of Dowe Lohnes Associates, Dr. Karen Paulson of the National Center for Higher Education Management Systems, Mr. Orville McTaggert of the College of the Caribbean, Dr. Pat Ford, Dr. Phil Ice, Ms. Phylise Banner, Mr. Dave Becher, Mr. Jack Ferraro, Dr. Chad Patrizi, Mr. Harry Wilkins, Ms. Terry Grant, Mr. Jim Sweizer and Mr. Michael White of the American Public University System,

Dr. Mark Stern of Shepherd University, Ms. Jennifer Waters of Columbia University, Mr. Tom Mauriello of Manhattan University, Dr. Karen Vignare of Michigan State University, Mr. Bill Thirsk of Marist College, Ms. Audrey Gramstad of Central New Mexico Community College, Dr. Nish Sonwalkar of MIT, Ms. Joy Colelli of the Polytechnic Institute of NYU, Mr. Gary Jansen of GWJ Consulting, Dr. Peter Shea of the State University of New York at Albany, Dr. Paula Penovich of the National Labor College, Mr. Daniel Gutierrez Sandoval of the American Political Science Association, Dr. Mark Milliron of Western Governors University, Dr. Michael Offerman of Capella University and Dr. Greg Von Lehman of the University of Maryland.

We thank our staff at the office in Delray Beach, Florida for their inspiration and motivation.

We thank Mr. George Lorenzo of the Source on Community College Issues journal for editorial assistance.

Our special thanks to Dr. Paul Rich, Life Governor of Harris Manchester College of the University of Oxford and President of the Policy Studies Organization for his wisdom and guidance.

We especially thank Dr. Wallace Boston of the American Public University System for supporting the research that made this work possible.

Again, all arguments or errors in this book are the authors' alone.

NOW, what I want is, Facts. Teach these boys and girls nothing but Facts. Facts alone are wanted in life. Plant nothing else, and root out everything else. You can only form the minds of reasoning animals upon Facts: nothing else will ever be of any service to them. This is the principle on which I bring up my own children, and this is the principle on which I bring up these children. Stick to Facts, sir!

– Charles Dickens, *Hard Times*

PART I

THE BEGINNING OF THE LIFE AND TIMES OF A DIGITAL REVOLUTION

We start with a brief review of John Cardinal Newman's philosophy rooted in "education for education's sake" versus the Utilitarian notions about a "useful" education. We explain how these views, dating back to the nineteenth century, are at the root of very similar debates about higher education occurring today. In particular, we show how Cardinal Newman's *The Idea of the University* still has a strong influence on the big picture of higher education. This much older backdrop sets the stage for a discussion through all five parts of this book about how we can apply these schools of thought to our current digital revolution – a revolution that is shifting the very essence of what it means to be an institution of higher learning. We are seeing the birth of a new kind of university that brings dramatic change but also requires historic, already well-thought-out philosophies and truths that need to live on for the university to maintain its "heart."

We explain how the beginning of this change is affected by relatively new technologies that allow faculty, staff and administrators to analyze large amounts of course data and become more transparent in our teaching, learning and administrative practices overall. In

1

short, the digital revolution is dramatically affecting the way higher education functions as well as altering its entire power structure.

We also refer to the digital revolution as a second Industrial Revolution, where the increasing power and intelligence of digital technologies have incurred unprecedented influences, affecting all sectors of business and society, in general. New ways of communicating and new ways of accessing more information have led to a new understanding of what constitutes higher education reform today.

A great disruption is rolling through higher education, causing faculty, administrators and staff to rethink what some believe is a "crisis" and what others think is an unprecedented period of time that can only bring about positive results. We conclude Part I by asking who will survive.

CHAPTER ONE
A NEW KIND OF UNIVERSITY

Don't fight forces, use them. – R. Buckminster Fuller

Our thesis is simple: The digital university is a fundamentally different institution from the traditional university. We are seeing the birth of a new kind of institution. We argue, however, that while much has changed in universities in recent decades, there are elements that need to remain the same for the university to maintain its "heart."

Before we take an in-depth look into the digital university, we must explain how the university has traditionally defined itself. In public policy debates around higher education, nostalgia for the past often plays an important but underestimated role in the modern discourse (Hass and Fishman 2010). We begin, therefore, with an examination into some of the key ideas formed by the seminal work of a thinker who played a pivotal role in defining higher education: John Cardinal Newman.

CARDINAL NEWMAN'S IDEAS

In 1852, Cardinal Newman delivered a series of lectures in Dublin that were collected in the book *The Idea of the University* (Newman 2002). This work has been a required reading for all those who think about college life ever since. It lays out some of the key concepts that still animate today's discourse about higher education (Dawson 2001). In short, *The Idea of the University* is a book in praise of education for education's sake.

3

At the same time when Cardinal Newman was writing, the Utilitarian philosophy of Jeremy Bentham and John Stuart Mill was dominating the discourse about higher education in England and Ireland. While it is a grave injustice to reduce the Utilitarian philosophical system to a single statement of "what is good is what is useful," this simplistic formula of Utilitarianism led to political pressures to reform higher education and make it more responsive. We will see that often in the history of the university, a one-size-fits-all solution that is politically driven has had far-reaching and often-unintended consequences. Utilitarian thinking stressed that an education should be judged by its usefulness to the graduate, along with its capability to enhance one's happiness and economic well-being through a course of study.

Cardinal Newman had a longer view. He wanted education for its own sake, with the final result being a citizen who was a critical thinker, ethical actor, and someone who understood science and had a certain store of classical cultural ideas. *The Idea of the University* was not just about the *trivium* and *quadrivium* of the liberal arts; it was also very modern in its estimation of the role of the sciences. Cardinal Newman thought the study of sciences would enlarge the mind and help the student become an analytical thinker. He urged students to rely on each other, not just their professors.

He believed that student interactions formed knowledge networks that could grow and feed off each other. Cardinal Newman saw the university as a learning community fully engaged in the pursuit of both knowledge and wisdom. Anyone who has spent one single day in Oxford, where Cardinal Newman spent much of his life, can feel the predominance of learning that still exists in that city today.

Other concepts presented by Cardinal Newman in this influential work are still animating discussions about the modern university today (Watson 200 In Discourse V of *The Idea of the University*, for instance, he argued that the university should teach a wide variety of subjects. Students would obviously benefit from a university where many subjects were studied and discussed. In our own time where more and more students are majoring in fewer more practical disciplines like business and computer science, this should be kept in mind. The growing absence of literature and philosophy majors has an impact on university life. The broad education advocated by

Newman would insure a wide range of opinions and approaches to problems. In Discourse VI, he promoted the study of the liberal arts. While this work ranges over many subjects, its focus is how to prepare students to be useful and happy citizens. John Cardinal Newman was not very interested in gainful employment. He wanted a graduate to be someone who could think, communicate and lead. In our own time, we could not wish for more.

Cardinal Newman was more a conserver of tradition than an innovator (Dawson 2001). From the founding of every great European university, most often in the shadows of a great cathedral, to the time when Cardinal Newman was writing his book, the essential nature of the university had not changed much. It was true that the role of theology had been diminished, and alchemy had given way to chemistry, but much remained the same. Even in North America, new campus buildings were built in imitation of the architecture of Oxford, Cambridge and Edinburgh (Tolles 2011). There is a nostalgic and conscious effort to link modern universities to more ancient traditions. This link to the past plays a key role in higher education's storied resistance to change (Hass and Fishman 2010). But change is inevitable, and the digital revolution is shifting the very essence of what it means to be an institution of higher learning.

COMMUNICATION CHANGES EVERYTHING

In his 1948 lectures at Oxford, Harold Innis, who spent most of his life at the University of Toronto, speculated that it was impossible to understand the history of the British Empire without understanding the changes in communication technology that accompanied its rise and fall (Innis 2007). His writings looked at the role media played in both ancient and modern societies. He saw the shift from oral to written communication as leading to the golden age of Greece. Innis also saw contemporary civilization as being driven by advertising and marketing media that focused only on the present and future, while obliterating the past. He warned of a "continuous, systematic, ruthless destruction of the elements of permanence essential to cultural activity" (Innis 1952). We can remember this in the context of the novel *1984* where the destruction of the past is essential to the control of the populace.

Innis's work was carried forward by two of his students: Walter Ong, a Jesuit who wrote about the shift from orality to literacy, and Marshall McLuhan, a media theorist. They were both part of the so-called Toronto School whose research showed how changes in communication technology influenced every aspect of society (Watson and Blondheim 2011). The most remembered statement of the Toronto School is, of course, McLuhan's pithy "The medium is the message," which tells us that if the medium changes, the very content of what is communicated will change (McLuhan 2005). The loss of adverbs and adjectives in the universe of texting is a good example of how the medium changes the content that is communicated. LOL!

Scholars from the Toronto School argued that changes in communication influenced the evolution of the British Empire, Greek Golden Age, Renaissance and the Protestant Reformation. The same holds true for our Digital Age, where a new revolution backed by communication technologies has already taken hold and brought about a new world.

Getting back to Cardinal Newman, and to what many educators are concerned about today, he believed that liberal arts and sciences were losing their position in the university to more practical studies. He thought education was not just about getting a job. He was resisting the pressures that modernity had brought to the university. If Cardinal Newman had walked into a faculty meeting today, he would have found the cultural wars that he engaged in have not subsided. The debate about the usefulness of a college degree had not advanced very far. The question of the liberal arts and sciences is still on the floor of many faculty senates.

Moving forward to the second decade of the new millennium, we cannot be overly confident in our understanding of the changes occurring in higher education being wrought by the digital revolution. Much of the debate about the so-called crisis in higher education, voiced by such diverse thinkers as E.D. Hirsch, Alan Bloom, Margaret Spellings and Senator Tom Harkin, has to be understood in the context of a communication revolution that has impacted every other type of institution in our society. The unfolding of new forms of media and new methods of communication has changed everything.

ENTER THE DIGITAL COURSE
AND "BIG DATA"

The in-person lecture method of instruction that was at the center of university life from the lectures of Peter Abelard and William of Occam to the present day has, for the first time, encountered a competing model, an alternative to the physical classroom – the digital, online course. In fully online courses, every keystroke is recorded.

What makes the online course so different? When the semester is finished, there is a record of every interaction, every question and every event that occurred in the digital course. There was no such record with the traditional classroom. For hundreds of years, a single professor would close the door; class would begin; and there was no oversight, record or map of what had happened. We did not have the tools to determine if a class was well taught. Many teachers never entered the classrooms where their colleagues taught. Professors taught in isolation. Comparisons between each other did not occur or if they did, it was a subjective interpretation. While there were occasional efforts at team-teaching and collaboration, teaching was an individual matter that was not recorded.

In addition, the rules related to academic freedom made it difficult to assess a professor's impact. In Part III, we explore the topic of academic freedom. For now, however, we duly note that many departments have only a single expert in a single area who may rightly argue that even their peers in the same department do not have the expertise or experience to judge their teaching.

A small philosophy department in a state university can be considered a typical example. There may be five faculty; one teaching ancient and medieval philosophy; another teaching modern philosophy; a third teaching philosophy of science; a fourth teaching symbolic logic, ethics; and a fifth whose specialty is women's issues. Is someone who spent an entire graduate career studying logic able to judge someone who teaches ancient philosophy? How could someone whose expertise is in women's issues be asked to judge someone teaching philosophy of science? In short, when it is time for a decision about tenure, the department may be able to clearly see the quantity of publications of one of their colleagues, but who among them can judge the quality?

Assessing good teaching is a slippery activity for college administrators (Tinto 1994). If a professor has high dropout, failure, and withdrawal rates, does that automatically mean he is *de facto* a poor teacher? If a second faculty is very popular with the students, and a large number of those students are receiving high grades, does that automatically mean that this faculty member is a good teacher? What are the hallmarks of a good class or bad class? With the door closed and teaching being an ephemeral event that ends when the class is over, it is difficult to answer such questions.

An online course, however, is very different from an on-ground class. In effect, the door of an online course is always open. When the semester is over, an online course leaves a map showing where students had questions, where learning was taking place and where lessons were difficult. These points of interest can be mapped out just as surely as rivers or highways (Boston, Diaz, Ice, Gibson, Richardson and Swan 2010). Suddenly, by looking at the data from an online course, we can see where educational activities picked up and/or lagged behind.

For example, take a hypothetical International Relations course. Imagine that there are 15 students in the course and a single instructor. Looking at the course data from weeks one through three, we can see that there were an average of five posts in the discussion board per student. Imagine that the instructor in this course is a sophisticated and experienced online instructor. Imagine that she has coached her students, in a very detailed syllabus, on what constitutes a good post. She instructed her students that a well-constructed post should be grammatically correct, have a premise and a conclusion, be argued carefully and should encourage replies.

Let us further imagine that the administration ran a semantic analysis on these student posts using a sophisticated software program. The program determined that most of the adverbs and adjectives used during the first few weeks of the course were positive in nature. In week four, however, something changed. The data from week four revealed that the number of posts per student slipped by 50%, and there were words such as "difficult," "don't understand," and "cannot" in the messages. While these measures do not provide a full picture of what happened (for example, week four may have been the week when quantitative methods were introduced in the class), they do give rise to some questions. We will point out throughout this work that data does not tell the whole story but it is a way to begin the conversation. The analysis of data must be tempered by an understanding of the school, students and subject matter. A class in music appreciation is something very different from a chemistry class. We must be careful in analyzing both and not put them in the same meat grinder where everything comes out sausage.

This kind of data is the starting point for a conversation about what can be improved in the class. We could never do this in a traditional classroom. If the enthusiasm died between weeks three and four in a brick-and-mortar class, only the instructor would know. The traditional form of instruction left no record that we could learn from.

When data leaves a fingerprint, the classroom is no longer the province of the professor alone. There is now data that can be sliced and diced. In the past, it was difficult to make sense out of such large amounts of seemingly chaotic data. However, with the advent of tools to deal with what is referred to as "Big Data," we can now make sense of what was formerly an incoherent jumble (Manyika and Chui 2011).

Big Data consists of data sets that have grown to such a size that they can no longer be handled by traditional database software and hardware sets. It is only recently that we have the software and hardware tools to handle such massive amounts of data. In short, Big Data sees patterns that were previously invisible (Ratner 2011).

TRANSPARENCY CHANGES EVERYTHING

The weekly journal, *Inside Higher Ed*, reported on one of the largest and most controversial uses of Big Data in academia to date: The Predictive Analytics Reporting Framework, known as PAR (Fain 2012). PAR is a research project supported by the Bill and Melinda Gates Foundation. PAR consists of six higher education systems that are pooling data from their online learning classes to see patterns that may not have been evident in smaller data sets. Under the leadership of Dr. Phil Ice, the initial members of this grant included two state colleges (The University of Illinois at Springfield and The University of Hawaii System), two community colleges (Rio Salado Community College and The Community College System of

Colorado), as well as two for-profit online colleges (The American Public University System and The University of Phoenix).

To insure the independence and accuracy of the data sets for the PAR project, the Gates Foundation brought in the Western Interstate Commission for Higher Education (WICHE) to broker the data and insure a fair result. With millions of bits of data, there is a huge pool to draw from. This project has required the partners to be honest and clear about what is working and what is not and show where they are failing, where students are not learning and where the warts are located. In the past, many colleges were unwilling to do this. But with government and the public demanding greater transparency, data analyses like this will become more commonplace. When colleges share data that reveal progress, attrition and graduation rates, there is always some trepidation on the part of administrators. What if the data makes the school or program look bad? What if the comparison is not flattering? These schools are to be commended for risking this. Transparency leads to the ability to learn, change, and make improvements.

As the PAR project progressed, researchers have created a database that measures 33 variables for online course work for 640,000 students. This tracks student retention and performance across a wide range of demographic factors. The data set from the PAR project will show what works at a specific type of institution and what does not (Fain 2012). In phase two of the project set to kick off in 2013, a number of other schools are being added to the data set and other variables will be included.

Perhaps more interesting, however, is that the *Inside Higher Ed* article on the PAR generated a good number of comments posted by professors who gave their two cents on this kind of data collection in higher education (Fain 2012). The less-than-enthusiastic comments often came from professors in traditional universities. Many traditional brick-and-mortar professors have viewed online learning as a threat to their profession and their world. We will see why they are quite right to worry. What they do can never be measured. What an online class does can be measured. It is that simple.

Analyses like this are changing the conversation. Several decades ago, the focus changed from teaching to learning. Consultants were brought into faculty retreats to discuss active learning, problem-based education, constructivism and effective pedagogy. It has always been difficult to say what constitutes good teaching. But we can do a much better job of measuring whether or not students are learning. Projects like PAR will give us great transparency into the process of learning. While there have been some notable critics of this shift (Bloom 1988), the conversation has moved more toward a focus on learning theory (Illeris 2009).

The analogy we like to use to describe this facet of change can be found in the story of the Nazca Lines. The Nazca Desert in southern Peru has a series of lines carved in rocks that are known as geoglyphs. For centuries, no one knew what the lines meant. Then, in the 1930s, a plane was flying over the area and noticed that the geoglyphs were actually huge drawings that could only be seen in their entirety from the air. Suddenly, a series of random lines formed images and pictures that were so amazing that in 1994 the Nazca Lines were declared a UNESCO World Heritage Site. There are images of human beings, birds and animals that can only be seen from the air. Data can show us what was in front of us for years, but in a form we could not understand until now.

THE NEW LIBRARY

The classroom is not the only place where the digital revolution is changing the very DNA of higher education. Every aspect of the university has been impacted, including college libraries, where the digital revolution has already had a profound effect.

For generations, universities were built around libraries. The layout of the traditional university was often around a quad with the library centrally located. Great universities have many libraries or a library system to house books, manuscripts and other collections. Often, professors and scholars would travel far and wide to use collections available only at specific universities. Because some books were rare and collections one of a kind, scholars and students would travel to a university just to use its library collection. There was a time, for instance, when the papers of James Joyce could only be viewed at the special collection libraries of Cornell University or the State University of New York at

11

Buffalo. Today, we have the James Joyce Scholars Collection of documents that are easily accessible online, edited by the very capable David Harmon at the University of Wisconsin.

The digital revolution has obviously changed the way students use libraries. Students today have a very different understanding about how to use library materials for reference (Applegate 2007). The rapid growth of online, democratic encyclopedias, such as Wikipedia, for instance, has changed the way students look for, retrieve and use information (Lim and Simon 2011). Whole library collections are being digitized, rapidly altering the way academic libraries are accessed by students and utilized by faculty members for scholarly research.

There was a time when great libraries attracted great minds and great teachers. Albertus Magnus taught in Paris, attracted there, in part, by the University at Paris library. Isaac Newton was a great patron of the libraries of Cambridge University (Coplestone 2003). Perhaps it is fitting that the online digital library catalog of Cambridge University is now named "Newton." Yale University, which can boast both the Sterling Library and Beinecke Rare Book and Manuscript Collection, among others, attracted faculty such as Jacques Derrida, Peter Gay, and Benoit Mandelbrot, the mathematician who invented fractal geometry. Yale traditionally attracted scholars who came to use the library and learn from its faculty. The Beinecke collection is now going online. As the collection is digitized, its roles change.

Suddenly, students and faculty can access the great libraries of the world from the Hogs Breath Saloon in Key West, where Ernest Hemingway did some of his best work. The great universities no longer have the singular pleasure of having great collections that scholars needed to visit for their research.

Efforts by the Gutenberg project, Google Books and the Library of Congress have worked to make extensive collections of texts available in fully digital form. An interesting question has come from these mass-digitization projects: Are e-books really books? Without binding and paper, are e-books so different that they can no longer be called books?

THE NEW MACHINE

So far, we have briefly shown that the classroom and library have undergone dramatic changes in higher education. The impact of the digital revolution on higher education, however, does not end there. The greatest change to the university in the past quarter century has been brought about by the unification of all of its systems and decision points on one piece of software that cannot be easily altered once it is set in motion. When colleges centralized all of their computer functions for the ease of administrative functionality, the machine became the focal point of what could or could not be completed. However, technology is never neutral, and there is a price to be paid for every advance it brings in speed and efficiency (Rojcewicz 2006).

Almost every college in America is now "run" by software, not humans. A software–hardware configuration, usually under the control of the Information Technology Department, typically runs the guts of the university. Called an Enterprise Resource Planning (ERP) system, this software–hardware configuration tells us when semesters start, when grades are due, how grade point averages are calculated, who should be denied financial aid, who should go on probation and a thousand other check boxes that were previously negotiated with a human being.

The names of the companies that provide ERP systems are well known to those who work in education: Banner and Datatel (now Ellucian) SAP, PeopleSoft, Jenzabar and CampusView, to mention a handful. The flexibility and power that individual faculty members, registrars and advisers once owned have been taken away by the standardized mechanism of the software. Like the introduction of the time clock in the factory, where the worker must punch in or out, the ERP system now makes exceptions to rules all but impossible. The software–hardware array links up a student's personal information, grades and financial aid information and binds it all together. To make one change is to have changes ripple through the whole system. This often makes registrars, financial aid officers, advisers and deans look inflexible. But, in reality, it is the program naming the tune, not the administration or faculty.

The digital revolution impacted certain fields earlier than others. The conservative element of higher education caused many institutions to resist the implementation of technology that arrived under the disguise of "improved efficiencies." There were good reasons to resist these changes. The machine now does the scheduling. Grades are now due at a certain time to be entered into the machine. A student is locked out of class or let in by a non-human-generated calculation. Faculty members have become cogs in the machine built to make the lives of administrators easier.

Some may object to this line of reasoning by saying that these elements are not essential to higher education. It could be argued that the key decisions are still made in the faculty senate or some similar body. But if the machine gives us the parameters within which we must color, and it is costly and complex to move outside of them, are we still as free?

REGRETTABLY RELINQUISHING POWER TO THE ERP SYSTEM

The science fiction movie *Blade Runner* takes place in a future dystopia where humans have created replicant humans to run their businesses, do their work and fight their wars. These replicants are stronger, smarter and more relentless than humans. But there is price in turning your power over to something stronger and smarter than you and does not need to eat or sleep. In the end, it could take over everything.

Nonetheless, as a result of all decisions being software dependent, university information technology departments have become incredible centers of power and control. With this new control, it becomes imperative to ask who is really running our universities. It is important to discuss the relationship between the faculty senate and the chief information officer. Who does the CIO report to? Who is she responsible to? How responsive is she to faculty concerns and not merely administrative systems?

ERP systems are controlling all aspects of college life, running the vast majority of America's colleges. ERP systems are not neutral. These systems dictate the pace of the modern university, just as the looms did in the textile factories in the first Industrial Revolution.

These programs bring together data for student enrollment, admissions, payroll, various computer systems and any other data used by the university. Once the whole campus is under the control of a computer system, certain decisions become forced. It needs timelines, and it dictates changes in behavior. The introduction of ERP systems has changed higher education just as profoundly as robotics changed the assembly line. Once all systems are linked, there is no longer room for the exception and, sadly, there is no longer room for the exceptional. Once the algorithm is set, we all must dance to its tune.

Certain departments in the university felt these changes early on. Once the computer demanded conformity of records, the registrar could no longer do someone a favor outside the confines of the program. Once financial aid and registrations were linked, it was harder for the dean of students to say, "just sit in class and we will work it out later." Faculty members now have to turn in grades by a certain date or the entire program cannot run. All sorts of calculations can be run on these massive brains that tell us the graduation rates, retention rates, withdrawal rates, drop-out rates and even grade distribution. Do any of these rates indicate good or bad teaching? Do any of these rates tell us if a class is a success or not? It is tempting for administrators and data geeks to use quantitative data to develop models that define quality education. In addition, it is all handed to us neatly packaged by the software that runs silently in the background. We have to be careful and realize that some things that go on in a university may not be quantifiable. It may be that some elements of mentorship or learning occur in a more circuitous or non-linear ways. Data is the beginning of our journey but wisdom and experience must temper what we do with this data.

It has often been argued that faculty governance should not extend to areas outside of its expertise, such as information technology, because they do not have the expertise. But if faculty members do not control information technology, the information technology department will control the faculty members. This is a question about the very heart and soul of the university. This is a question about the future of the university. It is a binary question. It is that simple.

We have laid out the new challenges that the digital revolution has brought to the classroom, the library and university management.

Our task now is to see how far we drifted from the blueprint laid down by Cardinal Newman more than 150 years ago. Are we in harmony with the classical nature of the university, or is it destroying what is essential to the university? We will explore what the university of the future will look like and how can we prepare for it. To do this, we will take some historical side trips (particularly in Part II but also throughout every part) where we discover the essence of the digital revolution and how it has impacted the university, as well as how the university has evolved and adapted over its long life. We will look at issues related to academic freedom, shared governance and curriculum (Part III). We will talk about how the digital revolution has brought new opportunities and redefined the higher education workforce (Part IV), and we will wrap everything up with in-depth conclusions rooted in traditional philosophies and supported by modern technologies (Part V).

CHAPTER TWO
A NEW SCRIPT FOR WORK, PLAY AND EDUCATION

There are only 10 kinds of people in this world, those that understand binary and those that don't.

— Anonymous

THE SECOND INDUSTRIAL REVOLUTION

For a variety of reasons, the digital revolution can be thought of as a second Industrial Revolution. Like the Industrial Revolution, the digital revolution has changed the relation between people and work (Riordan and Hoddeson 1998). However, the changes already wrought by the digital revolution have not been evenly felt by all sectors of society and the economy. Some have felt the tsunami of change earlier than others. Industries that used technology more heavily felt the changes first.

At the outset of the first Industrial Revolution, a large percentage of the population was agrarian, making their living off the land. That kind of work required the skills of a farmer or herder and the complex knowledge handed down orally for generations associated with these occupations. No formal education was required (Hepplewhite 2009).

The Industrial Revolution disrupted our agrarian society, causing large social displacements and societal change. Populations shifted, new jobs were created and new job skills were needed. A mass exodus from the country to the city swelled urban centers. During this time,

Karl Marx and Friedrich Engels documented how capital became highly concentrated in the upper classes (Marx 1978), while Charles Dickens and Victor Hugo showed us how the introduction of new industrial technologies brought suffering and anguish to the proletariat.

A good historical representation of this transformation can be found in *A Christmas Carol*, by Charles Dickens, which detailed the new relationship between work and leisure happening during the nineteenth century (Dickens 2004). The still infamous Mr. Scrooge works relentlessly to keep up with his business while his humble and loyal employee, Bob Cratchit, gets caught between his duties at work and his desire for leisure time at home. Scrooge's nephew Fred represents the freedom and pleasure wealth promises and many seek out. All these characters were created out of the upheaval of the Industrial Revolution.

Today, the digital revolution is rewriting this script yet again. Even though this second revolution is very young, it has already impacted every aspect of our social and working lives.

What exactly is the digital revolution? The short answer is that it is defined by the dropping cost and increasing deployment of microchips across all sectors of society. The digital revolution's pre-birth started with the transistor, developed at Bell Labs in 1947 (there is still debate on who invented it). In 1954, Texas Instruments began to mass produce transistors, resulting in an immediate and very significant impact on our culture (Riordan and Hoddeson 1998). This led to smaller, faster and cheaper appliances. During the last half of the twentieth century and into the twenty-first century, the introduction of digital devices changed how work was completed and commodities produced.

The banking industry is a good example of how the digital revolution shocked its workforce. In 1954, when Texas Instruments was bringing its first transistor off the assembly line, there were banks everywhere in America that had offices on the second and third floors of large marble-and-brick buildings filled with clerks who wrote down transactions, balanced accounts and kept records. In 1954, the proverbial Bob Cratchit was still alive and doing manual calculations at his job. On the ground floor of the same bank, there were windows full of bank tellers who took paper, wrote down what it meant, and gave the customer cash or some other paper to record the transaction. There were human beings making a good living at every stage of this process.

Fast forward to the twenty-first century. We now have Automated Teller Machines (ATMs) where customers can deposit money or obtain money. Our paychecks are automatically deposited into our checking accounts, so we no longer have to walk into a bank and wait in long lines on payday. Today, a bank teller's window is often empty, replaced with a "Please Go to the Next Window" sign. The second or third floor of this same bank is rented out to some other company, as the armies of bank employees have been put out of work by automated digital technologies (Kozak 2005). What humans once did, computers now do better, most of the time. Consequently, the number of jobs that have been lost in banking, insurance, finance and similar areas due to automation has been astronomical. In almost every field the increasing power and intelligence of the computer chip has begun to have powerful and unprecedented influences.

In 1980, the personal computer came into our lives. In the mid-1990s, the World Wide Web began its incredible transformation of our global society. Robots build cars and computers fly planes. Many tasks that took skill and a trained human being to accomplish have been taken over by machines run with a digital brain.

Banks of machines in subways, train stations and other locations have replaced the booths where tickets were purchased. The impact of smart tags on toll collectors has been immense. A very large chunk of our workforce has been displaced. In addition, wages for middle-class workers have stagnated, and high unemployment rates remain unchanged and worrisome in our national discussion. The rule is simple. If your job does not involve significant creativity, a machine will eventually do it for you. Bob Cratchit has been out of work for two years, and he is behind on his mortgage payment and running out of unemployment benefits.

HIGHER ED'S NEW
COMMUNICATION MODALITY

All of these changes have pushed more and more Americans into thinking that they need a college education. In some cities, a minimum level of higher education is required by candidates for a job in fire services, emergency medical services or as a police officer. In the armed forces, college degrees are necessary for advancement beyond a certain rank. A computer genius with fantastic skills but no college degree would have to be lucky or know someone to find a good job.

The digital revolution has changed the way human beings work, play, relate, date and even marry. A 2010 study funded by match. com found that one in five relationships and one in six marriages came about through online dating. It has been speculated that by 2020, more than two in five marriages will begin online. With the advent of smart-phones, tablet technologies and computers, handwriting has deteriorated to the point where there is concern about whether or not it will survive. New technologies and communication modalities are changing every element of human society.

The university has also been transformed by the digital revolution. Until now, the university was able to keep its basic form consistent with its well-established, lecture-based origins from places like Bologna, Salamanca, Paris and Oxford. As far back as the thirteenth century, Albertus Magnus, Thomas Aquinas, and Duns Scotus all stood in front of rows of students and expounded in lectures using their notes (Hunt 2008). In the nineteenth century, George Hegel and Arthur Schopenhauer stood before similar rows of students at the University of Berlin and lectured from their notes. Today, all over America, professors are still walking into classes, facing rows of students, and lecturing from their notes. But this lecture-based, sage-on-the-stage teaching and learning modality is changing dramatically due to the digital revolution.

The mode of communication influences every institution in a society (Innis 2007). In our own time the digital revolution has made the wisdom of the ages available to anyone who can afford a digital phone. Over its short history to date, online learning has become the preferred method of instruction by college students.

When asked about their preferred method of study, students overwhelmingly chose online learning over the traditional physical classroom (Sloan 2011). In a survey of college presidents sponsored by the Pew Foundation, it was revealed that more than three quarters of college presidents have embraced online learning as a significant part of their strategic plans (Parker, Lenhart and Moore 2011).

Online learning has moved teaching outside of the traditional brick-and-mortar classroom. Radical teachers have always escaped the brick-and-mortar classroom by taking their students outdoors, going under the oak tree on the first hot day of summer. That hippie English teacher or Marxist sociologist holding class outside still exists, but they are the exception and not the norm. In towns that grew up around universities such as Oxford, England or Cambridge, Massachusetts, you will still find learning going on after hours in the pubs and coffee houses, with scholars and students extending the conversation. Be it at the Eagle and Child Pub on Saint Giles in Oxford where C.S. Lewis and J.R.R. Tolkien held court, or the John Harvard Pub, the conversations are similar. But now the conversation also lives in the air. Learning and communicating happen over the waves or, as we say, in "cyberspace."

Teachers are no longer bound to or limited by the physical classroom, and the primacy of the lecture has been challenged (Collins 2009). Students can learn outside of the classroom anywhere they can get a digital connection. In the universities of the United Kingdom, the lecture it is not as prominent as it used to be under the tradition of German research universities, marked by a focus on the educational theories of Kant and Humboldt (Kant 2011). When the Johns Hopkins University was under the guidance of the Germanophile and former president of the University of California System, Daniel Coit Gilman, the German model-dominated American higher educational thinking. But again, all this is undergoing rapid change.

The online course, various forms of social media and chat rooms now allow learning to occur at our own pace, in places of our own choosing and at the times we find most convenient. Students can also access other points of view, other lectures from other professors at other colleges, as well as any kind of contrary information they may seek, all instantaneously.

ACCESS TO INFORMATION GONE WILD

While the classroom, library and lecture have undergone dramatic change, so has access to information itself. In the 1960s, there were three networks in the United States that attracted and split up the nation's television audience. CBS, NBC and ABC had a virtual monopoly on what the public viewed. There were few other avenues that had such a wide popular influence. For example, many stories about the private lives of presidents and public figures were kept out of the news by a gentleman's agreement with the three networks and a handful of national papers. The close relationship between Washington politicians and the Washington news bureaus of the three networks insured a consistency of information.

Today, there are countless ways to access information. There can no longer be consensus or control. This has fragmented our news coverage and given us television, radio and satellite channels that are progressive, conservative, libertarian, gay, African American, Hispanic, Haitian, Jewish and Christian, to name but a few. The consequences of this fragmentation of information may not be understood for a generation. The common language of the big three networks that held us in a common spell no longer exists. The Walter Cronkites are gone, perhaps never to return.

In the education sector, like in all other sectors of our society, the Internet has changed how information is accessed and utilized. This change has brought disruption and differing points of view that have yet to be resolved. Faculty members, for instance, were skeptical of students who used tools such as Wikipedia for class assignments and research. While the scholarship on student use of Wikipedia and similar tools is in its early stages, studies in such peer-reviewed journals as *First Monday* reveal initial student-use patterns as well as changes in their concepts of verification that help us understand the validity of such online resources (Lim and Simon 2011).

In 2005, the journal *Nature* conducted a noteworthy study about Wikipedia, claiming that Wikipedia articles had a level of accuracy comparable to the *Encyclopedia Britannica*, which had the same number of serious errors, if not more, than Wikipedia (Lim and Simon 2011). When the editors and publishers of *Britannica* objected, *Nature* responded in an editorial in 2006 with a point-by-point rebuttal that ended the debate and changed the way we thought about online encyclopedias.

Also in 2005, the British newspaper *The Guardian* published a story headlined "Can You Trust Wikipedia?" Seven experts were asked to review articles and score them on a scale of zero to eight for accuracy (Lim and Simon 2011). Most of the articles received a score between five and eight. This put them on a par with edited and vetted traditional encyclopedias.

How significant was this study? It could be compared to the Judgment of Paris in 1976 when the French were shocked to find out that in a blind taste test the two most drinkable wines were not from Burgundy or Bordeaux but were instead a Chateau Montelena and Stags' Leap, both from California.

The digital revolution has touched and transformed every aspect of human experience. It has changed the way we travel, keep track of our children, keep our recipes, take pictures, date, marry, and stay in touch with old friends. The digital revolution has wreaked havoc on almost all institutions in our society. It has impacted the post office, the local library, the local bookstore, and countless other institutions and industries.

Just as the fundamentals of communication, work, leisure and even religion have been impacted by the digital revolution, the university has also been impacted. This has raised questions concerning every aspect of the university. What is the role of the lecture in the digital age (Brown and Rice 2008)? What is the role of the library when students can access materials from home (Collins 2009)? Is online communication inferior to classroom interaction? Can costs be held down by online instruction (Finkelstein 2000)? Does electronic publishing water down scholarly research? What does it mean to have faculty off campus? All of these questions are relatively new, and it will take time to see all of the unintended consequences that flow from them.

CHAPTER THREE
IS HIGHER EDUCATION
EXPERIENCING A CRISIS?

All history is nothing but a succession of crises – of rupture, repudiation and resistance. When there is no crisis, there is stagnation, petrifaction and death.

— Eugene Ionesco

The digital revolution changed how we obtain, use, share and store information. Colleges are places where information is obtained, used, shared and stored. It is natural that this change in communication technologies would change higher education at its core. It is too early in the digital revolution to understand all of the unintentional consequences that will result in time. But the transformation of the university is already well underway. But does this transformation constitute a crisis?

Some thinkers have questioned if there really is a crisis in higher education in America (Searle 1993). If there is a crisis, what exactly is it a crisis of? Is there more than one kind of crisis in higher education? Does the government need to fix it? Does the professoriate need to be reformed? Should colleges operate more like businesses? Should there be greater accountability? Are our college students unfit to compete in the global marketplace (Lewin 2010)? All of these questions have escaped the faculty senate and the Academy and have reached a point of heated debate in the public media and government.

UNDERSTANDING THE BACKGROUND
OF EDUCATION REFORM

There is now pressure from the Department of Education to change how higher education is funded and reports its data. The federal government is very active in its attempts to regulate higher education (Miller 2010). Before we ask how to fix and reform higher education, we must understand the question in its historical context.

Many people are not aware that the word "education" does not appear in either the Declaration of Independence or the Constitution. Additionally, the Tenth Amendment to the Constitution, which was part of the Bill of Rights ratified in 1791, reserves all powers not granted explicitly to the federal government to the states or the people. The powers of the federal government are limited to those things the Founding Fathers saw as essential to the smooth functioning of a republic. So, constitutionally, education was not seen by the Founding Fathers as something that needed "regulating" by the federal government.

During the early years of the United States of America, there were only private colleges funded by various religious groups. The University of Pennsylvania founded by Benjamin Franklin in 1749 and the University of Virginia founded in 1818 by Thomas Jefferson were the forerunners of what we today call public institutions (Hitchcock 2012). There was no momentum to establish national education standards, a ministry of education, or some governing body to set the rules for higher education.

We often talk of the "genius" of the Founding Fathers. If they were, in fact, geniuses, why did they leave out the government's role in the regulation of higher education? How could they have missed something so essential? Do we know something they did not know? Their genius was that they did not try to regulate education, resulting in a system that is both wonderful and troubled. It is wonderful because there is no cap on its greatness placed on it by government. It is troubled because, with no national standards of quality, higher education has been driven more by changes in culture and the market than federal policy. We have some of the best universities on the planet yet many of our college graduates are not properly educated. How can this be? The freedom of the American system is its glory and Achilles' heel.

GLOBALIZATION'S IMPACT AND ECONOMIC REALITIES

We live in a hyper-connected world (Friedman 2007) where globalization has had a negative impact on the American workforce. The exporting of jobs, first in manufacturing and now in management and design, to nations outside of the United States, has led to increased unemployment and the suppression of wages. With inflation outpacing growth in wages, a whole generation of American workers has lowered their expectations for a better life (Brown and Lauder 2010).

Our democracy depends upon a strong middle class, and this class has seen its wages stagnate as prices have continued to rise. Higher education has always been recognized as a way to improve one's economic condition and prospects for a better life (Brown and Lauder 2010). But as wages and income have stagnated for a large portion of our population, the price of college has continued to rise, often faster than the rate of inflation. So, students graduate, often saddled by a huge amount of debt, to find they cannot pay back student loans that have been guaranteed by taxpayer dollars.

THE GREAT DISRUPTION OF HIGHER EDUCATION

In addition to the problems of college affordability, coupled with the extraordinary growth of debilitating student-loan debt and the lack of good-paying jobs, there is a disturbing college-completion problem in the United States. Each year The College Board ranks countries in terms of what percentage of their population completes college. The College Board measures in each nation the percentage of its population, age 25–34, who has a college degree. At one time, the United States led this survey. In 2010, Russia led the world in college graduation rates at 54%. Canada came in second at 48.3%. The United States was in twelfth place in the world with 40.4% of its citizens having earned an associate or bachelor's degree (Huffington Post 2010). These kinds of statistics point to a "crisis" in higher education in the United States.

For more than a century, there has been a public debate about the "crisis" in higher education. Pundits on both the left and right continue to decry the state of higher education (Bloom 1988). In study after study it is pointed out that our students are not globally competitive in math and science. America ranks low when it comes to learning foreign languages. Foreign languages are among the first programs to be cut at the secondary level during a budget crisis. College graduates flunk tests on their knowledge of American history and the basics of high school civics (Arum and Roksa 2011).

The crisis in higher education could be looked at as a subset of the crisis in our culture and the growth of our global society. The hyper-connected world has spread wealth from the first world to countries that we previously dominated economically. As more Indians and Chinese have risen out of poverty into the middle class, there has been a corresponding decline in the earning power of the American middle class (Friedman 2007).

In 1945, at the end World War II, the economies and manufacturing capabilities of Japan, Germany, England, France and Russia had been decimated. The United States was the sole economic power. Every car, refrigerator, television set or radio was manufactured in the United States and exported to the rest of the world. States like Michigan and Ohio boomed and could not keep up with the demand for skilled labor. The middle class grew as more Americans were able to achieve the "American Dream."

By the 1970s, the major countries of the world had rebuilt their economies and built new factories with modern manufacturing and management strategies. America began to slip from its number one position in all sorts of surveys. Questions began to arise as to how this could happen, leading to debates on numerous issues, including poverty, equality of income, crime and immigration (Brown and Lauder 2010). But these are variations on the same theme. When income stagnates, tax revenues go down. When tax revenues go down, we are not able to support federal and state government-funded education programs. When the government cannot fund programs, stress is placed on the safety net, civic organizations and our ability to fund our defense. So, the debate about higher education is really a debate about numerous issues and challenges and how we can remain competitive in a global society.

RETHINKING THE "CRISIS"

The word "crisis" has an interesting etymology that may help us rethink higher education. It comes from the Greek word "krisis" that was first used as a medical term by thinkers such as Hippocrates and Galen. For the Greek thinkers, a krisis was that point at which a fever broke or subsided, a sore healed or multiplied or that point at which the patient lived or died (Nutton 2005). In the seventeenth century, the word gained wider use by describing those situations that could lead to instability, danger and ultimately destruction.

In their 1998 paper, "Communication, Organization and Crisis," Seeger, Sellnow and Ulmer defined "crisis" as "specific, unexpected and non-routine events or series of events that create high levels of uncertainty and threat or perceived threat to an organization's high priority goals" (Seeger, Sellnow and Ulmer 1998).

Based on the definition cited above, we are compelled to ask if the changes in higher education caused by the digital revolution have created a true crisis. First, are these changes "unexpected?" If we were attentive to Marshall McLuhan and other members of the Toronto School in the 1960s, we would not now be shocked and surprised by the events impacting the university (McLuhan 2005). The Toronto School had its origins a series of lectures delivered by Harold Innis at Oxford in 1948, which later became the basis for his book *Empire and Communication* (Innis 2007). Innis also studied how different mediums of writing, stone carving, mud tablets, papyrus, parchment, writing on hides and eventually paper changed not only how writing happened but the very subjects of writing. Each medium shaped both the form and content of what was written. Social forms and mechanisms changed as well. Read a love letter written by your great grandparents during the First World War. Read the flowery prose, the well-constructed sentences, the liberal use of adverbs and adjectives. Today, one youngster texts a joke to another and the second replies LOL, which stands for "laughing out loud." How did this shorthand ever drive out adverbs and adjectives? Innis had great influence on McLuhan who acknowledges this in his book *The Gutenberg Galaxy* (McLuhan 2011).

McLuhan expanded and popularized the work begun by Innis. McLuhan claimed that the medium was the message (McLuhan 2005). When the medium of communication changes, so does the content. Changes in communication technologies impact every aspect of society. The work of McLuhan was taken to another level in the work of his doctoral student Walter Ong. Walter Ong was a Jesuit priest who worked on the fault lines where different kinds of communication clashed. His most important work was on the transition from an oral culture to a literate culture in ancient Greece (Ong 2002). Father Ong, following McLuhan and Innis, argued that communication plays a more fundamental role than previously realized.

FROM ORAL TO WRITING TO PRINTING TO DIGITAL

The shift from orality to literacy gave birth to all of the disciplines Athens bequeathed to future generations. Father Ong noted that philosophy, psychology, logic, astronomy, mathematics, geometry, drama, comedy, poetry, epic literature, political, economic and historical theories were all born during this transition. Similar to the transition from orality to literacy, the shift from an analog culture to digital culture has not occurred in a simple step-by-step manner. The cultural shift has hit some aspects of society earlier than others. By looking at this transition, we can understand more about the transitions in our own time.

Plato, that greatest of writers, was conflicted about writing and how it was surpassing speech. Plato was the student of Socrates, the man Nietzsche called "he who did not write" (Derrida 1998). Socrates was a man of the spoken word, of the situation, of the here and now in which all orality lives. Plato is remembered both for the beauty of his writing and for being a critic of writing.

In his dialogue, *The Phaedrus*, Plato contrasts good and bad writing (Plato 1928). He uses a myth to tell his story. He places his tale in ancient Egypt. He tells of the gift of the god Theuth to Pharaoh Thamus who was to share these gifts with his people. Writing is presented in this myth as a remedy for the holes and gaps in memory. Theuth promises to restore memory and keep them complete. But Thamus realizes that writing, instead of restoring memory, was likely to have the opposite impact. With the advent of writing, memory weakens; stories no longer need to be remembered *in toto*. When something is written, it can be read by anyone. You cannot ask questions to a written text. Once something is written, it cannot be rethought, rewritten or improved. Writing cannot defend itself. It is dumb in every sense of the word.

Plato's ambivalence about writing and the damage it was doing to morality, discourse and society was his reaction to the changes that follow a shift in the medium of communication (Ong 2002). The move from speaking to writing threatened traditional values, religion, social order and political structures.

The pioneering work of Fred Stielow in the area of digital libraries and digitalized collections shows us a new direction. Stielow noted that the pace of digitization will only increase as both the majority of faculty and students prefer digital archives over their physical cousins (Stielow 2003). This may seem a distant future, however we have seen the creation and adoption of cloud storage technologies. There was initial mistrust and skepticism about this technology but time has led to massive adoption of the technology. In his collaboration with Mary Bundy, Stielow claimed that the library is no longer just a place for books. It has become a social gathering place that has a political function as well. The change in media changed the whole function of the library (Bundy and Stielow 1987). Those who are optimistic argue that libraries were forced to adapt more rapidly to the digital revolution than other aspects of the university.

WHO WILL SURVIVE?

Finally, we posit that there is not a crisis in higher education. The etymology of the term tells us that a crisis is a point where the patient lives or dies. The patient here is not going to die, but the python is halfway through the process of shedding its skin. The top-tier colleges will survive and, in many ways, they will survive with little impact (DeMillo 2011). There may be no crisis in funding at the top-tier universities, but for the vast majority of colleges there is a sense that something is wrong (DeMillo 2011). This may be the beginning of a consolidation of institutions for economic reasons (DeMillo 2011). This has happened in other sectors and has sometimes been called a "shaking out" process.

The rise of the huge online for-profits was made possible by the digital revolution. The growing role of information technology departments on college campuses is highlighting how this change is taking place. The introduction of these technologies has changed not only the use and sharing of knowledge on college campuses but has altered the very structures of governance as we will see later.

By our earlier definition, crisis is an unexpected or surprising disruption. For those of us who have paid attention to the digital revolution, what has happened in the past quarter century should be not be unexpected or a surprise. The university will not die. But something new has been born.

PART II

THE STORY OF HIGHER EDUCATION:
A HISTORIC OVERVIEW

Our historic overview of higher education is more clearly detailed in Part II, although we draw on important historical influences throughout the book.

We posit that some of the roots of American higher education
are ensconced in the European university system, and especially in
the German university model. We present a sweeping chronological
description of these influences, starting with medieval universities
up through modern times.

This conversation about the nature and purpose of the university continued to meander and become energized throughout every
new development in our higher education system. We show how
the birth of land-grant universities and community colleges, for
instance, brought new ideas; how the G.I. Bill, the Cold War, the
Higher Education Act and much more influenced the heart and soul
of higher education in the United States.

We then go back to a history lesson that emphasizes how these
influences are really much more of a reinterpretation of the same
philosophical debates that existed long ago and still carries through
today. We also show how the so-called democratization of higher

education continues to be a great theme that still has a widespread altering effect on the future of higher education.

We stress how the debates on the failure of higher education have often mirrored larger political and economic issues, such as the Cold War and the recession that started in 2008.

We then take another step back in time, particularly in Chapter Six, showing how a complex and diverse "quarrel between ancients and moderns" brings diverse philosophies that can all find their place somewhere within the huge and varied elements of thinking that exist within higher education today.

And we conclude Part II with a short treatise about how the professoriate has historically conducted their work. We will discuss the impact of the digital revolution on the professoriate and its future.

CHAPTER FOUR
MEDIEVAL EUROPE TO COLONIAL
AMERICA TO LAND-GRANT UNIVERSITIES

History should be written as philosophy. – Voltaire

Learning has existed throughout time. Plato's Academy, Aristotle's Lycium and The Library of Alexandria are all known to Western readers. But great bodies of learning also existed at the Shang Xiang school founded in the Yu Shun Era in China, the textual education of noble youths that took place during the reign of Darius the Great in Persepolis and the University of Timbuktu, which was reputed to be the largest university in the world in the twelfth century (Brook and Webb 1999).

NOSTALGIA RUNS DEEP

American universities have their roots in the European university system, and especially in the German university model. Clearly understanding the culture or our modern university system requires that we know its rich and varied history. For instance, it is important to note that nostalgia for the European university runs deep in American higher education. This can be seen in the design of college buildings that harkens back to the great universities of Europe. In a wonderfully illustrated book, *Architecture and Academe: College Buildings in New England Before 1860*, Bryant Franklin Tolles shows us, page after page, how the design and execution of college buildings in America copied the European model (Tolles 2011). But this nostalgia does not end with architecture. The founders of America's earliest universities also copied the curriculum of Oxford and Cambridge. In addition, our earliest research universities, such as Johns Hopkins, were consciously founded on the German university model (Thom 2009).

FOUNDATIONS OF MEDIEVAL EUROPEAN UNIVERSITIES TO COLONIAL AMERICA

Our journey begins with the foundation of the Medieval European universities. We then proceed to the American colonial experience and founding of our earliest colleges. From there we follow the various social and educational revolutions that have impacted the American university.

The first European university is often thought to be the University of Paris, founded in 1190. Although the University of Bologna claims to be founded much earlier, in 1088, there is a distinct reason for putting Paris first. Bologna was founded by a student guild, whereas Paris was run by a faculty guild (Rashdall 2010). While there were numerous institutions that educated young men, it was the formulation of faculty governance that gave the modern university its present form. The model of faculty governance, which has been so much at the heart of the modern university, is today under attack, and some see it in full retreat (Donoghue 2008).

The application of digital technologies and the impact they have had on university culture is one reason why faculty power has declined. The rise in the percentage of online courses and the increased percentage of adjunct faculty teaching in universities may also be related to this power shift (Schrecker 2010).

The current debate about the crisis in higher education is a variation on questions that predate the founding of our Republic. Gerald Graff wrote a wonderful history of college English departments that went back to colonial times. In his research, he found that even before America declared its independence, there were questions about the quality and usefulness of a college education (Graff 1989). For those of us who are immersed in these kinds of questions every day, passing the political football called "higher education," it is refreshing to know that 250 years ago, the public and press were worried about what was going on at those questionable new institutions like Harvard, Yale and William and Mary.

In colonial times, higher education was much easier to define because it was much smaller, with less than 1% of the population enrolled in college (Cremin 1970). At that time the vast majority of college students were from the upper classes. While there were exceptions, this should not confuse us to think that college in the earliest days of our Republic was egalitarian. It was not. For this reason it was easier to find a consistency of purpose in the university and the values it was trying to pass along.

As more students with different backgrounds and levels of preparation entered college, the system became stressed with more things for more people. With each movement toward greater inclusion, the purpose and aim of higher education became both more confused and more controversial. With every expansion of opportunity came new challenges that made the old guard nostalgic for the earlier, and clearer, version of the university. From the inclusion of women, Jews and Blacks, to the founding of the land-grant colleges, to the G.I. Bill, to the explosion of community colleges, to the rise of the for-profit online universities – each of these expansions made college a little more complicated and the goals of a college education a little less clear. Every one of these changes in higher education has been met by ferocious resistance that saw the change as a blow to the quality of higher education.

Most of the earliest universities in America were church supported, and one of their earliest missions was to produce ministers for the growing colonies. The curriculum of Christian scriptures and Latin and Greek classics were presented as a combination of memorization and ethical examples meant to improve character (Kraus 1961).

As time went by, the early universities became schools where the sons of the elite could get the education needed to be a gentleman. Colleges for women were not founded until many years later, and the specter of gender inequality is still an issue of discussion in higher education.

At college, the elite could sharpen their connections and leadership skills. In a sense, this legacy haunts the university to this day and clouds our thinking about what it is and what it does. There is a nostalgia for those elitist days that is grounded more in the heart than the head in our thinking about higher education (Hass and Fishman 2010).

There is a common mythology that years ago students were brighter, and the curriculum was more enlightened. There is no data to support this claim. In the colonial period, college was often a deadly combination of rote memorization in dead languages (Graff 1989). For example, when Thomas Jefferson founded the University of Virginia, he did so because he felt his own alma mater, William and Mary, did not teach enough science and progressive education. The same thing happened when William Barton Rogers founded MIT because the citizens of Massachusetts felt that Harvard was behind the curve in science and technology (Killian 1957). My, how times have changed!

Harvard was founded to educate ministers of the Puritan faith while Princeton produced Presbyterian ministers. One of the earliest crises in Harvard's long and distinguished history happened in 1653 when its first president, Henry Dunster, left the Puritan faith and converted to the Baptist faith (Hall 1988). This conversion from one Protestant denomination to another cost him the presidency. Harvard's second president, a devout Puritan, named Increase Matther, followed him. Matther's first act was to get rid of pagan authors such as Plato, Pliny and Cicero and replace them with Christian authors (Hall 1988). The battle over which texts should belong in the college curriculum in America had begun. The culture wars, still discussed today, have been an ongoing skirmish started long before our Republic was founded.

These early universities had a more coherent student body, staff and faculty who all shared similar values, similar backgrounds as well as the same religion. But it was also a time of sectarianism where what was good for the Quakers in Pennsylvania would never do for the Presbyterians in New Jersey.

Why is this conversation relevant here? We believe that the longing for a lost golden age has historically been at the heart of conservative educational theory for centuries. Nostalgia frequently exists in debates about government, monetary policy, public morality or education. We have to understand the role nostalgia plays in our current debate.

Questions about quality in American higher education became increasingly louder as it became more and more inclusive. The history of higher education in America moves one step forward toward greater inclusion, followed by two steps back driven by conservative elements in higher education and society who have seen these inclusions as weakening the quality and standards of higher education.

The digital revolution is in the same tradition of the following disruptions: the inclusion of women and minorities; the advent of technical colleges, community colleges and land-grant universities; and the implementation of the G.I. Bill. The move from a few small elite colleges to the massive education industry today has not been smooth or easy. Every inclusion has made the concept of the "university" more difficult to define.

In addition to the battle between inclusion and excellence, we add a third spice to this stew, which will make it particularly and distinctively American: the tradition of anti-intellectualism in our country. In his excellent book, *Anti-Intellectualism in American Life*, Richard Hofstadter showed that from our Puritan origins there has been a mistrust of intellectuals, book learning and higher education. There have been whole periods in American history, such as during the Jacksonian democracy, where the very values of education came under scrutiny (Hofstadter 1963). Combine this with our confusion about the priorities of both inclusion and excellence, and we can see why what pleases one audience will at the same time infuriate another.

In the beginning, higher education in the colonies was mainly an affair for white males. But women in the colonies also needed higher education. Numerous women's academies popped up and died in the early history of our nation. One of the most famous was the Litchfield Female Academy in Connecticut founded by Ms. Sarah Peirce in 1792 (Pichnarcik 1996). Although the school offered courses in needlepoint and crocheting, it also taught history, composition, geography, ancient languages and literature. The Litchfield Female Academy also offered courses in Latin, philosophy, rhetoric and logic. College records show a wide diversity of economic classes represented at the Litchfield Female Academy.

But even in classes like painting and embroidery, the subject matter was often related to examples taken from the classics and literature that illustrated proper behavior for young ladies (Pichnarcik 1996). It was actually the suffrage movement that increased the expectations of women for a career outside of being a homemaker. The suffrage movement had a large impact on higher education and changed its population to be more inclusive of women. Over and over the battle lines in the history of higher education have been between those who defend the status quo and those who are seek more inclusion. The argument against inclusion has usually been framed as a "watering down" of quality. Be it women, Jews, African Americans or non-traditional working adults, the terms of the debate have not changed very much.

By the early 1920s, more Americans were enrolling in college, with almost 4% of the population attending a higher education institution. In a century and a half, the population of college students had almost quadrupled, and things were about to accelerate at unprecedented levels.

AMERICA'S LAND-GRANT COLLEGE SYSTEM

One of the greatest jolts to the higher education establishment in America were the Morrill Acts of 1862 and 1890, which created America's land-grant college system (James 1903). The Industrial Revolution and westward expansion called for an expansion of our idea of higher education. New skills were needed for the new economy, and American higher education was needed to boost the country's westward expansion. The federal government gave land to the states to raise funds for colleges that would teach agronomy, agriculture, engineering and the mechanical arts. While the traditional liberal arts were still taught, they took a backseat to more practical learning (Webb 2005). You can imagine the reaction of classics professors and the eastern elite to the creation of colleges whose course of study was more corn than Cicero, more agribusiness than Aristotle and more pigs than Plato. In schools where pickle technology and sheep breeding were subjects of study, the American university took a decidedly different turn.

This conversation about the nature and purpose of the university was charged with emotion at the birth of Michigan State University, Penn State University, Ohio State University, Oklahoma University, the University of Illinois and many other state institutions during the mid to late nineteenth century. The entry by state and federal government into education was necessary to create a skilled labor force, but it also brought an extension of governmental regulations, oversight and politics into higher education.

That conservatives greeted the founding of the land-grant colleges with skepticism is an understatement. Some thought that farmers did not want or need a college education. Take, for instance, an editorial in the *New York Times* from January 22, 1859:

> There is…an entire failure of evidence to show a desire on the part of the farming interest for this concession. The prejudice against book or scientific farming is certainly passing away; but in his weekly and monthly periodical devoted to agricultural topics, the farmer finds quite as much scientific farming as his leisure permits him to study, and his laboring hours to practice…

Things got more interesting when funds went out to land-grant colleges. When the state of Connecticut did not have an adequate institution to fill the role, Yale College generously volunteered and accepted funding to train farmers and mechanics. This offer, however, was not as generous and straightforward as it first seemed. Daniel Coit Gilman led the effort. He was the director of libraries at Yale who is credited for being one of the founders of the Skull and Bones, the secret society at Yale that has exercised a great deal of influence over America. He turned Yale's curriculum toward more science. Later, Gilman left Yale to become the first president of both the University of California and Johns Hopkins University (Franklin 2010). He can easily be likened to the Forrest Gump of American higher education in the nineteenth century. He was at the birth of many trends that have persisted long after his death. It may be no surprise to find that Gilman was also instrumental in the drafting of the Morrill Act (Franklin 2010).

For a quarter of a century, Yale received funding as a land-grant college. However, it was revealed that during that quarter of a century

Yale had graduated only seven students from their agricultural course of study, at a total cost of $180,000 or $25,700 per student (Thelin 2004). Those who had intended the land-grant colleges to expand access to American higher education met this revelation with anger. One organization that stood up for the farmers against the traditional establishment was the National Grange, which had an interest in educating and improving the lot of farmers. Because of Yale's lack of success educating farmers, there was pressure to create a new state-run institution that would focus more on agriculture and mechanics and less on knowledge that was of little use to working men.

Yale insisted they had the most experience and history in education in the state of Connecticut. This debate over the establishment of a state-run institution was known as the Yale–Storrs controversy. It eventually resulted in the creation of the University of Connecticut at Storrs, Connecticut (Stave and Burmeister 2005). Yale lost its status as a land-grant university. Dartmouth and Brown lost their land-grant status as well, as large land-grant state-run universities were born (Stave and Burmeister 2005).

GERMAN INFLUENCE IN THE NINETEENTH CENTURY

At the same time the land-grant colleges were being founded, a very different trend arose in American higher education. Daniel Coit Gilman used the monies from the Morrill Act, intended to educate farmers, to instead expand the natural science departments at Yale. This helped to form the modern university based on the German university, where Gilman had previously spent some time while in Europe.

It often comes as a surprise to many Americans that our universities owe more to Heidelberg than to Oxford. In the nineteenth century, German science and engineering was a model for the rest of the world. It was believed that their universities were the best in the world. Charles William Eliot, the progressive president of Harvard, also spent time in Germany. In short, during the nineteenth century, the German model had left its footprint on the American higher education system.

The German system has its philosophical roots in the writings of Immanuel Kant and Wilhelm von Humboldt, the founder of the

42

University of Berlin. The German model was a comprehensive research university, and its setup has influenced American universities even into our own time. After being passed over for the presidency of Yale College, Gilman became the president of the newly formed University of California for three short years from 1872 to 1875. His first speech as president of the California system had an obvious German influence and is a classic in the literature on the history and nature of the university. In this speech, Gilman emphasized the public good a university creates. He praised science and research almost as much as he spoke about pedagogy.

Not being a native Californian and a non-westerner as well, Gilman ran afoul of California politics and shortly left in 1875 to become the first president of the Johns Hopkins University, an elite research university based squarely on the German model (Hawkins 2002).

Johns Hopkins was a Quaker, a bachelor, an abolitionist and a philanthropist who made his fortune in railroads. As a life-long resident of Baltimore, Johns Hopkins wanted a modern university in his hometown (Thom 2009). He founded the Johns Hopkins Hospital and Johns Hopkins University, along with many other institutions. When Daniel Coit Gilman arrived, he used the German model with an aim more toward research and scholarship than at teaching. Johns Hopkins would focus more on graduate students and the creation of new knowledge. The mould of the modern American university was taking shape (Hawkins 2002).

So, we had two trends going in two opposite directions. The land-grant colleges were opening the doors to a new kind of college student, while schools like Johns Hopkins were focusing on graduate research. The land-grants were founded on the impulse of democracy and focused on the applied arts for practical ends. On the other hand, universities like Johns Hopkins, the first of the modern research universities (Hawkins 2002), focused on the creation of knowledge rather than its application through teaching. The aim of the Morrill Act was to create universities where American farmers and manufacturers could improve their skills. The impulse of the research university, or "schools of science," as Gilman called them, was to produce managers, not workers (Thom 2009). It is amazing that Gilman was present at the birth of each.

CHAPTER FIVE
THE TWENTIETH AND TWENTY-
FIRST CENTURIES

*Human history became more and more a race between education
and catastrophe.*

— H.G. Wells

THE BIRTH OF COMMUNITY COLLEGES

The land-grant colleges were not the only departure from the traditional study of the classics. Technical institutes began to pop
up in the 1890s to fulfill the need for workers with mechanical skills
that were at the heart of the Industrial Revolution. Today's Bradley
University, for instance, was formerly the Bradley Polytechnic
Institute (Bradley 2006). There was a proliferation of technical institutes and polytechnics around the turn of the nineteenth century.
Many of these institutions were short lived, and their quality was
often questioned. But it was clear that the nation needed to expand
the education of its workforce to stay competitive.

Between the end of the Civil War and the Roaring Twenties, there
was a steady stream of immigrants arriving in the major cities on both
the east and west coasts of the United States. This spurred the growth
of institutions that later became community colleges. These schools had
many names, such as junior colleges or normal schools. It was not until
the Truman Commission in 1947 that the name "community college"
came into fashion and commonly accepted usage (Hutcheson 2007a).

The educational needs and backgrounds of junior college students diversified as enrollments grew from the immigrant population. Our thinking about the role of the community college began in Chicago. The University of Chicago, with its roots in John Dewey's educational philosophy, has always been on the forefront of the revolutions in American higher education (Dewey 1997). In 1901, the University of Chicago attempted to clarify the future of the community college. The University of Chicago's president at the time, William Rainey Harper, worked to incorporate a more rigorous structure for American higher education. Like Daniel Coit Gilman, he followed the model of the German system of education. He envisioned junior colleges as connected to the university with the first two years of undergraduate study preparing students for the final two years on the university level (Beach and Grubb 2011). He wanted local denominational colleges to lower their curriculum from four years to two years and let the universities teach the final two years.

One of Harper's friends and a fellow parishioner was the superintendent of the Joliet, Illinois school district who helped set a plan in motion in 1901 to start a community college. Joliet Junior College has laid claim to be the first true American community college. Harper worked with other university presidents to define the difference between "collegiate work" and "university work" (Beach and Grubb 2011). Collegiate work is what we today may call the liberal arts and sciences, or general education, which provides the foundation for future study. University work entails the advancement of knowledge through research.

The founding of the American Association of Junior Colleges in 1921 gave these emerging institutions a voice (Beach and Grubb 2011). Many community colleges started their lives as normal schools that prepared teachers for the growing population. In the early part of the century, contemporary community colleges took their shape by providing the first two years of college but also began to expand their mission to include other kinds of training and certifications (Beach and Grubb 2011).

The Truman Commission of 1947 proposed the term "community college" for institutions designed to serve the local area's economic needs. The community college is an American phenomenon whose growth really started to take place mainly in the twentieth century. The terms "booster college," "normal school" and "preparatory school" have all disappeared, but the term "community college" has remained.

The opening of the land-grants, technical schools and community colleges all met with criticism, with claims they were watering down higher education and diluting the quality of education.

THE G.I. BILL

Probably the greatest shock to the system of American higher education happened with the passing of the Servicemen's Readjustment Act, known informally as the G.I. Bill. This was a law that provided higher education benefits to returning World War II soldiers. The flood of G.I.s into colleges transformed American higher education in many ways. Milton Greenberg, former Provost of American University, in his wonderful study of the impact of the G.I. Bill, showed what an earthquake this legislation shook up in higher education (Greenberg 1997).

The GI Bill became law on June 22, 1944, just 16 days after D-Day and the invasion of Normandy. Not everyone welcomed the G.I. Bill. As with earlier college movements, there were fears that it "watered down" a college degree. In today's language, this might translate into saying it "dumbed down" the college experience. Some of the movies during this time, such as *An Apartment for Peggy* (1948) show the culture clash that ensued when G.I.s showed up on the college quad. In this movie, a bunch of crass and rowdy G.I.s arrive on a serene and historic campus and start to turn the place upside down. College in 1947 was a totally different world from college in 1944. In a very short period of time many of the old institutions were doing things they could not imagine just a few years earlier.

The G.I. Bill was a tsunami for American higher education. The number of students enrolled in colleges and universities went from about 150,000 in 1940 to close to 500,000 in 1950 (Greenberg 1997). Not only did the numbers climb sky high, but the race, age and experience of the students radically shifted. This was a continuation of the democratization of higher education in the spirit of the Morrill Act that is still going on today. This growing tendency is still at the heart of the controversy about the definition of higher education.

THE DEBATE ABOUT ACCESS
AND RELEVANCE

In 1947, the Truman Commission on Higher Education stated national goals so forcefully that it began a debate whose echoes are still heard in discussions of higher education (Hutcheson 2002). The debate is about quality, excellence, cost and graduation rates. In 1947, it was access, relevance and opening the doors of higher education. The Commission recommended that the number of students in college should double by 1960. The plan was to go from 2.4 million in 1947 to 4.6 million in 1960. This radical ramping up of numbers was in the shadow of the surge of G.I.s just two years earlier that had radically transformed college life (Hutcheson 2002). The Commission reasoned that 49% of the American population were capable of, and could benefit from, a college education. This was a radical challenge to the higher education establishment that was asked to be more responsive than it had ever been in the past.

You may be surprised to know that as far back as 1947, college costs were seen as a barrier to those who were not in the upper echelons of society. The Truman Commission argued that college should be more affordable. Educators were also concerned that colleges could not grow fast enough to meet the demand needed for America's future. The Commission claimed that race, economic status, gender and religion were mitigating factors in limiting college enrollment.

In 1947, many minorities faced barriers not only to country clubs and entry-level jobs but also to the educational institutions that were seen as gateways to the professions. But it was not Blacks or Hispanics who were the central concern of the Commission. Their voices would not be a major issue in higher education for another generation. In 1947, it was the Jews who were kept out of the best schools and were limited in their educational choices because of their religion.

Women were also marginalized in higher education in America from its very beginnings. By 1947, not much had changed, and there was a widespread belief among many in higher education that women did not belong in college.

The Truman Commission also wanted future teachers with PhDs to be trained in the art of teaching. They recognized that while PhDs were trained to do research and write articles, they were not trained as classroom teachers, a question still alive today.

There has often been a national interest at work behind the scenes in our discussions of higher education. The land-grant colleges provided the labor for the new industrial age and the settlement of the West. This was necessary for America to compete. Part of the rationale for the G.I. Bill of 1944 was to avoid a repeat of the veteran's bonus riots following the First World War. So, education was important for national purposes. This has not changed in our time. In the digital revolution, the nation with the best educational system will be the most competitive. The talent wars have become global. The nation with the most educated citizenry will have a distinct advantage. So, it is crucial for the federal government to invest in higher education for the future of the Republic.

THE COLD WAR'S INFLUENCE ON HIGHER EDUCATION

During the Eisenhower administration, the concerns over higher education became more acute. President Eisenhower produced yet another commission to study the problem. However, the bigger event of the Eisenhower administration was the launch by the Soviet Union of the Sputnik satellite. The Cold War was at its peak, with both sides having enough nuclear weapons to deter the other. The policy was called MAD for "mutually assured destruction." The policy worked as long as one side did not have the advantage to make a decisive first strike that could paralyze the retaliatory ability of the other. When the Soviets showed they could put a satellite over our nation, it was interpreted as meaning that they could eventually arm those satellites with weapons. How did the Soviets beat us into space? How did they get this advantage? It was argued that the Soviets had beaten us into space because they had a superior educational system. The reaction by the United States was swift and focused (Hutcheson 2007b).

In 1958, the National Defense Education Act was passed to make sure our graduates could help us win the Cold War. You may be surprised to find the words "defense" and "education" in the title of the same law. It emphasized foreign languages, intelligence skills and science (Urban 2010). These were areas of competition between the United States and Russia.

The National Defense Education Act was controversial for a number of reasons (Urban 2010). In the previous year, Sputnik stunned the nation. In addition, the number of engineering and math graduates in America was not keeping up with the demands of our growing science and technology needs. The government used the carrot of funding to move colleges in the direction of better instruction in math and science. But there was also a stick attached to this Act. There was a loyalty oath included where colleges had to swear that if they accepted the funds, they would promise not to attempt the overthrow of the government of the United States. Some schools such as Yale refused the funds because of the onerous restrictions onacademic freedom (Urban 2010). The American Association of University Professors objected strongly to the language and restrictions of this Act.

The National Defense Education Act was repealed during the Kennedy administration, but Kennedy had another agenda and new concerns. Kennedy established his Task Force on Education in 1960 out of concern for the dropping scores of college graduates (Lyons and Drew 2006). But Kennedy's administration was cut short and it was up to the following president, Lyndon Johnson, to take the next step forward.

THE HIGHER EDUCATION ACT OF 1965

The next big event in the expansion of higher education was put forward by the Johnson administration in the form of the Higher Education Act of 1965, known popularly as the HEA. With the introduction of Title IV funding, the federal government sought to improve the output of college graduates. The HEA was part and parcel of Johnson's "Great Society" push. He saw education as catalyzing a movement of more Americans out of poverty and into affluence. The HEA has been so popular that it has been reauthorized many times since. But before it can be reauthorized, there is almost always a national debate on what is wrong with higher education and what needs to be improved. The next reauthorization will occur in 2013, and the conversations and skirmishes around this have been going strong.

The Act – signed into law 18 years after the Truman Commission – attempted to enact many of its recommendations by tying them into funding. Title IV funding, to a certain extent, was a way that the federal government could reach into colleges and use the funding as both a carrot and a stick to move higher education along the dual roads to excellence and equality (Hutcheson 2007b). With Title IV, the federal government went from offering recommendations to funding colleges, as long as they began to evolve to meet the social needs envisioned.

By 1970, at the height of the Vietnam War, when being enrolled in college could constitute a deferment that would keep a young man out of combat, the percentage of high school students attending college had risen to 53%. Currently, more than 60% of high school graduates go on to enroll in a college or university (Newfield 2008).

When the Higher Education Act was reauthorized in 1972, a major change occurred. Instead of giving funds directly to the university, the government guaranteed loans directly to the students. So, students had a greater choice about where they attend college. This huge investment of taxpayer dollars fueled an impulse in the federal government to assess higher education to see what they were getting for their investment. The strings attached to the federal funding would prove very important in American higher education as it gave the federal government a large say in what was being taught and how we were to measure success.

A NATION AT RISK IN THE 1980S AND 1990S

Democratic and Republican administrations have both agreed that higher education needs regulation and reform, but the aims and remedies they have sought are quite different. In 1983, President Reagan's National Commission on Excellence in Education produced the document "A Nation at Risk: The Imperative for Educational Reform." This report was written in such a way as to produce a lot of ink in the popular press and much political debate (Hutcheson 2007b). It saw our schools as falling behind and not being competitive. Reagan's Secretary of Education, T.H. Bell, was convinced that our higher education system was not competitive in a global economy.

The report expressed a concern about the effectiveness of pedagogy at all levels of American education, including college.

In the 1980s, the battle over the college curriculum took on a political flavor with the so-called culture wars or canon wars (Bolton 1992). This battle took the form of questions about which texts were selected and how they were taught. The conservative wing pointed back to a golden age when students were better educated and better prepared for the world of work. The liberal wing saw college as a way to advance the social agenda of inclusion advocated so many years ago by the Truman Commission. This was a time when questions of what should be included in liberal arts or general education requirements were reexamined. There was a movement for cultural literacy that would teach those things essential for us to share in order that we can form and sustain a democracy (Hirsch 1988). There were also assaults on the left as having an overly strong influence upon higher education (Bloom 1988). Bloom and company worried that ideas like "relevance" and "inclusion" were having a negative impact on the teaching of philosophy, the classics and great books (Bloom 1988). Questions were raised as to what constitutes the great books and whether or not they included more women authors, people of color and other groups that had previously been marginalized in the canon.

THE 2005 SPELLINGS COMMISSION

Things got more interesting in 2005 with the Commission on the Future of Higher Education, also known as the Spellings Commission, named after George W. Bush's Secretary of Education, Margaret Spellings. The Spellings Commission got the attention of the higher education community by the force of its rhetoric and focus of its questions. The Commission continued the same line of questioning that the Truman Commission of 1947 had articulated so clearly, but now the focus was not so much on affordability and access. It had shifted the focus to accountability and quality (Ruben 2008).

It is important to see the Spellings Commission in the shadow of the culture wars of the 1980s and 1990s. The same conservative critics that saw higher education as deviating from fundamental American values now had the power of the pulpit. Globalization was much on the minds of politicians who found statistic after statistic to support their view that America was falling behind and not staying competitive.

THE ECONOMIC MELTDOWN OF 2008

The debates on the failure of higher education have often mirrored larger political issues. In the age of Sputnik, it was the failure of science education. In the Reagan revolution, it was the failure of the liberal professoriate. In the economic meltdown of 2008, the focus became the question of cost. In 2008, the so-called housing bubble began a series of financial crises that impacted our financial institutions and spread to availability of credit and then to the whole society. Articles began to appear on students who had taken out large college loans, were now unemployed and could not repay their loans. In simple terms, people began to question if college was worth the price. For many years, the economics of universities were such that the price of tuition and fees rose faster than the price of inflation. Combine this with the stagnation of middle-class wages against price inflation, and you have the perfect storm.

As the middle class has seen their lifestyle and prospects slip, there is a lot of anger and blame to go around. The outsourcing of jobs overseas did not help. The concentration of wealth in the top tier did not help. But many people blamed their college education for costing too much and not delivering the lifestyle they expected. For a long time, part of the myth of social mobility was that a college education gave you a ticket to a certain lifestyle. For the first time, a generation of Americans would not be as rich and secure as their parents. This called into question the American Dream and with it the value of a college education.

FOCUS ON FOR-PROFITS

Cost continued to be a factor as the Obama administration came into office in 2009. But its focus was narrower. Members of the Obama administration's Education Department, such as Robert Shireman, had a history of criticism of for-profit higher education. Studies have shown that shortly after Obama came into office, the number of negative articles on for-profit education increased substantially (Gramling 2011). Much of their energies were focused on correcting the abuses of this sector, egged on by the state and non-profit colleges that had borne the brunt of the same criticism in so many past commissions.

Shortly after Obama's Department of Education began to take a close look at the for-profits, the Senate Committee on Health, Education, Labor and Pensions, known as the HELP Committee, under the direction of Iowa Senator Tom Harkin, began a series of hearings focused on the for-profits, which took a very hard line on their performance and value. Suddenly the critique of higher education as costly and not delivering what it promised since colonial times was laid at the door of a sector that educated only 11% of the students. The hearings began with testimony from short seller hedge fund manager Steven Eisman, who is famous for profiting on other sectors that had collapsed. Eisman was given the national spotlight to attack an industry he was widely believed to have shorted right before the Democrats gave him the national spotlight. It has never been disclosed how much he shorted the stocks or when he did it. There were claims he had secret meetings ahead of the hearings to get inside information to make his trades. He never had to reveal what his positions were in the industry he was given the spotlight to attack. But the Senate gave him the bully pulpit, and only he and the Senate staff knew it was coming.

A NEW DEBATE ABOUT INCLUSION AND QUALITY

The history of higher education in America is a tug of war between the desire for inclusion and the desire to maintain quality. One of the most maddening aspects of higher education in America is the lack of oversight that has allowed for abuses of the system. At the same time, this lack of oversight has allowed for the diversity of American institutions to flourish.

We believe the lack of central standards is a good thing. A freshman engineering student at MIT has different needs than a 35-year-old single mother starting a nursing degree at night at a community college. Any talk of national standards, comparing numbers or common comparisons, misses this fundamental truth. The richness of our system has been the direct result of its unregulated diversity. To repeat what we noted earlier, the word "education" is not mentioned in the Constitution. Maybe the Founding Fathers knew something we did not know.

CHAPTER SIX
THE QUARREL BETWEEN THE
ANCIENTS AND MODERNS

Remembrance of things past is not necessarily the remembrance of things as they were.

– Marcel Proust

Following in a historical sense about how our higher education system has evolved, we think it is important to review a classic argument that goes back to ancient Greece and is still on the hearts and minds of educators today. We start this review, however, during the Renaissance, when a debate broke out between the sciences and humanities. This debate began with the rediscovery of ancient sources of wisdom, when at the very same time a new scientific spirit was rising. During the Renaissance, there were great scientific advances in astronomy, physics and what later became known as chemistry.

THE HISTORIC DEBATE BETWEEN THE SCIENCES AND THE HUMANITIES

In 1959, C.P. Snow gave the influential, annual Rede Lecture at the University of Cambridge in which he talked about two cultures that divided higher education. The two cultures were the sciences and the humanities. It was his thesis that this bifurcated way of thinking got in the way of how we understood things. Was one superior to the other? Should science always be our guide? Are there things learned from the humanities that cannot be obtained in other ways?

The question here is a simple and historic one. Did the ancients have some profound and esoteric wisdom that we cannot hope to understand or approximate, or has science and progress made us much smarter than they were? This *Querelle des Anciens et des Modernes* began in the seventeenth century, and its impact has been felt every single day in discussions about the use and future of the university (Levine 1999).

We start in 1687, when Charles Perrault read a poem at the French Academy. The work *Le Siecle de Louis le Grand* argued that the modern world had produced great things that were equal to anything the ancients had produced, most notably Homer (Levine 1999). A heated argument ensued, and a number of eminent members of the *Academie Francaise*, including Jean Racine, walked out in protest. A series of books and pamphlets followed, taking sides with either the ancients or the moderns. In the end, a kind of truce was achieved by granting superiority in science to the moderns and superiority in art to the ancients (Levine 1999).

A similar battle broke out in England a few years later in 1690 that has been remembered as the "Battle of the Books." It began when Sir William Temple published *An Essay upon the Ancient and Modern Learning* where he praised the ancients and denigrated modern writing (Levine 1999).

As we have noted, nostalgia is present in many of the debates about the role and future of higher education (Hass and Fishman 2010). The debates around the "Quarrel" and the "Battle of the Books" reveal that when background noise comes to the foreground, so does the role of nostalgia come into the debate about higher education.

A DETOUR THROUGH ATHENS, ROME AND THE ARAB WORLD

The quarrel between the ancients and the moderns has its roots in the loss and recovery of certain key works, mainly by Greek and Roman authors (Yates 1991). To understand this dispute and its bearing on the modern university, we must take a detour into texts, empires, translations and heresy.

In the chaos that followed the fall of the Roman Empire, many of the classic texts of literature, science and philosophy did not survive in the West. The burning and looting of libraries, both ecclesiastical and private, by Ostragoths, Visagoths, Huns and Vikings threatened to destroy any link to our ancient past. While a number of monasteries, especially around the great cathedrals that kept libraries and scriptoriums (literally "writing rooms"), kept many books alive, many others were lost in what Daniel Boorstin, the head of the Smithsonian, has called the "Great Interruption" (Boorstin 1985). In his wonderful work, *The Ancient Libraries of Canterbury and Dover*, Professor Montague Rhodes James gave us tour of what these libraries were like (James 1903). They have come more recently into American popular culture through the fictional book *The Name of the Rose* by Umberto Eco.

The monastic libraries existed within complex political positions. They existed in an age where the threat of heresy could mean torture and death, but the librarians of this time were men of learning who must have surely been curious. Imagine the tension that existed within those walls.

The Medieval period was not as simple and monolithic as we once thought. The ascension of faith meant that reason, logic and argument lost the place of prominence they had to the pagan thinkers of the classical world. The Carthaginian church father Quintus Septimius Florens Tertullian (160–225 A.D.) once famously asked, "What has Athens to do with Jerusalem?" and "What has the academy to do with the church?" The wisdom of Plato and Aristotle had no place in the life of the church or its faithful. Other early church fathers, such as Saint Jerome and Saint Augustine, were equally strong about their doubts about the usefulness of philosophy and the sciences (Coplestone 2003). The idea of tossing out the old because it has been replaced by something newer and more relevant occurs over and over again in the history of the academy.

The Catholic hierarchy, based in Rome, stunted the growth of the seven liberal arts which are divided into the Trivium and Quadrivium. The Trivium consists grammar, rhetoric and logic. The Quadrivium consists of arithmetic, geometry, music and astromomy. This slowed down scientific inquiry (Boorstin 1985). At the very same time in history, the so-called "barbarian" Tartars of the Mogul Empire encouraged speculation, scholarship and the exchange of ideas (Boorstin 1985). But the story is more complex. While the Roman church was slow to move, it also had an essential role in the preservation of texts and the conservation of ancient wisdom (Yates 1991). Its role increased dramatically after the fall of Rome that can be dated to 476 A.D. when the Germanic leader Odovacer replaced the last Roman Emperor, Romulus Augustulus.

In these trying and dark times, travel became unsafe and the empire broke into pieces. Knowledge of Greek declined and so did the care of Greek and Latin pagan texts. Many of these texts were written on papyrus that was degrading (much like microfiche and celluloid film in our day). These works needed to be copied onto parchment, which was not cheap, to be maintained. After the fall of Rome, the libraries of Byzantium were still operating, but they focused almost exclusively on religious texts (Murray 2009).

It was a very different story in the Arab world. In Damascus, under the control of the Umayyad, works were being studied and translated during the eighth century. During the first centuries of the Abbasid Caliphate (749–1258), translations of Greek into Arabic and the preservation of texts became a whole industry (Murray 2009). Many of the works of Aristotle, Plato, Plotinus and a host of others have been preserved and handed down to us thanks to the efforts of these libraries and translators. It may be noted in passing that the Arab leaders were much more tolerant than their Christian counterparts when these works were saved for posterity. Logical treatises such as Aristotle's *Categories*, *De Intepretatione*, *Prior Analytics*, *Topics*, *Physics* and *Rhetoric* were deemed worthy to be saved along with Porphyry's *Isagoge* and almost the entire corpus of Plato (Black 1990).

PLATO, ARISTOTLE AND THE NOTION OF IDEALISTS AND REALISTS

From the eleventh to the thirteenth centuries, Christians won back portions of Europe, Asia and Africa that were previously ruled by the Arabs. When the Christians arrived in Spain and Sicily, they discovered the great libraries with a treasure trove of texts in places such as Toledo, Salamanca, Palermo and Catania. Scholars such as William of Moerbeke (1215–1286) translated philosophical, scientific and medical texts directly into Latin, which sparked a revolution in thinking and learning in the West.

But it was a vegetarian priest from Florence who really helped reintroduce the works of the ancient philosophers to the Western tradition. Father Marsilio Ficino (1433–1499) translated the Platonic works into Latin under the patronage of the Medici family (Allen 1984). With the rediscovery of classic texts, the classic philosophers Plato and Aristotle again entered the conversation. It was said by Samuel Taylor Coleridge that everyone is born either a Platonist or Aristotelian. This is tantamount to saying we are instinctively either idealists or realists. The introduction of these works helped expand conversations about theology, theories of truth and the role of empirical investigation. At the same time, advances in astronomy, chemistry, physics and mathematics were also blossoming.

One of the ideas that Plato and Aristotle agreed upon was the value of the life of the mind and its superiority to the life of action. Thinking for its own sake was the goal, and any action done for other reasons is somehow less valuable (Coplestone 2003). Questions about the usefulness of a college degree, and how and why we emphasize research and questions about the application of knowledge in and out of the university all have their roots in the Platonic–Aristotelian theories about thinking and how it is superior to physical work.

How has the history of speculative thought played out over the past two thousand years? Both Plato and Aristotle wrote on education, and both had a profound effect on education as it evolved. Plato was the student of Socrates, and one could argue that education has not advanced far from the origins that Socrates provided for us. Based in the dialectical logic of argument, the Socratic method is still a powerful tool for teaching. Beginning with an empirical skepticism (Socrates claimed, somewhat ironically, that the only thing he knew was that he knew nothing) Socrates explored the assumptions of any claim made in his presence. The Socratic method began with a question. When the question was answered that answer was parsed for exceptions, contradictions, or misapplications. The burden is on the student and the teacher questions the student's answer and asks the student to articulate arguments to defend her position. The teacher is not central but the student is. In this way, it is not the transmission of facts from student to teacher but the teacher coaching the student to improve the argument and evidence. This technique is popular in many college classrooms to this day.

But Plato was not content to stay with the simple skepticism of his teacher. Plato went on to construct rather complex theories of metaphysics, epistemology, ethics and education that influenced his pupil Aristotle and all who came after. The Harvard Philosopher, Alfred North Whitehead, once said that all of Western Philosophy is nothing but a footnote to Plato (Whitehead 1970).

The core of Plato's educational philosophy is found in his work *The Republic*. The subtitle of the work is *On Justice*. Why would a work on justice devote most of the dialogue to education? Because the state is made of citizens, and the education of citizens is essential for the success of the state. While Plato did have a hierarchy of social classes, he understood each need to be educated so that the state could function harmoniously.

When he looked at the states that existed in his time in the ancient world, Plato could find no satisfactory model for a just state. Each of the existing states was based on some kind of unjust distribution of power or goods. So, he decided to produce an ideal state, what he called a "city in speech" wherein he would construct a society to his liking. Plato divided his city in speech into three classes named after metals; gold, silver and bronze. Citizens were born into these classes, and it was very hard to move from one class to the other. The bronze or lowest class was comprised of craftsmen, farmers and manual laborers. Their education was designed to give them the skills they needed to perform these tasks. The next level of education was the silver. This was the warrior class who guarded the state. They needed a different skill set. Out of the warrior class came the guardians or leaders of the society that Plato thought of as the gold class. The guardians or rulers were selected for their wisdom. Plato called them the philosopher kings. He famously said there would not be justice until the rulers become philosophers and the philosophers become the rulers. In short, in Plato's ideal city, the classes were not equal. The hierarchy went from the physical at the low end to the intellectual on the high end. To keep order, the philosopher kings used what Plato termed the "noble lie." The citizens were told that their status in three classes was natural and not a social arrangement.

Aristotle, on the other hand, did not deal with an ideal city in speech. Instead, he began from the history and practicalities of everyday existence (Aristotle 1984). He still agreed with his teacher Plato that there was an ascending hierarchy from the physical to the spiritual planes. The physical labor involved in farming or mining was often performed by slaves. The name given to these routine forms of doing was *techne*. This activity was seen as less valuable than those involving more thought. Further up the scale of activity was *praxis*, which was defined as meaningful action such as taking part in politics. Slaves and foreigners were excluded from the politics of Athens. It was thought because politics determines laws that govern our lives that making and interpreting these laws is a noble and valuable activity. This was seen as impacting more people and doing more good than techne or manual labor.

Freemen (women were excluded from most intellectual and political activities in Athenian society) were also educated in the arts of poetry and music. This was called "poesis." The creation of poetry or literature adds to and in some cases can define a culture. Contributing to culture was seen as something useful. The creation of art, literature and music has been at the heart of many of the great civilizations. To make and appreciate something beautiful is an end in itself. And finally, there was contemplation that the Greeks called "theoria," meaning speculation (Aristotle 1984). Theoria is what philosophers do when they think about things eternal and unchanging such as truth, justice or the good.

Today, the value of pure contemplation and thinking for its own sake is not as universally accepted. The relation between action and contemplation has been turned on its head. To understand what happened, we must look at how these classical terms changed in our modern world, along with what this has meant relative to the value and design of college curricula.

Aristotle followed Plato in assigning a hierarchy in the ways of knowing, where the more mental and abstract the knowing was, the more valuable it was. This meant that thinking was more valuable than doing. Meditation and contemplation were more valued than making things. Knowledge workers were to be more valued than those who did manual labor. We even see this in the etymology of the word "manual," which comes from the Latin root *manualis*, which means "belong to the hand." On the other end of the scale, we find that *episteme*, or scientific knowledge, was one of the highest forms of human activity because it was mental and had little practical application.

ON REVOLUTIONARY AND CONSERVATIVE THINKING

The university in the medieval world was a place of both revolution and conservatism. While Thomas Aquinas saw his theological writings based on Aristotelian thinking condemned in his lifetime, his own system of philosophy eventually became Catholic dogma. Members of the Dominican order to which Aquinas belonged were forced to follow his teaching or be dismissed from their posts at the University of Paris or at Oxford (Coplestone 2003). Even more interesting, however, the Dominican order that produced such thinkers as Albert the Great and Thomas Aquinas became the lead order in the notorious Inquisition that tried to stunt any strands of new thought for generations.

But the university was always a place where conflicts were played out. At the same time that dogma was being enforced by the church, such radical thinkers as William of Occam used the university to advance both revolutionary and controversial doctrines. But the dominant paradigm was combining Aristotle's philosophical system with the revelation of the Christian scriptures and the writings of the early Church fathers such as Augustine of Hippo. The power of the church was so strong that it could not only threaten excommunication that would ruin a leader or academic, but, via the Inquisition, they had the power of life and death. Giordano Bruno was burned alive for his views. When he was taken in a cart to be burned in the Campo de Fiori in Rome, a metal spike was driven through his tongue so he could not address the crowd. The same Inquisition silenced Galileo for his support of Copernicus. One can understand how careful thinkers had to be in this kind of environment.

It is also both important and interesting to note that much of the revolutionary thinking during the Renaissance and the Enlightenment actually took place outside of the university. Many of the thinkers we spend time with in this chapter lived and wrote outside of the university.

DESCARTES AND THE CARTESIAN METHOD

The tradition of favoring the mental over the physical held sway through the Middle Age, and even in the Enlightenment it was championed in the works of Rene Descartes (1596–1650), known as the Father of Modern Philosophy. While he advanced geometry, algebra and philosophy, it was his Cartesian method that impacted how people went about investigating claims. The Medieval world relied almost entirely on quoting precedent and harmonizing thinking with the scriptures or sages from the past, Descartes chucked it all and started over. Using radical doubt as a method, he discarded all he could not absolutely prove to be true. While he took this method to extremes to make his point, it was a clear triumph of the empirical over quoting of tradition (Coplestone 2003). This was the beginning of the scientific method that came to dominate modern thinking. Descartes is also remembered for taking Platonic dualism into the modern world. His mind–body problem defined the mental or spiritual as having wholly different attributes from the physical body with its own set of attributes. He saw the mind and body as two different substances that needed different kinds of science to understand each. In his famous dictum *Cogito Ergo Sum* or "I think therefore I am," he shows us how thinking is the place where we begin. We start in the mind and not in the physical world. Descartes distinction between the mind and body gave a clear advantage to the mental. It would be many centuries before scientists would reverse this and give precedence to what can be seen and measured over what can be thought.

LOCKE AND THE EMPIRICIST TRADITION

But the revolution did not stop there. While Descartes relied upon reason and logic to found his philosophy, John Locke relied on experience, which became the foundation of the Empiricist tradition in Great Britain. His idea of the blank slate or *tabula rasa* disputed all *a priori* knowledge and showed us a real democratic tendency. We are not born noblemen or peasants; we are born equal. When Locke argued that we are all born with the same empty mind, he laid the groundwork for the political thinking that would change the way people saw authority and political obligation. Locke's writings on politics and education are so profound and clear that some of them were copied almost verbatim into the American Declaration of Independence (Stanford Encyclopedia of Philosophy 2012). Following the educational theories of John Milton and his Puritan allies, John Locke created a useful body of knowledge where application was favored over speculation (Rauch 2001). The tide of Plato and Aristotle with the superiority of the mental was beginning to recede.

Locke thought education should have a practical end and not be based on any theoretical speculations. While theology played a key role in European universities, Locke urged the teaching of more geography, math, science and economics. Locke was also focused on the education of a gentleman (Locke 1996). England was a society in which social class mattered, and the education of the ruling class concerned him. In this way, Locke followed the model of Plato. Locke advocated an education that included ethical instruction, the manners of a gentleman and skills that would prepare the student to make a practical life in addition to being educated. Locke's ideas were carried on by fellow Empiricists George Bishop Berkeley in Ireland and David Hume in Scotland. Both applied skepticism in ways that began to undermine the traditional ways of thinking.

The tradition of the Empiricists was kept alive in the Utilitarianism of Jeremy Bentham and John Stewart Mill and the Pragmatism of American philosophers such as William James and Charles Saunders Peirce. The tradition that started with Plato about the superiority of the mental would be firmly reversed by the time we got to both Marx and Nietzsche (Coplestone 2003). Marx truly stands Plato on his head by beginning with the economics and showing how that drives more abstract and theoretical constructions. Nietzsche exalts the life of action and is suspicious of hermit monk philosophers who contemplate but never enter the fray of human conflict.

FROM ROUSSEAU TO ARENDT TO TODAY

Jean-Jacques Rousseau lived and wrote on the outskirts of European intellectualism, and he is noted for attacking the whole structure of current educational thought (Bloom 1979). His belief was that civilization corrupts and does not improve. Rousseau questioned the very ideas of progress and science. He claimed that the aim of education was the freedom of the student. He believed that the student should set the agenda. The teacher is not there to run things but to be a facilitator for the student's interests. While Rousseau's thought has been influential, his emphasis on the individualization of instruction never took hold in mainstream education (Rousseau 2003).

In our own time, the roles of contemplation and action have become reversed. The twentieth century philosopher Hannah Arendt formulated the distinction between theory and practice in her early work, *The Human Condition*. She made a distinction between the contemplative life (*vita contemplativa*), which the Greek philosophers had seen as the highest form of life, the so-called life of the mind, and the active life (*vita activa*) (Arendt 1958).

Arendt saw that the products that technology and politics had produced catalyzed the good life of the modern world. She felt that meaningful action in the realm of politics was a noble way of life, and thus she tried to reverse the Platonic–Aristotelian prejudice in favor of action over theory. For her, *praxis* or meaningful action was the highest level of the active life where we improve society and act in a way that is good. If praxis is what makes us fully human, then it was essential that there be a realm of politics in which rhetoric and action by citizens actually mattered. So, for Arendt it is not the individual thinker who contemplates in the tradition of Plato and Saint Augustine but a citizen of the world engaged in meaningful action that makes things better.

As a Jew, Arendt escaped Nazi Germany where the state used authority and bureaucracy to commit murder and destroy Europe (Buckler 2011). The Nazi state stood in sharp contrast to a political sphere were individual actors with a moral code act to bring about the common good. Arendt saw the roots of Nazism in ancient hierarchies. Arendt traced the prejudice against meaningful action in the world back to the glorification of pure thought by Plato and Aristotle, which was continued into the Western tradition via the Augustinian concept of "stillness of the soul." The early Christian theologians followed the Greeks (Plato, Aristotle, Pythagoras, Epicurus) in favoring the withdrawal from action for a life of pure thought (Arendt 1958).

Arendt, however, gave us a philosophical foundation for the *vita activa*, the life of meaningful action. In her writings from the 1957 book *The Human Condition* to her last work *The Life of the Mind*, published posthumously in 1981, Arendt consistently reminded us that we were born into a world of plurality that we must navigate. She once said we are not "in the world but of the world" (Arendt 1981). She rejected the Platonic tradition that we were spirits in the material world where thinking was valued more than acting. The philosopher withdrawing from the world was no longer her ideal.

Marx and Nietzsche valued a life of action. Both were in revolt against the speculative idealism of George Wilhelm Hegel. But, for many thinkers of the time, the hierarchies still existed. Arendt valued *praxis* over *poesis*. *Praxis* existed in a historical–social context and was action involving others. *Poesis* was a kind of making and could be done by the lone artist or craftsman. Praxis could do more good in the condition of plurality, which Arendt told us was the human condition.

In *The Life of the Mind*, Arendt began her analysis with the conditions of diversity and plurality (Arendt 1981). This was the opposite of Descartes who began inside the mind with *Cogito Ergo Sum*. For Arendt, we are born into the social world to see and be seen. Because of this starting point, politics took center stage. What must the individual do to act in a meaningful political manner? They must act with a view toward the good of the whole society, which entailed an understanding of our condition of plurality, which meant living in a world of irreducibly different and conflicting viewpoints.

Arendt noticed that in the male-dominated field of philosophy, death was an important concept. She, however, emphasized birth, the birth of something new. In looking at the great moments in history, we are impressed when something new is born. Her classic example was the American Revolution, where a nation was born by the praxis of a wise political class who used *phronesis*, or practical wisdom, to create *arete*, the good for all. Nothing like America had ever existed before. The founding of our country was truly a new beginning (Wellmer 2001).

So, the quarrel between the ancients and moderns has not yet been resolved. There are thinkers for whom the modern university is an engine of economic growth with a Utilitarian function (Smith 2010). There are others who look toward a wider education with a goal similar to Cardinal Newman's notion to educate the whole person for a higher end (Bloom 1988). We think the modern university can and must serve both of these ends. In the digital age, there is no reason to choose one at the expense of the other. The debate about the superiority of contemplation over technical skill has echoes in every modern debate about higher education. The running battle of the superiority of the most abstract subjects over applied knowledge was fought during the creation of the land-grant colleges, the G.I. Bill and the birth and growth of technical and community colleges.

Community colleges have a very different aim and mission than research universities. Technical colleges have a different mission than Ivy League schools. We should not vote in favor of one model to the exclusion of others. The information revolution made the need for more extensive learning a necessity in almost every field. These social concerns must be kept in mind as we rethink the modern university. In the technological age, more of the population needs more education to be successful in an increasingly complex and technological workplace. But more importantly we must tip our hats to Plato and Newman who realized that an educated citizenry is essential for a free and successful society. The success of our nation depends upon the success of our educational system. Our collective future depends on it.

CHAPTER SEVEN
THE PROFESSOR AS CRAFTSMAN
IN THE DIGITAL AGE

Teaching is not a lost art, but the regard for it is a lost tradition.
— Jacques Barzun

The architecture and social practices of the university classroom has remained very much the same since its beginning at the University of Bologna in 1088 to the present day (Hunt 2008). Contemporary American college or university classrooms resemble the classrooms of Salamanca or Oxford from a millennium ago. A medieval university had classrooms with teachers standing in front of students. The view from the lectern in the medieval university was rows and rows of students in desks taking notes about what the professor said. Things have not progressed very far, until now.

From the beginning, professors did their work in isolation from other professors. Professors were alone in a classroom with their students as they were alone in their research and scholarship. From the beginning of the European university, there was little team teaching and there was little evidence that teams created syllabi together (Hunt 2008). While a few classes used the Socratic method, science labs, periods of disputation and study groups, the main method of delivery in the university was the solo lecture (Brown and Rice 2008).

THE PROFESSOR AS LECTURER WORKING IN ISOLATION

Each professor is an individual craftsman, and one of the products he produces is the lecture. Like craftsmen who make pots, paintings or unique furniture pieces, lectures are the products of each individual professor's creation. They are solely responsible for the content and form of their lectures, which are not verified or checked by anyone else. Just as other craftsmen work in isolation as experts in their given field, so do professors.

The first faculty guild was thought to be at the University of Paris, where the faculty governed the university. From that time to the present, faculty governance has been an essential hallmark of institutions of higher education. Faculty members hold the power in higher education because they have the expertise manifested in their lectures. Students would come to universities to hear the lectures of famous professors. Thus, the professor as craftsman and the university as faculty governed are linked historically.

Even though the lecture is a solitary activity, a "good" lecturer is often thought of as a "good" teacher. Teaching was measured and valued in the early literature of the university (Graff 1989). The lecture was and still is a one-time event that has to be scheduled at a particular time and place. Three credit hours of a college class are typically three hours of lecture a week.

All lectures are similar to performance art that cannot be captured in writing because they vary from one class to another. A good cabinet-maker may be able to recognize the work of another craftsman in the same field. Great craftsmen leave their mark with their own distinctive style. In the long history of the university, there was no mass production of the lecture and there was no way to exactly capture the style of great lecturers.

PROFESSORS' UNIQUENESS

The professor's work is distinguished from all others by the uniqueness of her personality and style. Just as a woodworker is limited by the quality of the wood she works with or a sculptor by the quality of the marble, so must a teacher adapt to the quality of the student body. An English 101 course in the most elite Ivy League university is a very different course than English 101 in an urban community college weekend class for working adults.

A professor may teach the same course year after year as well as teach more than one section of the same course in the same semester. Professors often talk of the number of preparations they have, meaning number of unique courses that they are teaching. In a typical American college or university, a professor may teach four courses a semester, three sections of introduction to chemistry, for example, and one section of organic chemistry. Or a professor may teach three sections of introduction to art history and one section of the Impressionists. While professors often use notes, they vary the lectures within those notes (Brown and Rice 2008). Just as every chest of drawers a cabinet-maker constructs is unique and singular, so too each lecture a professor gives in each section of the same course is unique and singular. Because of this, the classroom is an ephemeral event that cannot be captured except in the notes of the teacher and students. This ephemeral event in time is the work of a singular artist. The great teachers had a unique style that might be compared to a chair designed by Frank Lloyd Wright that shows his unique artistic signature. So, professors deliver lectures in unique ways, and their work cannot be tampered with by anyone.

PROFESSORS NOT TRAINED TO TEACH

It is not commonly known by the public that many college professors arrive at the university with no training in pedagogy. Professors are trained to be researchers and not teachers. So, while there is training in how to do scholarship, footnote articles, solve problems and decipher texts, there is no formal training in pedagogy. Professors learn on the job as they teach. In most graduate schools, there is little or no discussion of grade books, classroom management or learning theory unless you take your degree in education, where it is the primary subject matter.

If professors are not trained to teach, how do they learn the craft of teaching? Most learn to teach through their work as a graduate assistant or through an informal apprenticeship during their first university or college position. But this is not quite the same as a typical on-the-job training exercise in business and industry. It may be wrong to even use the word "apprenticeship" in this context. The difficulty in calling it an apprenticeship is that from day one, each professor works mostly alone. From the first day they arrive at the university, professors are alone in class, beginning to develop their unique and singular teaching style. Even though most have not been formally trained in pedagogy, it is assumed they have the skills to teach.

NEW WAYS TO COMPARE
TEACHING AND LEARNING

This is how higher education evolved and has stayed for almost one thousand years, with nothing to compare the classroom to except another classroom. A professor could only be compared to another professor. Until just a few decades ago, this was how teaching and learning progressed. Until just a few decades ago, all discussions about teaching and learning were subjective. What was good teaching for one student, or at one institution, may not have been viewed similarly by another student, or at another institution. It was impossible to define a good class, a bad class or good versus bad teaching and learning. It was all a matter of opinion; as in the old Latin expression *De gustibus non disputandum est*: taste cannot be disputed.

With the creation of the online course, something very dramatic happened that can perhaps be considered the biggest revolution in the history of the university. With online learning came a new and different kind of classroom, a classroom without walls and with a dashboard that any member of the course could read from any location where there was an Internet connection. In addition, because the activities of the entire course could be recorded, the ability to compare one course to another became a distinct capability.

While there are similarities, there are also differences between the traditional brick-and-mortar classroom and the digital classroom. It is not our place here to review the extensive literature on the differences between the two and arguments over whether or not one is superior to the other. Instead, our focus is on one facet of the digital classroom: the digital classroom leaves a fingerprint of the activities of an entire class inside a public document in a way that the physical, traditional classroom was never capable of accomplishing.

Of course, it can be said that brick-and-mortar classrooms also leave a record, primarily in the form of the professor's notes, the class syllabi and/or student notes. However, no standard exists for either college syllabi or professor notes. If there are best practices in these areas, they are not widely known or widely followed. Further, student notes are notoriously unreliable, as anyone knows who has tried to reconstruct a professor's lecture by comparing different student notes. Student notes are oftentimes more about those subjects of interest to the student than an objective interpretation of the teacher's lecture.

Online courses leave a record of every interaction between both professors and students. With the arrival of online education, educators can now make efforts to measure the difference between physical classrooms and digital courses. For the first time in the history of the university, the course leaves a record that is an objective result of its many interactions.

What is the difference between the old traditional class and the new online course? A database from an online course features interaction from a discussion board, for example, where we can easily find patterns. In week one of an online course, for instance, 100 discussion posts between students and an instructor were displayed and easily viewed electronically. Let us say in week two we found a similar number of posts. Imagine that in week three the number discussion posts dropped to less than 25. While the sheer quantitative data did not provide a definitive answer as to why interactions declined, it did provide an indication that something changed. While it may have been exam week or Spring break, it may also have been an indication that the lecture was not structured correctly, or that the students were having difficulty with the material or some other issue that could be analyzed and corrected for future courses. This kind of granularity was not possible in the traditional brick-and-mortar classroom.

ON DATA TRAILS AND MORE

But this is only the beginning of the difference between physical classrooms and digital courses. With the growth of data collection and predictive analytics, we are now able to take the data from the online course, analyze that data and draw a variety of conclusions and prognostications. We can map out the interactions between teachers and students, apply them to complex data gathering systems and ultimately see where students are succeeding and failing (Huba 2000). The data trail shows us where and how students respond to questions, the elements of tests where the vast majority of students have difficulty and where the instruction could be clearer for the benefit of the learning. Assessment in digital courses can be done with more rigor because there is more data. All this leads to new questions. What does the birth of the online course mean for the future of the university? How will it impact the role of the professor?

For the first time, what is being taught and learned can be looked at by a number of people using data, not opinion. With the digital course, the focus has turned from teaching, which is ephemeral and subjective, to learning, which can be measured in a more rigorous way. As Robert Barr explained:

> A paradigm shift is taking hold in American higher education. In its briefest form, the paradigm that has governed our colleges is this: A college is an institution that exists to provide instruction. Subtly but profoundly we are shifting to a new paradigm: A college is an institution that exists to produce learning. This shift changes everything (Barr and Tagg 1995).

FROM LONELY CRAFTSMAN
TO TEAM MEMBER

The Industrial Revolution brought the move from individual craftsman to factory worker and changed the whole concept of work. The craftsman no longer worked alone in his shop. He had to commute to work. The concept of time changed, as now a team of workers had to begin and end at the same time of the day.

The change from professor as craftsman to professor as team member is, in part, a direct result of the digital revolution. The electronic record generated by an online course can be worked on by a team of experts and learning theorists who can use the data to ultimately create and implement new types of more effective teaching and learning environments.

AN EXAMPLE OF AN ONLINE FOR-PROFIT'S USE OF DATA

An example of how data can be used can be found at the American Public University System, where there are more than 100,000 students and 2,000 professors. The course delivery method at the American Public University System is 100% online. The online format provides the university with a large chunk of data that can be used to see how learning is progressing. The university uses analytics to analyze the number of drops, number of withdrawals and number of failures, class-by-class, program-by-program and school-by-school. They then compare these numbers to university averages, school averages and program averages. For example, the failure rate in Arabic I may be much higher than in a History of Popular Culture course, but that is not an indication of one course being superior to another. However, if we were to look at History 101 and discovered that in one section taught by one professor the number of drops, withdrawals and failing grades was triple the rest of the program, this would be a starting point for a discussion about the course.

A rigorous teacher is not necessarily a bad teacher, but we must keep in mind the goal of the course is student learning. If that is not taking place, it is the responsibility of the university to ask "why." In addition, the American Public University System uses national benchmarked tests by Princeton's Educational Testing Service (ETS), such as the Proficiency Profile, the Major Field Tests, in various majors as well as the National Survey of Student Engagement (NSSE). These national tests administered by a third party reveal how the American Public University System graduates and students stack up against other colleges and other programs.

At the end of each semester, the university uses the Community of Inquiry (COI) end-of-class survey to measure the indirect experience of the student. The COI is a scientifically validated instrument that has been taken by more than 500,000 online students and was designed to measure the efficacy of the online course (Boston, Diaz, Ice, Gibson, Richardson and Swan 2010). This instrument looks at three kinds of presences at work in the online classroom: social presence, teaching presence and cognitive presence. Social presence measures how much social engagement there is among students and faculty in the course as a learning environment. Teaching presence measures the student's perception of the effectiveness of the teacher as leader of the course. Cognitive presence measures the student's opinion of how successful the course has been designed and set up as a learning environment. By separating these three kinds of presence, we can see if any problems in the course are the result of the course design, the instructor or the content of the course. By looking at classroom drops, withdrawals and failing grades, the university gets the first view of the class. When they combine this with the ETS data and the COI data, the American Public University System begins to get a more complete picture of the online course. In addition, the school uses the National Survey of Student Engagement or NSSE to see how students perceive their educational experience. By mixing direct and indirect measures, we can come up with a picture of how students are doing and how they perceive they are doing, which is sometimes two very different things. The authors have had numerous conversations during the writing of this book with faculty who claim what is essential cannot be measured, and by measuring we are measuring the wrong things. We believe that data is the starting point and its interpretation must take into account the uniqueness of the institution, major and faculty member. Data cannot produce wisdom but it is a starting point.

The American Public University System's examination into effective online teaching and learning does not end here. Using IBM's SPSS Modeler and predictive analytics, the American Public University System has analyzed more than 50 variables of student data, such as gender, age, GPA, number of credits transferred in and so on. They can use this data to predict which students are likely to succeed and which need intervention. Other universities are using similar measures to manage student success with varying degrees of accuracy.

DECENTRALIZING THE PROFESSORSHIP

If, through data analysis, we are now able to challenge the idea that professors in biology, psychology and philosophy may not be experts in teaching, we also challenge the fundamental idea of the university. The digital course brings new tools and new roles for the professor (Christensen and Eyring 2011). The course as a communal document that can be shared and analyzed by non-experts in the field decentralizes the professor. As this happens, the very concept of the power of faculty is tested. Remember that the expertise of the professor and faculty governance have been historically linked. To challenge one is to challenge the other and this is a fundamental shift in our thinking about the university.

Since the birth of online education, there has been a significant hostility to digital courses by members of the professorship. Suddenly, cheating online has become an issue, when it has always been an issue throughout the history of higher education. Suddenly, there were questions about the quality of online learning, when such questions apply just as well to the traditional classroom.

For the first time in the history of the university, there is public record of the class that can be accessed by those who are not experts in the field. This changes the balance of power and the structure of teaching. It changes how we think about grading. It challenges some long held beliefs about academic freedom.

The digital universities have redefined the role of the traditional professor (Donoghue 2008). The digital revolution has redefined the role of faculty in assessing learning. We have looked at the metaphor of the professor as craftsman and his craft was teaching. There was no objective measure to compare one craftsman to another. The online professor does something wholly different. He or she can be viewed as a digital collaborator who is a partner in a learning enterprise with measurable results that can be compared to other courses. This is a seismic revolution that has only begun to be felt in the academy and whose impact has only begun to be understood.

The professoriate has been decimated in recent decades. In searching for a heart and soul of a university, it cannot be found anywhere but in a strong faculty voice and shared governance. We do not believe that the change in classroom practice should be the end of faculty governance involving academic decisions. We think there should be a Chinese Wall between administrative functions involving the business of a modern complex university and its academic life. Ops, CIOs and CFOs have to be free to make decisions that involve complex computer programs or tax codes. But when their influence extends into matters academic, we are no longer talking about a university but a business. Faculty governance can and must survive in some form. There are experts on both sides but the university has suffered when one group or the other has the only say. We will flesh out these thoughts in the upcoming chapters.

PART III

HOW THE DIGITAL AGE CHANGED ACCREDITATION, ACADEMIC FREEDOM AND GOVERNANCE

*H*ere, we describe some of the very important factors that are defining the new digital university. For one, it is important to understand that many unique colleges and universities dot the American landscape. Most of their success is dependent upon their ability to garner accreditation status, most significantly regional accreditation status.

Regional accreditation, however, has recently been under attack, due to an ongoing debate between the federal government and academia that started with a kind of accreditation fiasco that happened at two for-profit institutions, the American Intercontinental University (AIU) and Bridgepoint Higher Education.

Again, we draw on many historical cases as well as current precedents to prove our point that higher education is dealing with some hefty issues and challenges because of the birth of the digital university. We proclaim that academic freedom and historic governance by faculty have been altered beyond recognition through the hiring of new business managers who use high-tech data analysis as the basis for enormous change.

The digital revolution has accelerated a decline in faculty power and created a new class of professional managers that has been empowered by their digital and managerial expertise. This has happened in all sectors of higher education, including for-profits, state universities and privates. Rethinking the university in the digital age will mean asking how faculty power can be preserved in an era of the establishment of a new managerial class that has its roots outside of the university.

What is needed now is a synthesis that respects the traditional role that faculty play in academic leadership while at the same time modernizing the university for the digital age.

We conclude Part III with a look inside what we call the BLT governance schema, which is defined by a Bureaucracy Centered Model (B-governance), a Learning Centered Model (L-governance), or a Teacher Centered Model (T-governance). L-governance is described in the most detail as the model for finding a much-needed balance between business and academia.

CHAPTER EIGHT
DIVERSITY AND OVERSIGHT
IN HIGHER EDUCATION

Education consists mainly of what we have unlearned.
— Mark Twain

There is an old story about a village in ancient India where six blind men lived. One day they heard there was an elephant in the village, and none of them had ever encountered an elephant. Because they could not see, each one touched a different part of the elephant. The first one felt his solid legs and said the elephant was like a column in a temple. The second man felt the tail and said the elephant seemed to him like a rope. The third one felt his swinging trunk and said it was like a snake and so on. They argued and could not decide who was right. A wise old Yogi came and told them that each of them was partly right. But the elephant was more than any of the parts they had touched.

Much of the confusion today in our approach to higher education is that we are thinking about it in the same way that the six blind men thought about the elephant. The term "higher education" is deceptive in that it looks like it means one thing when it should probably be "higher educationS" because it denotes so many things. When we hear prescriptions of what needs to be done to "fix" higher education, we are amazed, because prescriptions alone cannot take in the rich tapestry of American higher education.

There is no central Ministry of Education in America that insures quality and standards as there is in some other countries (Rudolph and Thelin 1991). Higher education in America has been a freewheeling affair and this has made it a knife that cuts both ways. We have some of the finest universities in the world, and, at the same time, the quality of our second- and third-tier colleges is often judged as below average. Any calls for national standards are almost impossible to implement in higher education today. However, this has not stopped state and federal agencies from calling for basic standards or outcomes without thinking through what this would entail.

With colleges not regulated by either the federal or state governments, there are few national standards or universal agreements on terms (Campbell and Boyd 1970). While there are state regulations and federal rules usually attached to such things as Title IV or Title IX funds some schools operate outside of these regulations. In our complex landscape of states, tribal colleges, religious schools and so on, it is hard to find any single point of agreement. In many countries, however, there are exams, degrees and standards set by a central ministry of education at the national level that guarantees a consistency of graduates.

Early in our history, academic standards were set by the individual colleges, which created a diversity of standards that differed from college to college and state to state. In one state, there is the requirement for a course in that state's history; in another, to graduate you need 6 hours of science and so on. This diversity of standards, which comes from the self-governance of colleges and universities, is still a sticking point in the discussion about the future of higher education today.

A LAND OF MANY UNIQUE COLLEGES AND UNIVERSITIES

There are many kinds of colleges and universities. To have one standard for all college graduates would be caustic to our diverse system. To have one scorecard for all colleges misses the essential diversity of American higher education. There are research universities, elite colleges, public institutions, private institutions and for-profit institutions. There are 64 tribal colleges that operate on or near Native

American reservations which have the status of sovereign nations (Warner and Gipp 2009). There are more than 100 Historically Black Colleges and Universities, some of which, such as West Virginia State University, are today more than 75% Caucasian (Betsey 2008).

There are bible colleges that are mostly undergraduate institutions. Some of these bible colleges are extremely small. There are rabbinical schools representing the various schools of Judaism. There are seminaries that are mostly graduate schools, training priests and ministers. A number of military services operate academies, such as West Point and the Air Force Academy, that teach leadership. Then there are the war colleges such as the Naval War College where the art of war is studied and researched. There are agricultural and mechanical colleges, such as Texas A&M, that teach, among other things, agronomy and animal husbandry. There are institutions like the National Fire Academy in Emmitsburg, Maryland which is an institution with a specific focus. In addition, there are culinary schools, polytechnic institutes, medical schools, law schools, holistic medicine colleges and schools of dance, just to mention a relatively small number of the many kinds of colleges that exist today.

THE GOVERNMENT'S RELATIONSHIPS WITH THE ACCREDITING AGENCIES

The U.S. government has intruded on all of higher education with funding, for a wide variety of reasons, over its long history. For example, the 1965 Higher Education Act funded Title IV, but the funds came with government oversight and accountability. Title IV funds, which ultimately come from the taxpayer, gave the government a stronger voice in higher education. Title IV funds are very important to higher education institutions because they allow students to take out loans to pay for college. Without Title IV, there are fewer options for students to fund their education.

How does the government decide who should or should not get Title IV funds? The Department of Education recognizes a number of accrediting agencies which certify that institutions are educating their students. What kind of agencies can accredit institutions and allow them to process Title IV funds? The list is long and varied.

There is The Association for Biblical Higher Education Commission on Accreditation, The Association of Advanced Rabbinical and Talmudic Schools Accreditation Commission, The Distance Education and Training Council, The Commission on Massage Therapy Accreditation, The Council on Chiropractic Education Commission on Accreditation, The Council on Accreditation of Nurse Anesthesia Educational Programs, Midwifery Accreditation Council, The National Association of Schools of Dance Commission on Accreditation, The National Association of Schools of Dance, The Accrediting Council for Continuing Education and Training, The American Bar Association Council of the Section of Legal Education and Admissions to the Bar and The American Board of Funeral Service Education Committee on Accreditation. As dizzying as this list is, there are more than we have room for here! So, the question "Are you accredited?" is more complex than many people realize. A college may be regionally accredited lbut their nursing program may not be by the agency that oversees nursing education. Because there may be dozens and dozens of accreditations a university holds and it can be hard to keep track of them.

Political and journalistic calls for national outcomes testing, agreement on curriculum or talk about common standards shows a lack of understanding of the complexity of our educational landscape. A simple political solution might be to ask for a common standard or common measure of success. But if urban community colleges and our most elite colleges must share learning outcomes, curriculum or even values shows a lack of historical and sociological knowledge about the differing aims of higher education in America.

If this stew is not spicy enough, many majors and programs within a college have their own specialized accrediting agencies that assure certain levels of excellence. In business programs, for example, there are two bodies that put their seal of approval on programs meeting certain standards: The Association to Advance Collegiate Schools of Business and The Accreditation Council for Business Schools and Programs. Provosts and deans in contemporary institutions spend much of their time not improving classes or looking at student outcomes but leapfrogging from preparations for one accreditation visit to another. There may be multiple accreditation visits in a single year. There is a nursing accreditation visit in September, business accreditation in November, dance in March and theater in April. To make matters even more cumbersome, every year a number of reports must be submitted to accrediting agencies, government agencies and, in some cases, state agencies.

All of the accrediting agencies mentioned here are peer organizations whose membership is voluntary. Institutions are granted accreditation usually by team visits consisting of members from peer institutions. By giving these agencies the power to put a stamp of approval on all kinds of institutions, the United States Department of Education trusted higher education to police itself. Peer review, which has been in place for more than a hundred years, is how higher education has been assessed in America. It had not been challenged in more than a hundred years and recently even that changed.

ABOUT REGIONAL ACCREDITING AGENCIES

Of all the agencies that the Department of Education recognizes for the accreditation of institutions, there are six regional accrediting agencies that represent the gold standard. The United States is divided into six geographic regions, and each region has its own criteria by which it judges institutions. These six regional accrediting agencies oversee thousands of institutions. Obtaining regional accreditation is important for many reasons. For one, it gives institutions a barometer that allows them to accept the transfer of student-earned credit between each other. Obtaining regional accreditation is also a badge of honor that signifies that an institution offers programs that are high in academic quality. The voice of the six regional accrediting agencies on national issues is stronger than any of the smaller accrediting agencies. For a long time if a college was not accredited by one of the regional accrediting agencies, other colleges would not accept their courses in transfer or recognize their degrees. While there have been efforts to change this practice, regional accreditation is still the gold standard by which colleges are measured. There is extensive literature about the cost of obtaining and retaining accreditation and the impact this has on institutions who must bear this cost. Membership is voluntary and peer review is the norm. Each regional accrediting agency has its own history and culture. The New England Association, where American higher education was born, was founded in 1885. The Middle States Association, which governs the Mid-Atlantic States, was founded in 1887. The Southern Association and the North Central Association were both founded in 1895. The Northwestern Association started in 1917. The Western Association is the youngest, founded in 1923. Because they came into existence at different times they have different cultures and standards. For example, the New England Association has many of the oldest ivies. The Western Association has the California schools that are new, progressive and have been a hotbed of innovation and protest. These different cultures have impacted how the regionals look at higher education and how they measure it.

DISRUPTIVE ACCREDITATION

Two events that happened during the first decade of the twenty-first century threatened the autonomy of American higher education because they brought on the possibility of a government takeover of accreditation: the accreditation review of AIU and the accreditation review of Bridgepoint Higher Education, both for-profit institutions (Lederman 2010). These two events resulted in questions about higher education's ability to govern itself. The profiling of these events was so high that the United States Department of Education threatened to decertify the North Central Association and take over accreditation, whipping up a storm of controversy that has not yet subsided (Miller 2010).

All this occurred within the context of the Obama administration's almost exclusive focus on for-profit higher education as being inferior to non-profit higher education. It was shown, for instance, that while for-profit education accounted for less than 10% of students in American higher education, a large percentage of federal student aid was allocated to the for-profits. The default rates, dropout rates and withdrawal rates in the for-profit sector were also high. Consequently, all of the questions about cost of tuition, academic quality and administrative oversight in higher education were focused on the for-profit sector. While every administration from Truman to Bush talked about the failures of higher education as a whole, the Obama administration focused on the for-profits for their lack of quality and cost ineffectiveness (Gramling 2011).

In his work on disruptive technologies, Clayton Christenson of Harvard explained that disruption to any sector happens by doing something new and different. His definition of a disruptive technology is worth quoting in full:

Generally, disruptive innovations were technologically straightforward, consisting of off-the-shelf components put together in a product architecture that was often simpler than prior approaches. They offered less of what customers in established markets wanted and so they could rarely be initially employed there. They offered a different package of attributes valued only in emerging markets remote from, and unimportant to, the mainstream (Christensen 1997).

What the big online for-profits did was so simple that it seems amazing that traditional colleges did not do it first. Online learning was available to all schools in the early 1990s, but there was resistance to its deployment in many traditional universities. There were questions about the effectiveness of an online learning environment. There were questions about faculty workload. Some thought it was far inferior to face-to-face instruction. The for-profits saw the need to serve a non-traditional population using non-traditional means and this meant embracing online learning and digital technologies early.

The shared governance that was the major force in higher education slowed down the adoption of new technologies in many traditional universities. The big online for-profits, however, grasped that these same technologies allowed them to reach a whole new class of users that were not on the horizon of most of higher education. These new students were working adults who had a hard time driving to night school after a long day on their feet; stay-at-home moms who needed child care, which is expensive, to attend a brick-and-mortar college; and military students who moved around a great deal and had a hard time completing a degree in only one on-the-ground college. The big online for-profits recognized that this was another step in the inclusive journey of American higher education.

These new institutions did not set out to compete with Harvard or Yale. Instead, they offered the bricklayer, the stay-at-home mom and the marine in Korea a way to go to college while they lived their lives. Variables that tell us in advance why a student may not be successful in college include the following trends: being an adult, working, being a parent, being out of school for a while and not taking SATs. This new class of students was not as well prepared for college as traditional freshman several generations ago. In addition, they had life circumstances that might mean they could not finish a semester or program. A worker could be laid off, a mother could have a sick child or a marine could be deployed to the front lines. Admitting these students into college meant taking in students with a far worse chance of success than traditional students. If one looks at the number of drops or withdrawals in urban community colleges over the past quarter century, the numbers are not much different as compared with the for-profits. These non-traditional students constitute a new class in higher education. The for-profits combined online learning, wholly digital backbones, and then they marketed their courses and programs to students who did not previously think of attending college. They made it easy for a new population to enter college. They also operated more like efficient businesses.

Because many of the students they aimed at were low-income individuals, the for-profits relied heavily on federal student aid – what their critics would term "taxpayer dollars." Of course we can say that all colleges that take federal student aid are funded by "taxpayer dollars." In addition, it might be noted that for-profits pay state and federal taxes while non-profits do not. Insiders in the for-profit industry have suggested that in place of the terms "for-profit" and "non-profit," we use the terms "tax paying" and "non-tax paying." We can go further to say that community colleges and state colleges are funded almost exclusively by taxpayer dollars. But the online for-profits were capitalist organizations where the executives were often very well paid. In addition, some of these institutions, such as the University of Phoenix, Capella University, Kaplan University and the American Public University System, were owned by publicly traded companies. So, the idea of taxpayer monies funding a for-profit institution did not sit right with many people.

Some traditional colleges experimented with spinning off their own for-profit wings. NYU Online and Fathom of Columbia University were both spectacular failures because they were not clear about what they were trying to accomplish (Washburn 2006). More recently, the University of Illinois folded a large and expensive online venture.

In short, a new marketing space was opened. A new class of students was brought into the university and a new way of doing things was born.

CONFRONTATIONS WITH THE NORTH CENTRAL ASSOCIATION OF COLLEGES AND SCHOOLS

A crisis in higher education accreditation was ignited over an accreditation visit in 2006. This visit and its result triggered a confrontation between the Higher Learning Commission of the North Central Association of Colleges and Schools and the Department of Education over the accreditation of for-profits. The accreditation decision regarding AIU was so controversial that it triggered a crisis in American higher education whereby the United States Department of Education threatened, in a public memo, for the first time in history, to strip the North Central Association of its ability to accredit colleges and instead make the federal government the arbiter of college excellence in America (Miller 2010). Calls for government oversight of higher education evoked memories of McCarthyism. In the entire history of regional accreditation, the Department of Education had never reacted with such speed and rancor as in the case of the AIU visit (Miller 2010). By threatening to replace the voluntary peer review system of regional accreditation with professional bureaucrats and political appointees from the Department of Education, the whole edifice of higher education in America was called into question.

What caught the attention of the Department of Education and caused such a furor in higher education policy? An accreditation team was sent to AIU for the start of its first application for regional accreditation status through the Higher Learning Commission. This was not a renewal of previous accreditation, known as "reaccreditation," but an application to, so to speak, "get into the club." AIU was a for-profit university that had previously been in the southern region where it had experienced numerous difficulties and questions. Consequently, AIU switched regions. Why would a college switch regions? Each of the six regionally accrediting agencies has their own standards. Almost all of the large online for-profit institutions, such as the University of Phoenix, Capella University, Kaplan University, Walden University, American Public University and a good number of others, are in one region, the Higher Learning Commission's North Central Association. Why would all of these large online universities congregate in the North Central region? Historically, this organization has been more liberal about innovations in higher education, especially online learning and the application of other digital technologies. Under the longtime leadership of Dr. Steven Crow, the Higher Learning Commission of the North Central Association welcomed many of the innovations of the digital revolution. For this reason, the Higher Learning Commission has been the most controversial and has often been questioned about their standards. But it can also be said that they welcomed innovation and were on the cutting edge in how they saw things.

While digital learning was welcomed by the North Central Association, other regional accrediting agencies have been much more conservative in their reception and accrediting of online learning. We support this notion by making note of the fact that at the time of this writing there are no large online for-profits accredited by the southern region.

In the case of AIU, the accrediting team for North Central focused on how the university calculated a credit hour. The credit hour, sometimes called the Carnegie unit, is how most colleges assign credits. If you complete about 60 credits, you earn an associate degree, and with 120 credits or thereabouts you earn a bachelor's degree. This calculation is important in providing a government standing for Title IV funds. So, not meeting credit hour requirements is defrauding the government. While there has been a vague understanding of the credit hour; it was never clearly defined in such a way that it would restrict how professors teach. However, with the AIU visit, the team wrote that the university was offering more credit than the Carnegie unit should have allowed. The team found that the award of academic credit was so flawed that it was "egregious," a word repeated in dozens of articles about this historic confrontation between the federal government and the North Central Association (Miller 2010). For the first time, the report tried to define what academic credit is and tied that definition to an accreditation document.

The word "egregious" was un-redacted by the Department of Education in response to a Freedom of Information request as the media tried to follow the battle that was unfolding. The university was judged "outstandingly bad" and at the same time, "meeting all standards."

It was perceived that AIU clearly did not meet the standards of regional accreditation and many thought there were clearly issues of quality control and academic integrity. However, AIU was accredited, which allowed them to receive Title IV funds from American taxpayers.

The storm around this regional accreditation raised a flag for the future of higher education in America. Colleges and universities reacted strongly against the federal government's threat to remove the North Central Association from its list of accreditors and somehow allow Washington bureaucrats to become the arbiters of educational quality. This was a historic confrontation.

The federal government began to ask for a closer definition of a credit hour or Carnegie unit (Fryshman 2010). This was seen as a huge intrusion into higher education by the federal government. An hour of teaching a physics lab is not the same as an hour of lecture in a philosophy class, and is not the same as an hour of group work in a counseling class. To start counting seat time with a spreadsheet would kill academic freedom in America. Nonetheless, since the AIU decision, colleges all over the nation have begun, sadly, to make these calculations. The AIU visit had damaged academic freedom and peer review in the United States. The Higher Learning Commission of the North Central Association of Colleges and Schools was back on its heels. It seemed things could not get worse. But suddenly they did.

The second disaster that befell the North Central Association involved another institution that they accredited shortly after AIU, Bridgepoint Higher Education, a publicly traded for-profit company made up of two schools, Ashford University and The College of the Rockies (Lederman 2010). Bridgepoint was a combination of some small, on-the-ground colleges hooked up with a huge online learning operation. Ashford University maintained a small on-the-ground campus in Iowa that is in the North Central Region. But its corporate offices and most many of the executive offices were located in San Diego, California, which is in the Western Region. When North Central gave Bridgepoint accreditation in 2006, the visiting team report questioned if they had a "substantial presence" in the region. So, the team had doubts that they were even legally operating in the North Central Region but decided to accredit them anyway. This was the second red flag in the disruption of American higher education. When the college was accredited by the North Central Association, there were so many questions that the head of the North Central Association, Dr. Sylvia Manning, was asked to appear before the Senate Health, Education, Labor and Pension Committee (HELP), chaired by Senate Democrat Tom Harkin of Iowa, to be grilled about how this could have happened.

Some saw the Bridgepoint hearing by the HELP committee as politically motivated. The Obama administration had already made a point of targeting the for-profits, and this gave them the ammunition they needed to begin to remake higher education law in America. For most of the three-hour hearing, Senator Harkin alone appeared in the chamber. Republicans such as Senator Michael Enzi, the ranking Republican from Wyoming, appeared only to criticize the hearings as an "agenda-driven rush to judgment" and described the whole for-profit hearings as "the most biased and poorly executed hearings in my nearly 15 years in the Senate" (Lederman 2011).

But it was Senator Harkin who got the headlines and the sound bites. His critique went as follows: "The question I would ask is, in their current state, are our accreditation agencies equipped to oversee billion-dollar, multi-state corporations?" As is common on Capitol Hill, he did not wait for an answer from Dr. Manning and instead provided his own: "I don't think so," Harkin said. "I don't think accrediting agencies have the wherewithal" (Lederman 2010).
Rethinking Accreditation

There have been tens of thousands of peer review visits in the history of higher education over more than a hundred years. No two visits have shipwrecked the reputation of accreditation more than the AIU and Bridgepoint Higher Education visits. Because of these two incidents, there has been a rethinking of accreditation by all regional and national accrediting agencies. This increased scrutiny will have some positive results as the AIU and Bridgepoint visits have shown us how accreditation should not be done. But there are always unintended consequences to any decision. This confrontation has raised questions about online learning, questions about the liberal transfer of credit, questions about independent study and non-standard semesters. The impact of these is to wipe out much of the innovation that was made possible by the introduction of digital technologies. It was an accepted whiplash against all of the innovations that have battered higher education. It has sent a chill throughout higher education.

The damage had been done, and the federal government wanted a stronger say in higher education. The federal government now wanted a definition of the credit hour and a way to track it. They want a say in how colleges gain accreditation. There have been calls in both the Senate and the Department of Education for more government oversight and improvements to the accreditation process.

As a result of this visit, Bridgepoint Higher Education attempted to get accredited in the Western Region where the corporate offices are. It was no surprise when the Western Association denied them accreditation in a scathing report. This triggered another visit by North Central that many expect will try to redo the flawed 2006 report in way that makes more sense. One more result of the Bridgepoint visit was that when the Western Association released their full accreditation report, for the first time, they published it on its website with the names of the accrediting team. This was another first in the history of accreditation. Until now, reports had been confidential and team member names not revealed. Accreditors were supposed to keep things they learned quiet. It was peer review by old standards. But Bridgepoint gave us the first published report for all to see, question and criticize. Now there will be pressure to make all reports and team membership lists public. This greater transparency will mean more publicity, more controversy and more room for political intrusion into the process. When Bridgepoint was refused accreditation by the Western Association, the stock value of it and the whole sector took a hit. The value of the for-profit education companies had declined significantly during the Obama administration and the publicity around American Intercontinental and Bridgepoint.

In the summer of 2012, Senator Harkin and the Democrats on the HELP Committee released a report of more than 5,000 pages that sought to put the nail in the coffin of for-profit higher education in America. In a 2012 article in *Inside Higher Ed*, educational reporter Paul Fain summed up what Harkin's concerns were about the future of accreditation:

"As for accreditation, the report said both national accreditors that focus specifically on for-profit institutions and regional accrediting agencies have at times been unable to keep up with the industry's growth. It singled out the Higher Learning Commission of the North Central Association of Colleges and Schools for allegedly failing to properly review Bridgepoint Education's Ashford University and American Intercontinental University, which is owned by Career Education Corporation."

In response to these two events, a college scorecard has been proposed by the Department of Education, which would pull data from all colleges to show their progress and graduation rates. Colleges were asked to track their graduates to see if they are "gainfully employed" in the field for which they studied. Colleges now had to do a better job at data collection, assessment and analysis of learning outcomes. The relationship between the accrediting agencies and the government has been forever altered.

CHAPTER NINE
ACADEMIC FREEDOM, GOVERNANCE AND CHANGE

To live is to change, and to be perfect is to have changed often.
— John Cardinal Newman

A CONSERVATIVE AND REVOLUTIONARY MOVEMENT

For a variety of reasons, the university has come late to the digital revolution. First, the university has always had a conservative tendency (Graff 1989). There are many reasons for this. Higher education is by its nature both conservative and revolutionary (Postman 1987). It has been accused on both the left and the right of being prejudiced against the other side. It is conservative in that it employs professionals in fields where there is an established methodology, paradigm and theory, making it natural for the authorities in the established paradigm to be fully invested in defending it (Kuhn 1996). It is revolutionary because it is a place historically isolated from accountability and profit. It is a place where trial balloons can be floated and new theories tested. This tension between the conserving nature of the academy and the revolutionary nature of the academy has been exacerbated by the digital revolution that has sped up everything. Now the focus is on the question of how the university has changed and what we need to do to insure its future.

This guiding question is one way of thinking about how good can come from the current chaos.

The formulation of faculty governance that came out of the University of Paris in the thirteenth century gave the modern university its present form. Most institutions in the middle ages were similar to institutions that exist today where one person made the decisions for the business and everyone else followed that chain of command. Government was top-heavy with the king, prince or duke having un-limited power over the masses. Religion was also a top-down affair from the pope to the parish priest. The university, from its origins, operated on a very different model that was freer and at the same time more controversial. Shared governance has its advantages and disadvantages. These have been debated for centuries.

The first universities were founded long before theories of so-cial contract were articulated (Strauss and Cropsey 1987). Having a faculty guild, however, where the model was shared governance, was something very different. Much of the debate about the future of the university today is around the survival of shared governance (Donoghue 2008). Many of the assaults on the university have been around the real cost of shared governance (Riley 2011). Has the digital revolution made shared governance obsolete? How is faculty governance different in the digital age? Before we can answer these questions, we have to ask if faculty governance is really part of the essence of higher education rather than a historical accident.

A CHAOTIC DEMOCRACY WITH FACULTY AND STUDENT EMPOWERMENT

In our own time, it has become fashionable to criticize faculty governance and what appears to be the chaotic democracy of the university. Academic freedom has undergone a series of attacks from conservative theorists and columnists (Riley 2011). There are also economic questions about the cost and productivity of a large body of tenured faculty (Finkelstein 2011). At the birth of the university, however, there were compelling reasons for empowering the faculty. The thirteenth century was a time of unbridled power of the Catholic Church and the nobility. There was no free press, no opposition party and no rights to a lawyer or trial. Torture and execution were common and accepted elements of the justice system. So, it was important to have protections by decree, papal bull or law for faculty and students in the city in which they studied. In the history of the university, there were times when the pope protected the university against the wishes of the king, and there were other times when the king protected universities against the wishes of the pope. With a nod toward the power of both church and state to crush dissent, the university was a relatively free place to think and discuss issues.

The guilds of both students and faculty were modeled on the older guilds in Europe. A craftsman such as a stonemason could work on a cathedral in York and then go to work building the cathedral at Chartres and his "education" would be vouched for by his guild status. It is not surprising that many of the secret societies so important in the American and French Revolutions, such as the Free Masons, modeled themselves on these medieval guilds in their governance structure. The University of Paris was known as a "Universitas Magistorum et Scholarium" (a guild of professors and scholars). This showed that power was not concentrated in any one person or office but spread throughout the university. It was a faculty guild, but this expression showed that the voices of the students were also heard. The expressions "shared governance" or "faculty governance" have been at the heart of academic discourse ever since.

ACADEMIC FREEDOM AND FREE SPEECH

In the early history of the university, through various alliances, the faculty and students won protection so that they could be free to teach and think. There were battles between the crown and the papacy over the freedom of the university. For example, in 1229, the French crown suspended courses at the University of Paris. Pope Gregory IX intervened with a Papal Bull. Although the negotiations took a good amount of time, courses were restored in 1231. But this was not the end of conflicts between the government and the university. We can also recall that the French revolution began in Paris and transformed the role of the monarchy in Europe. The revolt of 1848, the Paris Commune of 1870 and the riots of 1968 revealed that the University of Paris, now reborn as the Sorbonne, had always been at the heart of social and political change (Hazen and Fernbach 2011). Ever since their founding, universities have been centers of unrest during times of political turmoil. In the current conservative political environment in America, the university and its professors are often seen as unpatriotic.

From Berkeley to Buenos Aires to Tokyo to Tripoli, students and faculty have been on the forefront of social revolutions. The suppression of free speech and radical thought has been a top priority of regimes all over the planet that have seen it as a threat to the status quo. For this reason, faculty have always been ferocious in their defense of academic freedom and free speech. Restrictions on academic freedom often begin with small skirmishes (Wilson 2008). Faculty often sees stopping the suppression at this point as imperative to preventing a much greater restriction in the future. The principle is what philosophers call the "slippery slope argument." If one gets to the top of an icy slope on a pair of skis, one is likely to end up at the bottom of the mountain whether they intended to or not. Thus, any attempt to reign in faculty freedom or shared governance is often met with resistance early on (McLemmee 2005).

One of the classic examples of what can happen when the university faculty loses its independence is in the story of a biology professor in the Soviet Union under Stalin. A Soviet Professor named Trofirm Denisovich Lysenko, who focused his research almost exclusively on genetics and genetic engineering, thought that biological science had it all wrong (Roll-Hansen 2004). From his experiments on *Drosophila melanogaster*, also known as the common fruit fly, he made analogies to the rest of society. He combined this genetic speculation with the Marxist theory of dialectical materialism. His theories won favor with Stalin and influenced, it turns out disastrously, farming, food production, agriculture, social organization and agronomy. He eventually was made head of the Soviet Academy of Science (Roll-Hansen 2004). His theories were called Michurinism but have come to be known later, and with a much different connotation, as Lysenkoism.

Any academic who opposed Lysenko was purged, and some were even imprisoned and killed. All academic opposition was silenced, and there was total accord with the new biology throughout the Soviet university system. Academic freedom had to be crushed totally and completely. The results were starvation and famine. The case of Lysenko showed what happens when the forces of politics or even popular opinion intrude into university life. The troublesome and unpatriotic professors were gone and with them went a check on madness.

There have been numerous times in our own history when academic freedom has been threatened. Being a democracy protected by the Constitution and the First Amendment has not protected the university from the creation of such threats. For example, the House Committee on Un-American Activities (HCUA) that ran from 1938 to 1975 often focused on academics and questioned their loyalty (McCormick 1989). In addition, a high water mark of this kind of interrogation happened during the early 1950s when Senator Joe McCarthy from Wisconsin looked to root out the communists and anti-Americanism in our colleges.

What was the actual upshot of McCarthyism on college campuses? An example of the impact of this type of thinking was revealed in what happened in 1951 to a college professor named Dr. Luella Mundel, who taught at Fairmont State University in central West Virginia (McCormick 1989). While the famous Army-McCarthy hearings did not start until 1954, McCarthy was beating the drum of "a communist under every bed" for many years before. Luella Mundel was a professor of art history and head of the department. She asked several questions at a meeting on "Americanism" at a local American Legion forum. Her remarks at that meeting led to her being fired from Fairmont State College for being a "security risk" and "atheist" whose views were anti-American.

It was the view of some at the American Legion that day in the heart of patriotic West Virginia that Fairmont State College was a hotbed of communism (McCormick 1989). When Professor Mundel could not find other employment because of the circumstances of her firing, she attempted suicide and was then hospitalized for "lunacy." Her career was destroyed, and her life was ruined for asking questions.

College professors are very sure they do not want a repeat of McCarthyism-like thinking. So, they have drawn bright lines to prevent it from happening again. For example, in a recent newspaper survey, it was found that more than half of Americans in 2012 believed that dinosaurs and humans lived at the same time. As the comedian Lewis Black joked, "when they watch the Flintstones, they think they are watching a documentary." More than half of Americans believe the world is less than 10,000 years old (Lagemann and Lewis 2012). But in our colleges, evolutionary theory and the scientific evidence that supports it tells a very different story. How can the university protect its expertise from popular opinion and the political pressures they can bring? If taxpayers are supporting a university, how can the university teach things that go against the beliefs of those same taxpayers? Out in the heartland or in rural Appalachia, how can a school be assured of that independence to teach things that many prominent citizens and community members think may be against their religion or patriotic beliefs? How can the university be a place of truth when that truth is unpopular and they rely on the citizens around them to support this endeavor? Even in the twenty-first century, questions of patriotism and faith are behind political attempts to reign in teaching at the university (Wilson 2008).

Even after the disbanding of the Committee on Un-American Activities, there have been continuing conversations about the patriotism of our professoriate. Historically, there were important reasons for the strong role of the faculty. It insured that politics would not intrude into academic life. It made sure that the pursuit of truth was not subjected to the vicissitudes of politics. But in addition to political, ideological and religious attacks on the power of the professoriate, there is another trend that is impacting the power of the faculty that came from a whole new place. The rise of the digital university has necessitated the creation of a manager class of programmers, registrars, COOs and others who now are in decision-making roles (Ginsberg 2011). This makes the university (including technical colleges, community colleges, non-profits, for-profits, polytechnics and even research universities) look more like a business than a traditional university run by faculty consensus.

THE GROWTH OF BUSINESS MANAGERS AND DECLINE OF FACULTY GOVERNANCE

The growing power of a professional management class has been necessitated by the increase in expertise required for computer hardware, software systems and for dealing with complex governmental and accreditation requirements. The complexities of financial aid, governmental reporting and data requirements have empowered a new class of college professionals that have never been faculty. In different types of colleges, the growth of a pure management class has happened at different rates (Birnbaum 1988). Today, a class of professional managers, who are often uninformed about the history of the university, have more say than the faculty.

One of the concerns in recent literature from the academy is the erosion of the faculty member's voice and their power (Donoghue 2008). The digital revolution has intensified this debate about faculty power and shared governance in ways that are new and not anticipated.

The power of faculty is rooted in their status as experts. The prestige of a university, before the advent of big-time college sports, was the number of well-known professors who were members of its faculty. In the high Middle Ages, there was a competition for well-known professors among the great universities of Salamanca, Oxford and Paris (Coplestone 2003). This has continued to the present day when universities compete for those scholars who can attract attention, alumni dollars and students (Kirp 2003).

The faculty's role in all of the institution's crucial decisions is a hallmark of higher education. Recent studies, however, have chronicled the declining power of the faculty, showing that professional managers and the application of business models to the university as the cause for this decline (Donoghue 2008). Other studies have followed a change in credentials of college administrators as professors of humanities and science with PhDs were being replaced by MBAs and CPAs. More terrifying for professors and the university are those newly arrived administrators and consultants armed with "efficiency theories," such as Total Quality Management and Six Sigma. Faculty are rightly suspicious of terms such as "organizational development," "organizational behavior," "organizational effectiveness" and "organizational leadership." They see them as code words for destroying faculty-shared governance.

In short, Thomas Mann has given way to Tom Peters. Why is this terrifying? Six Sigma is applied to all businesses equally, from making widgets to selling ice cream to universities. This kind of thinking, which is ahistorical, does not take into account the special history of the university and its need to preserve shared decision making and academic freedom. Yet, the arrival of managers whose only experience has been in business is an important change in the university. From the CEO, COO and CIOs, a top-down model exists today that treats the university as if it were just another widget-producing business. More and more college presidents have JDs and MBAs, and less and less have a traditional PhD or EdD who came up through ranks and were seasoned in faculty senates (Ginsberg 2011).

This transition from faculty governance to professional managers did not happen smoothly in American higher education. Robert Birnbaum, in his essential book *How Colleges Work: The Cybernetics of Academic Organization and Leadership*, noted that different types of colleges have different types of governance and decision making. He showed how an elite private traditional liberal arts college differs in governance and organization structure from a large state college (Birnbaum 1988).

In summary, academic freedom has traditionally been based on the power of the faculty in all of the key decisions in the university. From the earliest days of the university, academic freedom and shared governance have been assaulted and challenged by forces both inside and outside of the university. The digital revolution has accelerated a decline in faculty power and necessitated a new class of professional managers that has been empowered by their digital and managerial expertise. This has happened in all sectors of higher education, including for-profit, state universities and privates. Rethinking the university in the digital age will mean asking how faculty power can be preserved in an era of the establishment of a new managerial class that has its roots outside of the university.

COMBINING QUALITY ACADEMICS
AND HIGH-TECH BUSINESS PRACTICES
INTO THE MODERN UNIVERSITY

The university of tomorrow must combine shared governance in academic matters with the expertise needed to run a modern high-tech business that our universities have become. After the 1929 stock market crash, it was revealed that there was a great deal of insider trading that was unknown to most public investors. To prevent this from happening in the future, the curious term "Chinese Wall" was invented. This meant that information about one part of the business was to be walled off from another part of the business. This model must be applied to higher education for the university to survive. Academics needs to be independent from the business processes. Professionals not beholding to a faculty senate must manage the complex digital business of the modern university. A Chinese Wall needs to be formed and it is the job of the president and board to see that the interests of both sides are protected. The school is about academics, so academics is the end that everything else serves. But that end must be served by the cooperation of faculty and staff in service of the education of the students and success of its graduates.

We have argued here and elsewhere that the university of the future must combine both kinds of management (McCluskey 2012b). A strong academic voice, free to express dissent, is key to having academic quality and keeping alive the centrality of learning. At the same time, a strong managerial team must be free to make business and technology decisions that can position university growth and stability. The gray line will be between decisions that are academic and decisions that are business related. This is the conversation that must take place at the birth of something new: something neither for-profit nor traditionally not-for-profit, but a digital university that is simultaneously strong in academics as well as managerially efficient. In recent decades, the power of the faculty has declined. This power has not gone away but has been transferred to a class of professional managers. Over time there are less tenure lines, less full-time faculty positions and less protections for faculty dissent (Ginsberg 2011). At the same time, there has been a growth in the number and pay of professional administrators. It is time to stop this slide. There should be a full-time faculty who are invested in the university and its future. Part-time or adjunct faculty are often not paid to have office hours or paid to participate in the life of the campus. They are paid class by class, and this means they are not really included in the full life of the college. While there are many great adjuncts (the authors have been adjunct faculty), it is no substitute for a full-time faculty who are there to spend time mentoring and sustaining a campus life. An adjunct may have three or four different jobs and some have called themselves "Road Scholars" for all of the time they spent driving from gig to gig. Tenure has gotten a bad name for many. It has been argued that tenure supports lazy, unethical and incompetent faculty. This does not mean that tenure should be done away with. If they are not involved in some grant or research, it is the role of faculty to teach. But not just teach. Their job is actually to make certain that their students learn. We will suggest that the digital age has given us the tools to measure learning and student success. As long as these benchmarks are met, faculty should be free to express opinions, determine curriculum and help guide the future of the university.

CHAPTER TEN
DIGITAL FINGERPRINTS

Education is not the filling of a pail but the lighting of a fire.
— W.B. Yeats

Academic freedom is protected under the First Amendment to the Constitution. The history and evolution of judicial precedent around issues of academic freedom is a long and complex story (Wilson 2008). It is important to keep in mind that in discussions about academic freedom, in particular, or about the First Amendment, in general, we must remember that there is no absolute freedom of speech, but there is freedom of speech within certain limitations. For example, "treasonous speech" and "fighting words" do not have absolute protection under the First Amendment (Teschner and McCluskey 1988).

HOW THE HEART OF HIGHER EDUCATION HAS BEEN ATTACKED

At the heart of American higher education is the idea of academic freedom (McLemmee 2005). This concept is what makes a university different from a business. In a business or a corporation, once the CEO or board makes a decision, it is supposed to be executed without question down the chain of command. A business is not a democracy. With few exceptions, such as some Madison

Avenue advertising firms or some Silicon Valley software firms, American business has historically been hierarchical.

What makes the university such a difficult and wonderful place is the concept of shared governance, and this is underpinned by the idea of academic freedom. There have been numerous studies and books on the corporatization of higher education and how this has hurt the university (Schrecker 2010).

Colleges have attempted to become more like businesses (Ginsberg 2011). To do this they have brought in business types and adopted business principles. They have adopted Deming's Total Quality Management, Six Sigma and a host of other management theories in an attempt to reform or repackage higher education. The goals of many of these new managers are efficiency, improving cash flow and streamlining management systems. Many have had no previous academic experience where one comes up through the ascending apprenticeship of faculty rank. Often they do not understandwhat makes a university unique.

In the past, college administrators who mainly came from the ranks of the faculty took a long time to be promoted into an administrative position (Birnbaum 1988). A typical rise to college president often took decades and followed the path from adjunct to instructor to assistant professor to associate professor to tenure as a full professor to assistant department chair to associate department chair to department chair to school dean to provost to president. This is a long process, similar in length of upward mobility that stretches from the apprenticeship level to a master mason degree. In this long apprenticeship, the traditions and unique elements of the university are learned slowly.

There are a many points up the ladder to a college presidency where someone can fall off and not reach the next rung. In many schools, the faculty elects deans and department chairs. With elections due every few years, the department chair must be responsive to the faculty that must reelect her. Today, however, we have a class of managers and executives, in both the for-profit and the non-profit sectors, that arrive at the top of the administration without ever having to go through tenure review or learned the lessons and culture of the academy. They bring with them the idea of making a decision and having it carried out by "subordinates" (a term not very popular with college professors). There are advantages and disadvantages to bringing in fresh talent. But that "fresh talent" should not be allowed to monkey with pedagogy and academic content, things with which they have little experience.

Let us take another example. Let us suppose the reader is a relatively bright person with some life experience. Now, tomorrow you are made head of a jet engine plant, or a hotel in Key West or you are suddenly made a fire chief in a busy fire district. What could you teach those who had worked there for 20 years that they had not thought of before you arrived? What would you say to the firefighters who had done that job every day for 20 years? How could you make the jet engine assembly line more efficient? This kind of scenario is what happens in academia over and over.

ACADEMIC FREEDOM AND TENURE

Before we can reform higher education, we must understand what it is and what that reform will change. For a thousand years, faculty members have debated and voted on all key decisions (Ridder-Symoens 2003). Faculty governance and shared governance rest upon the twin pillars of academic freedom and tenure. Yet, in the history of the university, faculty have been censured and dismissed for heretical views on theology, science, art, politics, philosophy and social issues (Wilson 2008).

As unpopular as tenure is in the press, we argue that it must survive in some form. Without protection there cannot be honest criticism, and without honest criticism there cannot be faculty freedom. Academic freedom insures the professor is free to speak the truth. In America, the defense of academic freedom has been tied into discussions about tenure. Tenure is the system that makes it harder for administrators to silence a faculty member who may be expressing heretical views. But tenure has been under assault for a long time. Conservative critics of higher education see it as protection for a faculty whose liberal views put them out of touch with mainstream America (Nash, Crabtree and Dunn 2000). Tenure began to disappear for librarians long ago and that trend shows no sign of abating. When librarians lost their tenure, this was not the red flag it should have been because some professors did not see them as "real academics". This was a huge mistake because the loss of faculty status of librarians was the first erosion of faculty tenure and power that is now moving at full speed. Librarians see themselves as academics and do need protection just as a faculty member does. The move to eliminate tenure is popular with taxpayers, politicians and the media. Many who call for it to be abolished do not understand what it protects.There has been governmental pressure from both liberals and conservatives that has sought to influence college teaching and policy. The history of the university has been rife with conflicts between university management and faculty who are expressing unpopular views. In the United States, there have been battles around racism, the teaching of evolution, perceived anti-American views and opposition to military campaigns, to name just a few.

In a 1915 statement later modified in 1940, the American Association of University Professors joined the Association of American Colleges (now called the Association of American Colleges and Universities) to issue the "1940 Statement of Principles on Academic Freedom and Tenure." The aim of this statement was to allow professors freedom in their classrooms when discussing their subjects. That is what academic freedom is really all about. The statement understood the complexity of higher education in America and it did make exceptions, such as the right of religious schools to limit faculty speech that came into conflict with the doctrines of their faith. The aim of the statement was to ensure that political views or powerful forces in the university or society did not hamper free inquiry. It is important to remember this was not a national law but an agreement among higher education institutions. Organizations such as the American Philosophical Association, American Psychological Association and the American Historical Association would note these sanctions in job postings. So, there were teeth in these recommendations even if they were not the law of the land.

PROTECTING FACULTY GOVERNANCE AND FREEDOM

Academic freedom is also protected by the regional accrediting agencies. As we noted earlier, institutions depend on regional accreditation so that courses transfer to other schools and degree programs are appropriately recognized between institutions. For this reason, regional accrediting agencies have power over the colleges. If the American Association of University Professors sanctions a school for violations of academic freedom, it could possibly impact their regional accreditation. The regional accrediting agencies work with the American Association of University Professors and the Association of American Colleges and Universities to make sure that academic freedom and faculty governance are protected. It is important to remember that academic freedom is not absolute, and there is plenty of case law about faculty who have sued universities for violations of their academic freedom (McLemmee 2005). There are numerous cases today that are testing the limits of academic freedom. These issues will be ongoing as the lines of this fault are constantly shifting.

We are going to look at a few examples of battles around academic freedom. The list we are going to present is neither authoritative nor exhaustive. It is meant merely to show several of the milestone cases where academic freedom was an issue. With hundreds of cases to choose from, we have selected a few that have gotten our attention.

Long before the 1940 Statement by the American Association of University Professors, there were struggles about what could and could not be taught in the university. One of the earliest examples was the Bassett Affair at Duke in 1903. Professor John Bassett publicly questioned racism in the Democratic Party. The president of Duke came under fire from the board, and there was pressure to get rid of Bassett. The entire faculty voted to resign *en masse* if the board of trustees gave into public pressure to fire Professor Bassett. In the end, Professor Bassett kept his job and a milestone was achieved for academic freedom. As far back as 1903, the faculty of a university in the former confederacy knew enough to stand up for academic freedom.

1957 saw one of the most historic cases involving academic freedom. This case involved an admitted Marxist and progressive professor who on several occasions gave speeches. The attorney general of New Hampshire wanted Professor Paul Sweezy to testify about the content of his lectures. Professor Sweezy refused, sighting academic freedom and his First Amendment rights. The case was eventually brought to the United States Supreme Court (Barendt 2010). The court ruled in Professor Sweezy's favor, and this set a precedent for a long time. Earl Warren wrote the majority opinion for the court but Justice Felix Frankfurter also joined in the opinion. In this case, the Supreme Court recognized academic freedom as a special instance of the First Amendment (Barendt 2010). Frankfurter had been a professor at the Harvard Law School and had been active in the American Association of University Professors. Frankfurter wrote that any intrusion by the government into the classroom was dangerous to the First Amendment and the idea of academic freedom.

Another milestone case where academic freedom became an issue happened in 1967 during the case of Keyishian vs. The New York State Board of Regents. This case also made it all the way to the Supreme Court. Relying on the principles of Sweezy, the court found that New York State's attempt to prevent people with "subversive views" from obtaining state employment was unconstitutional. The professor was seeking employment in a state university and the state wanted to determine who was politically fit to teach. You can imagine the repercussions if this law was enacted in all 50 states. What is patriotic in New York might not be in Wyoming. What is considered science in Massachusetts might not be acceptable in Texas. The slippery slope was there and we did not venture out on it.

After the attacks on September 11, 2001, a University of Colorado Professor, Ward Churchill, came under attack for statements he made that were taken to be critical of the United States and the victims of the attacks. Public pressure mounted against Professor Churchill, and he eventually lost his position. This case is not a particularly good example concerning academic freedom in that Professor Churchill had allegedly lied on his vita and violated other rules of the university. Had the good professor been more of a model citizen of the university, this case might have been much more interesting. In the immediate aftermath of the September 11 attack on America, there was a patriotic fever that swept the nation. Laws were enacted very rapidly and a sense of urgency made dissent very unpopular. It is during these times when academic freedom is most important.

More recently in 2008, there was a case that caused much reaction in higher education. The case was a U.S. Circuit Court case of Stronach vs. Virginia State University (VSU). This involved someone other than a professor changing a student grade that the professor had given. Professor Carey Stronach had taught at VSU for more than 40 years in the physics department. He gave a student a grade of D based on the fact the student failed several quizzes. The student claimed he had gotten an A on two of the tests and faxed them to Professor Stonach. The professor felt the student had doctored the documents and stayed with his original grade. The student appealed to Professor Stonach's department chairman. The department chairman sided with the student and changed the grade. Professor Stronach felt this violated his academic freedom. The court ruled in this case that academic freedom did not reside with the professor but with the university. A fellow academic made the change in the same department who had management responsibility. Academic freedom is not absolute. It is not about doing whatever you want. It is the freedom to speak the truth without fear of punishment.

But the question of academic freedom has recently come under another kind of fire with the introduction of digital technology. In a previous chapter, we made an analogy between the classical idea of the college professor and a craftsman. The professor produces the artifacts of lecture and scholarship. Each lecture is unique and each class is a kind of performance. Because the professor was the craftsman, there was no way to mediate between him and his art. The individual freedom of the professor as a unique kind of craftsman underlies the whole university.

An important part of academic freedom is the freedom for the faculty to express themselves freely and teach without someone looking over his or her shoulder. This was fine in the age when chalk and talk governed classroom teaching. The digital age introduced online classrooms where students and teachers interact digitally. As opposed to the physical classroom, there is a physical record of every transaction that takes place in the classroom. Every discussion post, every essay, every teacher comment is captured for posterity. In hundreds of thousands of classes there is digital data being captured that can be analyzed and sorted. This means that for the first time there is a map of what happens in the classroom. Big Brother can now see everything. Does this mean it is the end of academic freedom?

THE DIGITAL ANALYSIS OF PATTERNS BRINGS A NEW WORLD

In the digital classroom, we have a record of where the student interaction was heavy and where student responses were lacking. We can see where student questions arise and where the material seems clear. We can see where the teacher must intervene. We can see patterns of confusion, enthusiasm and understanding. We can map it as we would a weather pattern or storm. We can find and analyze patterns of faculty interaction, encouragement and analysis. The interactions of a single faculty in a single class would not tell us much. But take a large number of classes and we begin to see patterns that we did not see before. Currently, there are projects underway that compare hundreds of thousands of records to see where activity rise and fall in online classes. We can now discover patterns that before may have seemed hidden.

This kind of data collection can present a challenge to academic freedom. A digital record that can be mapped, analyzed and compared with others has now replaced the individual performance of the craftsman. The shift in the university has been from teaching to learning. This means that the emphasis is no longer on good teaching and has focused back onto learning.

The existence of a map of the classroom is a significant change from all that had gone before. Once there is blueprint that can be compared to other blueprints, the role of the craftsman gets changed. We now have data that can be managed, manipulated and compared to other similar classes. This kind of talk has been an anathema to professors for as long as it has been going on.

Once there is digital map, all sorts of things follow. We can compare two sections of the same class taught by different teachers. We can analyze the patterns of interaction in different student populations. Now combine this data with the other data that universities keep. This kind of data might include high school class rank, SAT scores, GPA, ethnicity, gender, full- or part-time status, classroom attendance, major, age, economic status and countless other variables.

Combine this student data with our classroom map, and we are in a new and as yet uncharted territory. This territory is no longer the realm of the professor alone, sole craftsman of an art. It is now data to be assembled by a team, analyzed and looked at as the product of more than one person. With these new technologies, new kinds of professionals are needed in the university, such as data experts and instructional design professionals.

The classroom is now a place of collaboration and teamwork. It is where teams of professionals trained in the business of learning can intersect. It is a place where data can replace the expert judgment of the professor. It is important for us realize that professors are not trained to teach but to conduct research in a particular field. But now there is a science to the classroom, a record of success and failures and expertise for improving the odds for student success.

A new technology tends to favor some groups of people and harm other groups. Blacksmiths were made obsolete by the automobile; buggy makers were put out of business by the railroad; typesetters have been replaced by digital printing. With technological change, in other words, there are always winners and losers (Postman 1997). With that in mind, we must ask ourselves what the digital revolution will mean for the future of the professoriate and the university as a whole.

CHAPTER ELEVEN
RETHINKING COLLEGE STRUCTURE AND
GOVERNANCE FOR THE DIGITAL AGE

*All men who have turned out worth anything have had the chief
hand in their own education.*

— Sir Walter Scott

Numerous approaches have been taken to understand the complex governance structures of colleges (Kerr 1963). The BLT model is a simple scheme we developed to help us understand the organizational differences utilized by modern universities (McCluskey 2012c). Schools are governed by one of the three following models. While many schools have elements of each of the three, one model usually is dominant. A university can have a Bureaucracy Centered Model (B-governance), a Learning Centered Model (L-governance), or a Teacher Centered Model (T-governance).

The T-governance model is historically the most common in higher education. It refers to the teacher-centered college, and it was the norm a century ago. For a number of reasons as we will explore, many in higher education still see this as the ideal model.

THE SHIFT TO B-GOVERNANCE: MORE ADMINISTRATORS AND LESS FULL-TIME FACULTY

Universities are places of academic instruction, so who better to guide the institutions than the academics? We have mentioned that the University of Paris is often thought to be the first European University over others founded earlier because Paris was governed by a faculty guild, whereas the other schools, such as Bologna and Salamanca, were founded by student guilds. Today, much of the literature about the decline of the university connects this decline with the decline of faculty governance (Donoghue 2008). At the same time, there has been a growing backlash about the power of the faculty to block change and slow down progress (Hass and Fishman 2010).

The growth of full-time positions in modern universities has not occurred among the full-time tenured faculty. Instead, the growth has been at administrative levels. There has been some concern about the evolution toward what one author has called the "all administrative university" (Ginsberg 2011). In addition, the gridlock that can happen in faculty senates has been a source of frustration in efforts to modernize colleges (Rosen 2011).

A humorous story might help here. The president of a faculty senate once told us "if we dislike an idea, we form a committee to study it. If we really dislike it, we form an exploratory committee, and that is the end of it." Some argue that the pace of change in the modern digital university has become too rapid for the leisurely decision making of historic faculty senates. At the same time, the loss of tenure positions and the increase in adjunct faculty has weakened the power of the faculty. A number of faculty see the diminution of their role as one of the key reasons for the crisis in higher education (Lagemann and Lewis 2012). The resolution of this question is key for the future of higher education.

B-governance or a Bureaucracy Centered Model is when professional administrators or bureaucrats control the institution. For example, technical schools, normal schools and community colleges are often controlled more by a bureaucracy than a strong faculty union.

In particular, the complexity and size of many modern community colleges necessitates the need for a class of professional managers.

From a historical perspective, there are a number of reasons for this kind of governance. In 2011, the United States Department of Education listed some large community college systems, such as those in Houston, Miami-Dade and Northern Virginia, as being responsible for managing more than 50,000 students each. These same community college systems have long since departed from the three traditional semesters of Fall, Spring and Summer, which were based on the cycle of agricultural time where plants were planted and harvested.. Many modern community colleges now have more than 30 semester starts in the course of a single school year.

In modern community colleges, a large number of students are holding down full-time jobs. This means more courses are being offered in the evenings and on weekends, as well as online. Faculty alone cannot manage such a complex grid of students, colleagues, facilities and course schedules. Because of this new complexity and growth, an army of admissions professionals, registrars, course schedulers, room schedulers, financial aid professionals, librarians, bookstore personnel, institutional research teams, and more have been added to community college administrations.

All colleges (not just community colleges) now have powerful CFOs, CIOs and COOs who often have more power than the provosts, deans and faculty. Typically, faculty come and go to campus on their own schedules, taking time off for winter breaks or summer sessions. The B-governance team, the professional bureaucrats, is on campus all year round. For example, in many modern non-profit private colleges, it is not uncommon for faculty to be off campus from the end of exams in early December and do not return until sometime in January when a new term begins. During that time, however, the work of the modern college does not stop. It is the same with the end of class in spring term. Faculty are often gone when there is still much administrative work to do. Grades must be posted, courses for the summer semester need to be scheduled or canceled, new sections of popular courses for the fall semester may need to be created and staffed, rooms need to be assigned, academic standing computed, degrees conferred and grades disputed. Much of this activity is taking place when the majority of faculty members are off campus.

By making these decisions, the B-governance professional managers empowered themselves and began to make decisions that were in the past considered the province of the academics in the T-governance or Teacher Centered Model.

The organizational charts at most small or mid-sized colleges once consisted of professors who became deans and department chairs and are now provosts. These former professors often had more say about digital and data issues than librarians, registrars, institutional researchers, IT professionals and financial aid professionals.

Many of the complaints about changes in the modern university reflect the shift from T-governance where teachers made the decisions to B-governance where the bureaucrats have the power (Kirp 2003). Modern institutions can no longer be governed by the slow decision making that characterized T-governance institutions just a generation ago. The shift has been caused by both the increased number of students and the application of digital technologies that have taken decision making out of the hands of the faculty and placed it in the hands of professional managers. This battle between faculty and professional administrators has resulted in a number of conflicts that define higher education today (Ginsberg 2011).

Colleges are institutions designed to change slowly. We previously noted that MIT was founded because there was a widespread perception that Harvard was behind the times concerning science and progressive education (Killian 1957). In other revolutionary times, many thinkers such as Galileo, Da Vinci, Descartes, Leibniz and Copernicus did most of their work outside of the university. At the time when Descartes was revolutionizing geometry, Copernicus was challenging the heliocentric theory of the universe and Leibniz was inventing the calculus, there were universities filled with scholars. However, because of the church and its role, these great thinkers had to do most of their revolutionary work outside the walls of the university (Boorstin 1985).

The move from T-governance or Teacher Centered Model to B-governance or Bureaucracy Centered Model has not been popular with faculty. Many professors would like to see a return to

T-governance where faculty make all key decisions (Meiners 2004). But in reality, because of federal and state laws, reporting requirements, accreditation rules and new software running behind the scenes, events are moving too fast to vote on everything. This has forced a shift in decision making from T-governance or a Teacher Centered Model to B-governance or a Bureaucracy Centered Model. The return to T-governance or the Teacher Centered Model as it existed before the digital age is impossible. The increasing complexity of management challenges and computer systems have made it more difficult for faculty to function effectively as part-time administrators. The trick will be to make sure the college runs efficiently while at the same time preserving the power of faculty over academic matters. Before we examine L-governance or the Learning Centered Model, we must take a more in-depth look at challenges presented from the shift to the B-governance or Bureaucracy Centered Model.

A NEW CLASS OF MANAGERS AND CONFLICTS

The digital revolution has brought technology to the university and empowered those who program and direct that technology. This comes at a time of increased reporting to state and federal government agencies, accrediting agencies and the popularity of surveys such as those published by the U.S. News and World Report and Peterson's Guide. These activities separate a new class of manager from the old brand of faculty leadership that governed universities for generations.

While there has been hostility toward the for-profit sector for a number of reasons, the for-profit sector got out ahead of the non-profit sector in pursuing the adult and non-traditional student. How did these new schools with little academic reputation begin to beat long established brands? In some cases, it was through questionable recruiting techniques. At the same time, however, the for-profits implemented digital technologies more rapidly and became more efficient institutions (Rosen 2011). These institutions would not have been possible with the redesign of the entire college experience made possible by digital technologies (Ruch and Keller 2003).

121

The key point of conflict in many modern institutions is often between the faculty and the registrar, or, in larger institutions, between the faculty and what has come to be nicknamed "Ops" or operations. From a historical perspective, the registrar is often the keeper of the college seal who also heads the office where grade point averages are run, where records are kept about whether or not students make the honor roll or are placed on probation. The registrar is also responsible for maintaining the degree audit needed to determine who is eligible for degree conferral. Additionally, the registrar is responsible for the data used for generating reports that are submitted to accrediting agencies and state and federal governments (Birnbaum 1988).

The conflict between the faculty and the registrar is sometimes painted in the words of "academic freedom" or "faculty governance." The faculty see the registrar as intruding upon their freedom while the registrar attempts to straddle the academic and operations realms. The registrar is firmly rooted in both worlds and has a unique perspective due to their need to balance between these two areas. This conflict is rooted in the demands of external accrediting and legislative bodies that impose limitations on faculty. In the history of federal intrusion into higher education, for instance, a big step was taken in that direction when colleges began accepting federal funds for tuition (Schrader 1969). Once colleges began accepting Title IV funds, they had to meet a growing number of federal statutes and requirements. This meant that national and state politics began to play an increasing role in college governance. In conjunction with this increasing role, the price of college began to increase faster than the rate of inflation. If a college wanted to keep up with federal reporting and deadlines, they had to build an infrastructure to handle these demands. This led to more questions about how colleges spend their money and how they were governed.

THE BIRTH OF L-GOVERNANCE OR THE LEARNING CENTERED MODEL

While the push and pull between faculty governance and professional managers has dominated much of the press about college governance, we believe a third form of governance will trump this dichotomy. We can think about this in terms of Hegel's dialect of thesis, antithesis and synthesis (Hegel 1981). T-governance or the Teacher Centered Model is the thesis where the vast majority of colleges were just 50 years ago. The increasing complexity of institutions of higher learning gave rise to more efficient and agile B-governance or Bureaucracy Centered Model. But this efficiency and agility was bought at a steep price. Faculty complained that academic rigor and standards were being sacrificed for more short-term economic goals (Hess 2008). In comments echoing John Cardinal Newman's questioning of Utilitarianism, many academics see the institutions as sacrificing everything for simple economic gain (Nelson 1997). This has led to a deterioration of labor conditions for faculty and staff that some would say has all but destroyed the heart of the modern university (Fountain 2005). What is needed now is a synthesis that respects the traditional role that faculty play in academic leadership while at the same time modernizing the university for the digital age. This synthesis is the L-governance or Learning Centered Model where the learning organization uses feedback and data-driven decision making to balance economics and academic matters.

L-governance or the Learning Centered Model is, in our opinion, where the evolution of higher education has to go. L-governance does not mean that just the students learn, but the organization as a whole learns (Senge 2000). It is here we again find the impact of the digital revolution. The digital revolution has given us access to a great deal of data and provides ways to manipulate and learn from that data (Hentschke, Lechuga and Tierney 2010). Data-driven decision making means that we make policy decisions not on opinions, belief, tradition or theories. Instead, we make decisions based on data (Ratner 2011). This means that the administration, faculty, students, alumni and public must all be open to learn and be open to the fact that their cherished opinions or nostalgic memories may not be true.

DATA REVEALS TRUTHS AND CONSEQUENCES

Data-driven decision making can inform L-governance or the Learning Centered Model and change the way people behave. For an example of how this can happen, we point to a university we were familiar with that had a basic "College 100" course. These types of courses are common throughout the country because they are believed to improve retention while providing students with basic information and strategies for their academic career. While a small number of transfer students were exempted from this requirement, this particular university sought to channel all of their first-year students into their particular iteration of College 100. They did this on the basis of a belief that this would improve student retention. A great deal of time and attention was given to College 100 on this assumption. There was a College 100 committee, a faculty member who oversaw the curriculum and the best teachers who spent time on what was considered the pride of the college.

At one point, the institutional research team at this college ran a report that had a shocking conclusion. Students that successfully completed the course were less likely to graduate than those who avoided it or somehow missed it. Both faculty and administration challenged the data, so it was rerun to validate the results. It turns out the original report was correct. College 100 did not, in fact, contribute to better retention.

This story does not have a happy ending. This particular college had a strong dean and a strong academic voice. The college was T-governed not L-governed. The report was buried and the director of College 100 kept her job and the entire faculty kept theircourses and feet good about themselves. How many assumptions and consequent actions like this are impacting how we use the resources of our universities? One can only guess. We cannot know for sure because, to put it quiet bluntly, there is no data.

The information revolution can now provide data on faculty performance, student performance, learning objectives, student behavior and all sorts of other things. This provides the L-governance or Learning Centered Model with the tools it needs to be agile, smart and always learning. The move from T-governance or Teacher Centered Model to B-governance or Bureaucracy Centered Model has been painful and destabilizing for the faculty (Boyer 1997). When performance data is gathered and analyzed, the magic of teaching might be reduced to a series of metrics. So, the move to yet another model may be very difficult. While there may be unintended consequences, we believe this model will lead to a healthier faculty and student body in the end. We treasure what we measure and we should have started measuring learning in more rigorous ways long ago.

WHY L-GOVERNANCE IS NEEDED

Why do we need L-governance or the Learning Centered Model? Because institutions that fail to evolve into L-governance or the Learning Centered Model will be left behind. Because both T-governance or Teacher Centered Governance and B-governance or Bureaucracy Centered Model have been unable to contain the costs of higher education, and the issue of tuition has become a political football that is impacting the rest of the conversation. Even as the public began its outcry about the price of tuition and student debt colleges continued to raise their prices faster than the rate of inflation.

Years ago, the price of a college degree did not involve placing the student in lifelong debt (Brown and Lauder 2010). Today, the price of a college education has so outpaced inflation that questions have begun to be raised about the value of a college education. There are some who even advocate a do-it-yourself education where you can piece together your own degree (Kamenetz 2010). Under a 2011 grant from the Gates Foundation, Anya Kamenetz is currently writing a workbook on how to put together these credits gathered from various sources outside the university. In 2012, a number of books and articles appeared that advocated skipping college altogether and starting out your work life debt free.

The economic crisis in college debt will not be solved easily. Colleges raised costs without really thinking about a long-term goal or the public good. As the cost of college tuition outstripped inflation, it meant that college costs were rising faster than wages. This was driven by an expansion not in faculty or libraries but in the administration and infrastructure needed to keep up with changes in technology and reporting. The price of college even outstripped the rise in health care costs, which also rose faster than inflation (Brown and Lauder 2010). Why has this been the case? Were colleges not aware that their spending habits were straining the finances of their students and their

125

families? Did they not realize this was making them unpopular with their customers? Why could they not stop a trend that was opposed by the public, media and politicians? After a lifetime in higher education, our experience has been that colleges often would raise the tuition to cover any shortfalls or new projects they had on the books. There was obviously a lack of vision about where this train was headed. In 2011, with the economy still in recession, colleges announced their fall 2012 tuition increases, and numerous colleges announced double-digit tuition, some increases as high as 22% (Wolfgang 2011). Colleges perform a public function, contribute to the public good and educate our citizens, but we have lost sight of these goals as colleges have become too expensive for many Americans (Lagemann and Lewis 2012).

In short, colleges are historically inefficient, and this has been in large part due to their governance structures and a vagueness about their missions. Any talk about business or making colleges more efficient has been met with animosity by the professoriate (Donoghue 2008). In our experience in higher education, for example, any talk of equating "students" with "consumers" or worse yet, "customers" has met with strong objections because the analogy was not seen as ideal or perfect. A good analogy is one where the two terms being compared are more similar than dissimilar. While it is true that there are some differences, students have not been treated as customers. If they had been treated like customers, colleges would have found ways to avoid constant yearly tuition raises that hurt their customers and ultimately damaged the reputation of higher education. Overall, the end result has been that reckless tuition hikes have caused more people to question the value of a college education (Hacker 2010).

The L-governance college run by a Learning Centered Model is one where decisions are not made on what is best for the faculty or the administration or the students, but what is best for the university as a learning community as a whole. Think of the origin of the term. We have mentioned the University of Paris was a "Universitas Magistrorum et Scholarium." The key term here is the Latin word "Universus," which means "whole" or "aggregate." A university is a place where all learning and knowledge is included. It should also be a place where all voices can be heard and all points of view expressed.

To understand governance in the modern university, we must not look at the university as it exists today, but instead we must go back to fundamental questions about the nature of the university. We must ask the question "what is a university for?" We must ask "is there a public good that the university serves?" We must ask "is there a point where the financial inequality that colleges are heading toward becomes detrimental to the nation?"

CONTAINING THE COST OF TUITION AND TEXTBOOKS

L-governance or the Learning Centered Model allows us to abandon assumptions and let the data guide us. Buckminster Fuller once said "don't fight forces, use them." Does tuition have to be increased by 8, 10 or 15% every year? Some colleges have figured out how to keep tuition low. The American Public University System, a for-profit online university, did not raise undergraduate tuition or add any fees for a decade from 2001 to 2012 while at the same time growing from 5,000 students to 115,000 students. In addition, they included a book grant where students do not pay for textbooks. This also means the university has absorbed all of the raises in textbook costs, which are legendary (Allen 2008). Over the last decade, it has not been unusual for colleges to increase their tuition by 80%. In addition, the cost of textbooks the students are forced to buy has risen at similar rates. How then did one online for-profit not raise costs at all? In part, it is because of its commitment to being an L-governed or Learning Centered Model university. A budget was adopted and they committed to living within it to keep tuition costs flat. While there are many questions that can be asked about how they did this, the fact is that it is possible to hold down costs while building infrastructure at the same time. Colleges must learn and adapt to changes in the current culture and economy in order to change and adapt to the environment.

Take the price of textbooks as one example. In student surveys, the American Public University System discovered that the cost of textbooks was viewed as a burden. In ranking their concerns about college, the survey showed textbook costs near the top. So, the university made a commitment to pay for books without cost to the student. This had several unintended consequences. Some were seen as positive, and some have caused complaints by the students and faculty. First, it meant the professors would not require books that they would not use. The data revealed how many professors ordered "supplemental texts" that the students had to purchase, sometimes at great costs, and yet, these same textbooks were never used for their course.

At the same time, the university placed a maximum cap price on most necessary textbooks. This initially caused many clashes with professors, deans and program managers who argued that their academic freedoms were being impinged upon. However, this was not about the freedom of the faculty to order any book they wanted. It was more about the students' ability to pay. In the end, as an L-governance or Learning Centered Model organization, the university decided that the finances of the students outweighed the concerns of the faculty. The debating and politics of this decision is necessary in an L-governed institution. The L-governed institution must think about all sides of question and what is best for the university. In some cases, this may make the students or faculty unhappy but it is what is best for the whole.

While we have noted these two examples of cost containment, we are not arguing that all for-profits are L-governed and therefore superior, or even that all for-profits are well governed. We do nonetheless note that there is a great deal of animosity about for-profit education in general from the faculty because the for-profits have often weakened the voice of faculty in the total governance of the university (Sweeny 2011). As this shift in governance has happened, for-profits have often rightly been accused of weakening both academic freedom and academic quality. We have worked in several of the largest online for-profits and believe this to be true in many cases. At the same time, the for-profits used data and digital technologies to contain costs and, in some cases, lower tuition. In one recent hostile exchange, a traditional professor told us, "There is nothing to learn from the for-profits except how to lie and cheat." That professor, it turns out, holds tenure at a school with a 19% graduation rate after 6 years, and one that has raised its tuition by more than 100% in the last decade. The authors believe there are things to be learned from many

128

people. One of the reasons higher education has been slow to react to the coming storm is that, sadly, they thought they had all the answers and they were also dead certain they were the good guys.

FINDING A BALANCE BETWEEN BUSINESS EFFICIENCIES AND ACADEMIC STANDARDS AND QUALITY

We believe there is a way to balance the efficiency of the for-profits with the strong academic standards of some of the more traditional colleges. There needs to be a balancing of the voices of faculty members with the voices of administrators, alumni and students. But in this one case, the containing of textbook costs, the university asked the faculty to live within parameters dictated by the budgets of the students.

The two other unintended consequences were the turn to electronic texts and the creation of the university's own textbooks. While the price of print textbooks and publishing has gone up, e-books or electronic texts are less expensive. However, when the college started to move from print textbooks to e-books, there was great push back from both faculty and students, many of whom wanted the feel of a "real book." Because, in the first place, students were not paying for textbooks, there was little motivation to move them from the physical book to the e-book. There were many conversations around this issue. In an attempt to become an L-governed or Learning Centered Model university committed to data-driven decision making, the options were either to go to e-books or to pass the cost of textbooks onto the student by ending the textbook grant or raising tuition. In student and faculty surveys, it was determined that going to e-books, although not popular, was less disruptive than ending the book grant and ultimately increasing fees or raising tuition.

Finally, as the cost of textbooks continued to rise, a number of faculty began to produce their own e-books and materials from various sources on the web, saving more for the university and hence keeping tuition down. This L-governance or Learning Centered Model type of decision was not based on issues related to academic freedom, or even the demands of students. Instead, it was based on what was best for the university. The cost to the student was the driving factor here. But at the same time conversations with the faculty and an inclusion of their concerns and issues had to be part of the process. Ultimately, the issue of cost to the student overcame the objections by some faculty. But it may be in other cases that what the students want may not be good for the university. So, in the L-governed or Learning Centered Model university, the choice is made for the good of the whole and that means for the value of the degree and the education that is being provided.

The L-governance model promotes learning as the governing principle. In his groundbreaking work on learning organizations, Peter Senge is in the tradition of both systems theory and cybernetics theory, where feedback is incorporated into decisions (Von Bertalanffy 1969). The governance model of the future will be dictated not by faculty (T-governance) or bureaucracy (B-governance) but by the data that shows what is successful for the university as a whole.

Data-driven decision making has been applied to many businesses and industries, including education (Picciano 2005). Data-driven decision makes good use of the information gleaned from the institution to chart its future direction. The digital revolution has helped with this. In the digital university, many of the elements have become data points that we can learn from. The digital university has tools available to it that earlier iterations of college did not have access to. While the heart of the university must not change, how it does business must change in order to be more cost-efficient and effective. The evolution to L-governance will help this dual purpose.

This can be accomplished by the creation of a "Chinese Wall" between academics and professional administrators. A strong faculty, with significant protections, academic freedom and a secure economic future is essential to a healthy institution. Decisions about education should be made by the faculty in response to data in a way that supports an L-governed or Learning Centered Model university. Non-academic decisions, particularly those that impact a college's economic life, should not be the province of a faculty senate. Those decisions are in the domain of professional administrators who are influenced by data and feedback from students. Academics is the domain of professors and not the domain of bean counters. At the same time, we want to make sure that faculty do not need to approve all of the operations and functions needed in a modern university in terms of computer systems, data collection and federal reporting.

A committee of faculty who are voting on issues over which they may not have expertise cannot manage a complex institution in the digital age. The learning organization must be responsive to data that tells us our students are learning. It must show us where we can improve the learning. It must show us any gaps in retention and raise questions about fixing those gaps. The concerns of trustees, alumni, faculty, administrators, and future employers must all be balanced. External measures must be applied to make sure the education is taking hold and is effective for the students.

Being an L-governed institution helps to resolve questions about the focus of education. One of those foci is about providing degree programs that are useful in the pursuit of gainful employment for the many students whose sole aim in college is to improve their economic condition. Those who go to college for economic reasons are in the vast majority (Bok 2004). But many who attend college to improve their economic situation do not feel they have gotten their "money's worth" (an apt phrase for this population). A recent article in the *Chronicle of Higher Education* noted, for instance, that "over 317,000 waiters and waitresses have college degrees (over 8,000 of them have doctoral or professional degrees), along with over 80,000 bartenders, and over 18,000 parking lot attendants. All told, some 17,000,000 Americans with college degrees are doing jobs that the Bureau of Labor Statistics says require less than the skill levels associated with a bachelor's degree" (Vedder 2012).

There have been thinkers who have argued, by looking at the statistics aforementioned and similar data, that too many students are going to college (Murray 2008). The emphasis on the universality of a college degree may not have been the best idea. In 2012, it was widely reported in such publications as the *Washington Post* and the *New York Times* that college debt held by graduates is now in excess of one trillion dollars. That staggering sum can be written as $1,000,000,000,000.00. At the same time, wages have not risen at the same rate as college tuition, increasing the issues around student debt (Wolfgang 2011).

It may be that the media coverage around student debt and related issues could significantly reduce the number of students seeking higher education. If and when that happens, the bubble that is contemporary higher education may burst and many small and even mid-sized colleges may cease to exist. But the crisis is actually deeper. Whole public university systems as large as the California State System are on the verge of collapse (Scheper-Hughes 2011). Generations of students who have been all but guaranteed a cost-effective and quality education are now finding themselves with fewer options. In addition, there is a growing amount of literature indicating that the increasing number of adjuncts teaching at our colleges and universities today is having a negative impact on the quality of education (Sweeny 2011). There are more calls now for the unionization of adjuncts and an attempt to rectify the current situation (Berry 2005). But the causes go much deeper.

Marc Bousquet wrote an interesting analysis in which he tied the cheap underpaid labor of graduate assistants and adjuncts to a very stinging Marxist analysis of value theory. While he does not spare the for-profits, who have become whipping boys for the failure of the modern university, he notes that traditional colleges, state systems and community colleges are all in the same boat (Bousquet 2000). To call adjunct faculty "piece workers," "slave laborers" or "share croppers" is not unheard of (Fountain 2005).

Modern colleges and universities must understand the different motivations of their student bodies and realign their mission with this reality. Freshmen that arrive at Cal Polytechnic are most likely looking for something very different than those who arrive at Rochester Community College in southeastern Minnesota. Professor Vincent Tinto taught us all a great lesson when he showed us that students do not drop out of college, they drop out of a particular college (Tinto 1994). Students leave Harvard for very different reasons than they leave Rio Salado Community College in Phoenix. While there is some crossover, the vast majority of students in these two institutions have very different expectations about what their education should bring them. Understanding these populations and making adjustments through data-driven decision making will ultimately improve the whole university.

With falling scores in math and science, it is clear that the future of work is the future of technological innovation. Any job that does not require creativity has the possibility of being taken over by technology. For this reason, STEM subjects (science, technology, engineering and mathematics) must be brought back to the center of higher education. While the classics have their place and we in no way devalue the role of literature and art, STEM skills are an essential part of living in the digital age.

The digital university by its very nature has the ability to share information. When information is shared, there can be data-driven decision making. Faculty will have their role, administrators will have their role, student voices will be heard and other stakeholders will have input. Because data is collected and data can be shared and interpreted, this means information will be available to all. If knowledge is power, so is information. The sharing of this kind of information is the sharing of results, success and areas of concern. But the learning organization will be guided by what is best for the future and that, dear reader, is a philosophical issue.

PART IV

NEW WINDOWS OF OPPORTUNITY
AND REDEFINED JOBS

Big Data and predictive analytic tools can help higher education dissect teaching and learning like never before, but such new technologies require a step back that entails a deep understanding of the philosophical issues underlying higher education and the skills and values we seek to impart.

ERP systems have replaced paper and unified everything under one rather stilted umbrella that does not make any exceptions, causing distress between faculty and administrators. The registrar's office and its staff of today would be unrecognizable only a few years back. In conjunction with changes to the registrar's office, we note how the roles and duties of librarians have also been reoriented due to our digital revolution.

In the final chapter of Part IV, we explain how all of this change is more of the same theme of tradition and disruption in higher education locking horns. But then we throw in the birth of online education, and some even more amazing circumstances and disrupt-ers start to come to the forefront.

With the advent of online education beyond the course level and into the institutional level, the pace of decision making in fac-ulty senates, curriculum committees and other traditional decision-making bodies was unable to keep up with the rapid processing of data that arrived with this digital revolution.

However, we contend that the disruptions caused by the digi-tal revolution can, indeed, settle along with the continuity at the heart of the university.

CHAPTER TWELVE
BIG DATA AND THE FUTURE
OF HIGHER EDUCATION

Do not train a child to learn by force or harshness; but direct them
to it by what amuses their minds, so that you may be better able to
discover with accuracy the peculiar bent of the genius of each.

— Plato

Although the digital revolution has brought about great change
to institutions and industries throughout the world, higher
education, in many aspects, has been the slowest to change. Many
college-level classes taught today are still very much the same as they
were in 1120, when a Magister at Bologna taught a class (Rait 2010).

THE PROFESSOR AS PERFORMER

As we have noted earlier, teachers generally teach alone. When
the semester ends, the single-letter grade is the only record that
remains for the university. Words are ephemeral. The words of a
professor live and die in the moment and context of a class. The
professor is like a craftsman who makes pots or cups one at a time.
Every class is unique, each one a distinct artistic creation. The same
class can be taught over and over again by the same professor because each time it is a performance, like a live opera or a sporting
event with an uncertain score until the game is over. The professor
is paid, in part, for this performance that must be offered live every

time. Just as Medieval Europe had its bards, storytellers and trou-badours, the modern university has its professors. While it should be noted that many professors also teach by means other than the lecture, the lecture is still a dominant form of instruction in the university today (Brown and Rice 2008).

Using an analogy to musicianship, before the advent of musical recording, if you wanted to hear Mozart's latest creation, you had to hear it performed live. There was plenty of work for musicians in such a world. Before the dawn of recorded music, every coffee house, town square, church, bar or restaurant needed its own musicians. Before things were written down and recorded, every town had its bards, story tellers and historians.

The technologies of recording began modestly, with items such as the player piano. From there, more musical devices arrived over time (Milner 2009). The impact of technology in recorded music changed the need for live music, affecting the livelihoods of live musicians. Is something similar now happening to the college classroom? We must next ask what this means for the future of the professoriate. We must ask what this means for the future of the university.

THE MULTIVERSITY

In looking at an L-governed or Learning Centered Model, we must keep in mind that the university is a complex place with many stake-holders. This form of governance determines what is good for the university as a whole. The problem has been the university never was and never will be a monolithic institution driven by a single vision. A university is a place where different groups pursue different goals that are often at odds with each other. Historically, the university is where teaching, learning, researching, producing new knowledge, creating artistic productions and certifying what knowledge has been gained takes place. In addition, there are now college sports, fund-raising, social activities and service work on many campuses. Every one of these areas has been significantly impacted by the digital revolution.

In his 1963 Godkin Lectures at Harvard, Clark Kerr, the colorful president of the University of California, coined the term "multiver-sity" to cover all the various aims of the evolved modern college (Kerr

1973). Kerr once joked that the function of a university was to provide "sex for the students, sports for the alumni and parking for the faculty." The modern university (or multiversity) president must then satisfy many constituents, many of whom are at odds with each other.

We are just at the beginning of understanding the changes brought on by digital technology. How, for instance, has the relation between parents and children changed in the age of cell phones and social media? How has dating changed in the age of digital technology? How has our relationship to money changed in the digital world? What does it mean to be lonely or connected in the world of social media? Our new digital world will need psychologists, sociologists, anthropologists and economists, but most all it will need philosophers who can chart out our behaviors in tandem with the parameters of the digital world.

CAPTURING THE LECTURE AND ITS DATA

It is our belief that the same technologies that have loosened the underpinnings of the university can educate a larger number of students with more effective methods at a lower cost. We can rethink the university in light of the changes the digital revolution has wrought. To put it simply, knowledge and learning have escaped the campus. In our new digital age, great universities are no longer defined by the size of their physical libraries, special collections specific to that library and the focus of collections in certain subject matters. In addition, the live lecture is changing dramatically.

The lecture is often still a live performance that takes up a certain block of time for both performer (faculty) and audience (students). What is called a classroom hour or Carnegie Unit is a particular block of time shared by faculty and students. The Carnegie Unit, on which federal student aid and countless other government and accreditation metrics are based, does not measure learning, competency or even a basic grasp of concepts. It most often counts the time a live performance happens in the presence of an audience.

In the digital age, this live performance can be captured and replayed while the student is on a stair master or treadmill in their basement, on the beach in Florida or at their local Gold's Gym.

With the World Wide Web, students can now check other theories or interpretations almost instantly. The fact that many colleges and faculty did not allow commonly edited web encyclopedias, such as Wikipedia, as a scholarly footnote, showed the reluctance of faculty to cede their authority to amateurs. Faculty were concerned that without an expert editor the information may be wrong. There are those who argue that this undermines the very concepts of authority and expertise on which the university depends (Keen 2007).

In the Renaissance, much of the scientific advances did not take place in the universities, but outside them, often to the scorn of the universities and their faculty. Galileo, Leonardo di Vinci, Machiavelli, Descartes, Leibniz, Bacon, Locke, Hume and Kepler were not part of a university culture but thrived outside of it. When the Royal Society of England began a series of correspondences between independent thinkers, they came up with the concept of the *Invisible College* as a way of staking out a new kind of knowledge network outside of the university and other traditional centers of learning (Lomas 2002). Could it be that learning has once again escaped the walls of the cloistered college? With so much information available for free, what is the value of a college degree? These are questions that deserve to be pondered.

As we noted in Chapter One, Big Data finds the great currents that flow beneath the waves and reveals the deeper structure of things. To see more of the power of what Big Data can do, we refer to how one company used it to find patterns that, at first, were not obvious. A *New York Times* story by Charles Duhig in 2012 showed how the Target chain of department stores collects and analyzes data. Target begins with a guest ID process that allows them to gather all sorts of information about their customers. Because they sell everything from groceries to TVs, Target is able to obtain a keen understanding of their customers' buying patterns, and much more.

As noted in the article by Duhig, "Target can buy data about your ethnicity; job history; the magazines you read; if you've ever declared bankruptcy or got divorced; the year you bought (or lost) your house; where you went to college; what kinds of topics you talk about online; whether you prefer certain brands of coffee, paper towels, cereal or applesauce; your political leanings; reading habits; charitable giving and the number of cars you own. (In a statement, Target declined to identify what demographic information it collects or purchases.)" (Duhig 2012).

Marketers have figured out "that when someone marries, he or she is more likely to start buying a new type of coffee. When a couple moves into a new house, they're more apt to purchase a different kind of cereal. When they divorce, there's an increased chance they'll start buying different brands of beer" (Duhig 2012).

But the most amazing find was yet to come. They took a look at women who signed up on their baby registry and started to follow what they purchased and when. Patterns emerged that no one had noticed before. The data showed that women who were pregnant often switched from scented lotion to unscented lotion near the beginning of their second trimester. Target correlated this with other data that suggested that sometime during their first 20 weeks, pregnant women started to buy supplements like calcium, magnesium and zinc (Duhig 2012). When they got close to their delivery dates, these same women started to buy scent-free soap, hand sanitizers and large cotton balls.

As Target went through this data, they were able to identify about 25 products that, when analyzed together, allowed the store to assign each shopper a "pregnancy prediction" score. More important, they could also estimate a woman's due date to within a small window, so Target could send coupons timed to very specific stages of her pregnancy (Duhig 2012).

Now comes the payoff of this rather stuffy *New York Times* story that caught the public's attention and made it a much more personal story:

> A man walked into a Target outside Minneapolis and demanded to see the manager. He was clutching coupons that had been sent to his daughter, and he was angry, according to an employee who participated in the conversation.
>
> "My daughter got this in the mail!" he said. "She's still in high school, and you're sending her coupons for baby clothes and cribs? Are you trying to encourage her to get pregnant?"
>
> The manager didn't have any idea what the man was talking about. He looked at the mailer. Sure enough, it

was addressed to the man's daughter and contained advertisements for maternity clothing, nursery furniture and pictures of smiling infants. The manager apologized and then called a few days later to apologize again.

On the phone, though, the father was somewhat abashed. "I had a talk with my daughter," he said. "It turns out there's been some activities in my house I haven't been completely aware of. She's due in August. I owe you an apology" (Duhig 2012).

NEW WINDOWS OF OPPORTUNITY THROUGH DATA ANALYSIS

What does this have to do with higher education? The answer is simple. This kind of Big Data analysis has everything to do with the future of higher education but not too much to do with its present state. Big Data will impact how the university sees its students and their learning. It gives us a window into their behavior that we did not have before. Some may argue that this intrusion into the classroom can only have negative effects. But if we remember our Target story, we can see that they began to learn things about their customers that even their own family members had not guessed. Like the Nazca lines that could only be discovered in the air, there are things we will find out through data analysis that will enlighten us about teaching.

Big Data can help us see where students are learning, but it may not give us the full picture. For example, at the American Public University System, which has a large data team using predictive analytics, they looked at those courses where students were dropping, failing and withdrawing and asked the question "Why?" Traditionally, at American Public University, courses with a high dropout rate have been in areas such as mathematics and foreign languages. Does that mean the teaching needs to be improved, or does that tell us something about the difficulty of the subject? In figure skating, they judge the "degree of difficulty" of a jump or maneuver. More points are awarded to the more difficult jumps. The same leniency should be shown in college teaching. This requires that those who look at the bare data of dropouts, withdrawals and failures must have the wisdom and experience to know that not all classes in the university have the same degree of difficulty. These are not "widgets" meant to fit one inside the other. Teaching music appreciation is wholly different from teaching a biology lab, and that is wholly different from teaching differential calculus. This is something one learns as one grows through the apprenticeship ranks in a university. This is not something some vague management theory will provide a window into. For this reason, we recognize that gathering data is one thing and applying it correctly is something altogether different. One takes analysis and interpretation and the second one takes a kind of (are we so bold to say it?) wisdom.

The application of Big Data allows us, for the first time, to have a scientific way to see where education is succeeding and where we have work to do. It will open up doors to the sub-currents that impact how students learn. Earlier, we distinguished the BLT scheme for college governance. Colleges are governed by a B-governance or Bureaucracy Centered Model, L-governance or Learning Centered Model or T-governance or Teacher Centered Model. To move to the L-governance learning model, we need to break apart elements of the old governance structures. All organizations resist change, and colleges are no exception. Changing governance is really changing something essential about the university.

For the first time, Big Data gives the modern university the tools to separate what is essential from what is accidental. We can now see where we are successful and where we need to improve. We can see where students are having issues and where they are able to grasp and use concepts. But as we have cautioned before, data and statistics will not provide a direction to the university. Data and statistics will only guide us once we have a concept of what we are trying to accomplish and how we want to get there.

Cardinal Newman had it right. First, we must understand the philosophical issues underlying higher education and the skills and values we seek to impart. It is only then that the data can make sense. There is a difference between information and wisdom, and this is something we should never forget, even in the "information age."

CHAPTER THIRTEEN
THE CHANGING ROLES OF
REGISTRARS AND LIBRARIANS

I imagine paradise to be a kind of library.
— Jorge Luis Borges

As we noted in the first chapter, college registrars and college librarians have experienced profound shifts in the way they provide student and faculty services (Tierney and Hentschke 2007). The work, competencies and relationships of registrars and librarians have changed radically in the past few decades. These two positions have felt the impact of the digital revolution much earlier than most faculty members.

Issues related to academic freedom and control of the curriculum process continue to make it possible for many faculty members to resist the digital revolution. On the other hand, many registrars and librarians have already absorbed the digital revolution (Ruch and Keller 2003). The shift from the realm of paper to the digital universe has pulled the rug out from both of these roles as they were traditionally understood. But as these two positions have evolved, while in many colleges the faculty have remained relatively unaffected, a gulf has opened between the academic side of the house and the "student services" side of the house that adapted to technology much earlier (Parker, Lenhart and Moore 2011).

Colleges do two things for students, they educate and they certify that education. At one time, the college registrar was the keeper of the college seal and held the position that guaranteed that learning took place by ensuring that the transcripts were correct, grades were collected and students were on the proper path toward a degree. In short, the professor's main focus has historically been on educating, while the registrar's main focus has historically been on the certification or validation of that education in the form of a grade, certificate or degree.

FROM REGISTRAR AS GATEKEEPER TO IT DEPARTMENT PARTNER

In the universe that was ruled by paper, the registrar's office was the "holy of holies" where transcripts were kept, records secured, grades posted, letters in student files were placed and so on. It was the place where the college catalog and the academic policies insured the integrity of all academic decisions. It was the place where student and university records were protected (Lauren 2006). Because paper is a fragile thing, the office was set up to block student and faculty access directly to the records, so they could not be tampered with. Some colleges, such as Shenandoah University in Virginia, had bank vaults in which the paper student records were kept. Security and guarding the records was the job of the registrar who was the gatekeeper to graduation.

The digital revolution is in the process of taking that paper out of the registrar's hands. In more and more colleges, student records are now housed on servers maintained by the IT department instead of within the registrar's domain. ERP software now maintains all of the college's records, including the coding and validation of student grades, GPAs, financial aid data, and degree paths.

The ERP can display records in real time, so there is no longer a need for someone to locate and copy a piece of paper. The ERP has a common database, so that financial records are tied into grades, which are tied into student data, which are tied into satisfactory academic progress, which are tied into degree plans and so on (Bidgoli 2004).

There was a time when professors turned their grades into the registrar's office by hand. The professors would stand in line, and some clerk in the registrar's office would go over the grade sheet to make sure the writing was legible and all the grades were there. The registrar's office was the place where the grades were entered into the computer, numbers could be checked and issues may be found by manual intervention. That has all changed.

Because professors can enter grades directly into the system now, without the intervention of the registrar, the posting has become an issue between the professor and IT systems. The registrar, however, is still in the middle of the process because if the grades are not posted on time (and many professors do not post grades on time), the registrar is often the one in contact with the students, as well as a crucial intersection point for the operations of the rest of the university. So, while the registrars have surrendered control, they still have the responsibility to see that grades are "posted." Incidentally, "posted" is a word that comes from the time of cork boards where sheets of papers with students' names were tacked up to inform students of their grades.

If a student wants to alter a grade illegally, it is no longer necessary to break into the registrar's office like a cat burglar in the night and ink in changes. Instead, a student would have to hack into the system to alter a transcript. The registrar is technically no longer the keeper of the grades, no longer the guardian of paper and no longer the place where records are kept. All of this has been moved into the digital realm.

THE RECONCILIATION OF MULTIPLE SYSTEMS

When colleges first adopted ERPs, they began to link all of the data that belonged to the institution. Financial aid, student accounts, grades, grade point averages, satisfactory academic progress, catalog changes, degree plans and many other bits of data are now entered into the ERP. But this data needs to be interpreted and acted on for students to receive honors, and be placed on probation or certified for financial aid, tuition assistance or veteran's benefits.

The modern registrar now has the problem of reconciling system data and certifying their validity. Everything in the university has sped up with the digital revolution. In the world of paper, the university could only move as fast as that piece of paper could be processed. In the digital world, everything now moves at the speed of light.

147

There was a time when college catalogs changed every few years. The college catalog is the student's contract with the university and the student is held to the catalog under which they entered the university (Lauren 2006). Catalog changes are degree changes, and the various degree maps must be kept accurate. But with the digitization of the catalog, it became possible to put out catalogs more quickly along with reconciling new versions of the catalog (Bidgoli 2004). When colleges had to print and bind catalogs, it was prohibitively expensive. With digital catalogs, this is no longer the case. The digitization of catalogs has changed the pace of curricular changes at universities.

With the increased scrutiny of transfer credit, federal regulations surrounding student aid, questions about contact hours and multiplying session starts, it is up to the registrar to understand and harmonize these systems. For example, a student's academic progress and grade point average, which are both academic activities that determine if a student can receive financial aid, are usually handled by entirely different offices. Today, the registrar's office is the point at which both financial and academic data meet, ensuring that the student has registered for class and received his or her aid. Matching up these various parts is difficult because it entails harmonizing data from different sources, some controlled by finance, some controlled by IT and some controlled by academics. Thus, the modern registrar's office is the place where all of the contradictions of the modern university come to light.

THE DEATH OF PAPER

The registrar's office had a very different function before the digital age. In the past, the registrar's office was the place where paper was kept under lock and key. Grades, transcripts, student files, notes, catalogs, degree plans and all sorts of other information that validated the learning of the university were recorded on thousands of sheets of paper. Paper was the ship on which the university sailed. But that ship has sunk. The role of paper in the university and its undoing are at the heart of many modern university conflicts.

Paper has a long history in higher education. Paper made from pulp was first found in China in the second century A.D. It traveled to the Islamic world and arrived in Europe in the thirteenth century (Nakanishi 1990). The role of paper increased as Europe built water-powered paper mills to increase the production of paper. However, it was not the supply of paper that was the issue in the medieval world. It was how to get information onto paper.

The work of monks who copied manuscripts in scriptoriums was long and laborious. Because it took such intense labor, books were rare and expensive. For this reason, only a very small part of the population was literate. All of this was changed by a technology that revolutionized how documents were created. The pioneering work of Gutenberg and the Venetian Humanist Aldus Manutius made the mass production of paper documents possible (Ong 2002).

Paper grew up with the university. Evidence of this can be found in a 1970 novel by John Jay Osborn, Jr. titled *The Paper Chase*. This movie is about students in pursuit of a Harvard law degree. These students were studying from physical books in the library, writing their class notes in paper notebooks, and taking their professor's paper exams. Their ultimate goal and the end result of their labor was the paper diploma. Student advisers had paper; professors graded papers; and there were financial aid paper records. The registrar's office was at the heart of this paper empire (Birnbaum 1988). The registrar was the place where the learning was authenticated and student transcripts and degree plans were kept. When a student needed to transfer or graduate, the paper in the registrar's office was the passport out.

This empire of paper came to an abrupt end with the introduction of digital technology. The digital revolution brought all of the disparate systems of the university under one program that used its own iron universal logic to make decisions that could formally be appealed to human beings. Once the college became digital, the pace of its offerings, the ways it operated and how people interacted all underwent a dramatic change as transparency in all things was forced. All of the paper documents were sorted and joined by the ERP and were no longer under the domain of separate departments. The ERP forced decisions and made it much more difficult to make an exception.

This has created conflict between the registrar's office and faculty. In the past, a faculty member could amend a sheet of paper or trade a grade without creating too many problems. But once all of the systems have been tied together by the ERP, a change in a grade could mean a change in the student's satisfactory academic progress and could impact the student's financial aid and overall status. This unifying of systems has made the registrar's position more crucial in the university, while the status of this role has not been raised.

THE ROLE OF REGISTRAR REDEFINED

The registrar was often considered subservient to academics because the university itself was "academic" (Lauren 2006). But changes in technology have given the registrar more responsibility without giving the registrar more power. Conflicts in the rules governing financial aid, grades and programs impact classroom registrations, landing squarely in the registrar's office. This is where students find out that they are unable to register for a class or graduate from a program.

In some schools, the registrar has been placed under a COO and is now located somewhere down in the "Ops," or operations, portion of the organizational chart. We believe instead of being placed under a COO, the registrar's role should in fact be the COO's role at a university. The digitizing and linking of all systems now requires an expertise and technology savviness that a lot of faculty, deans and provosts do not possess because their career paths have not taken them over the rocky road of how computer systems and software programs actually work (Preinkert 2004). The linkage of systems has created the need for the registrar to understand not only the academic side of the university but also all of the business operations (financial aid, student accounts, admissions, etc.) as well. The domain of the registrar has increased in complexity and scope. For example, the registrar now interacts with the learning management system as data points such as registration and attendance flow over to those systems. Some colleges have even done away with the position of registrar. More people with management degrees, who have not come up through the apprenticeship of the registrar's office, are taking the place of registrars. Historically, because the role of the registrar was a complex mix of knowledge of degree programs, policies and university history, this position required a long period of apprenticeship within the academic world. But today there has been a move toward running the university more like a business using management theories (Ginsberg 2011). These changes have redefined the role of the registrar as a mediator between the faculty, IT and Ops, all of which have different cultures and often different goals (Deem 2008). The registrar has long been an educator, educating university students, faculty and staff about policy and processes. With the integration of institutional systems, the registrar becomes an educator in a new context as she/he must understand, on a fundamental level, all the systems and their interactions and thus, extending this knowledge and understanding to the rest of the university community as needed. Owing to the role change, we believe the registrar needs to have a higher-level role in the university and must bring a different skill set to the role as well. Skills would include project management and IT knowledge, as well as an understanding of the university as a complete system.

LIBRARIANS REDEFINED

The library has also been modified. With the advent of the Internet, the patterns of usage in academic libraries have changed (Applegate 2007). There was a time when the library closed at night and ended access to all materials. There was a time when students spent hours in the library among the stacks. There was a time when librarians would help students find information. Reference librarians were the search engines in the age of paper. But with the rise of the digital age, the role of librarians has changed. While librarians have not become irrelevant, their roles have shifted.

Because the technology of searching evolved faster than the technologies of classroom instruction, librarians arrived much earlier into the digital age than many other parts of the university (Stielow 2003). Librarians can now help students understand which online resources can be trusted and which should be questioned. Some have argued that the real role of librarians was never searching but educating (Stielow 2012). With the advent of search engines like Google and Yahoo, students are searching much differently today, and librarians are required to have information literacy skills to help students conduct meaningful research online.

In addition, voice recognition technologies and artificial intelligences are changing the way people interact with their digital devices and other people. Texting is changing how people communicate and use information. All of these technologies allow people to access information without the mediation of a reference librarian.

With all this change, more questions about our interactions with technology rise to the surface. Has the Internet made us all less intelligent? Will colleges survive the digital revolution? Will college libraries survive the digital revolution? The answer is yes, but they will survive in a different form. McLuhan told us that the medium is the message, and, as the medium changes, the message changes. As the technologies of communication change, we must expect what is studied to change and the very pathways of knowledge to change. The university itself must be reborn in the new age.

It is interesting to note that librarians were the first academics to face the loss of tenure. At one time, the role of a librarian was seen as an academic one, with librarians teaching bibliographic instruction classes to students. These classes taught students how to evaluate information sources as well as how to use libraries. Librarians also selected the materials in subject areas to be collected by a particular library. Librarians published papers and did research. Owing to the nature of their work, librarians were once seen as worthy of tenure but in the late twentieth century this idea of tenure for librarians was challenged. Most institutions began removing tenure status from the ranks of librarians. This change occurred as technological innovations and developments made information retrieval and management a different game. One can wonder if there is a relationship between the loss of tenure for librarians and the digitization of library resources.

Librarians need a new skill set for the digital age that involves much less specialization and a more rounded set of skills. For example, in the old world of libraries, there were books that needed to be cared for and managed by librarians. With one copy of one book, it was important to care for that book and track its use. Digital copies are different. Many people can use the same copy at the same time.

Academic libraries and public libraries have different missions and goals. In-person visits to public libraries in 2009 increased 10% compared with a 2006 ALA household survey. Seventy-six percent of Americans visited their local public library in the year preceding the survey, compared with 65.7% two years ago. Online visits to public libraries increased even more: 41% of library cardholders visited their library websites in the year before the poll, compared with 23.6% in 2006 (Jeffers 2010).

The web is increasingly fulfilling the promise of the library at Alexandria to capture and access all of the world's knowledge. Hence, the massive collections and delivery motifs of the university research library of the past century are largely obviated. Web search engines make obsolete the great Dewey and LC classification systems and allied retrieval mechanisms, which were once needed for searching and reference. Instead, the virtual academic library can only rise with the delivery of as-needed materials, which are tailored to the individual university's classrooms along with their departmental methodologies and research needs. This process switches the identity of the academic library from collections to services by librarians (Johnson 2009).

The public library has long been more about services than collections. The change is much easier for them. Their only battleground is trying to play bookstore by providing digital copies of best sellers. With the impact of large online book sellers and the move to e-books, where this battle will end is anyone's guess. Academic librarians face changes in other areas. One of the most important issues is the role of copyright and cases of "Fair Use" (McJohn 2009). The laws governing use of materials are more complex than many professors and most students can guess. One of the jobs of librarians has become educating the academic community about copyright law and the role it plays in the university.

It is not just the classroom but the whole university that has been impacted by the digital revolution. The changes are just now beginning to be felt, and professors, librarians and registrars are redefining their relationships and rethinking their roles. If the university is truly L-governed, it is what Peter Senge defines as a learning organization where every transaction must be a teaching and learning moment.

In the past, it was thought that teaching in the university was centered in the classroom. With the digital revolution, information and learning have escaped the classroom. When we rethink the university, rethinking the faculty, curriculum and classroom is only one part. For too long we have thought of "student services" as something outside of academics and thus in some ways ancillary to what is essential about the university. As the classroom went online, so did libraries and student records. This meant the skills of all the university professionals underwent a profound change. It impacted all of them but not at the same time. The new university is an organization that is whole, integrated and dedicated to teaching and learning. Thus, the "Universitatis" can be reborn as it was originally intended.

CHAPTER FOURTEEN
TRADITION VERSUS DISRUPTION AND THE BIRTH OF ONLINE EDUCATION

No man who worships education has got the best out of education ...Without a gentle contempt for education no man's education is complete.

– G.K. Chesterton

The university is a place of both the conservation of tradition and its disruption (Postman 1969). The conservative right wing tends to see the university as a hotbed of liberalism, anarchy and experimentation. A closer look inside higher education, however, shows that the university, in general, has often resisted many of the changes that have already impacted most other industries and sectors (Sampson 2012).

It has been decades since the banking industry embraced digital technologies to improve its business (Kozak 2005). Many other industries and sectors have changed dramatically through the adoption of digital technologies. Almost all assembly line plants, for instance, have adopted changes in management, labor and workflow due to the introduction of new digital technologies. Many colleges and universities, however, have resisted the introduction of digital technologies, especially for use in the classroom as well as for changing student services.

In retrospect, it could be that there was good reason for suspicion concerning how digital technologies would impact the classroom. An online course is very different from a traditional face-to-face class. While there have been studies to show that online teaching gives comparable test results that can be measured, who knows those things that cannot be measured that might be lost?

It is sometimes said we measure what we value. We have repeated the old adage "you treasure what you measure." But could it be that there are valuable things, events and processes that resist quantification? Is the university one of the few places where the magic cannot be bottled? Does the experience of the college student as a whole resist some kind of quantification and data collection? Will we miss what is essential if we attempt such quantification? Often the exchange between professor and student is more than an exchange of information or data. The professor may model the professional behavior the student may wish to emulate. There may be other exchanges not so easily reduced to a data set. It may be two or three generations of college students from now before we begin to notice changes we did not anticipate in the move from physical classroom to the online course. A virtual beer with someone is very different from sitting with your professor for a few hours and having a couple of real ones. While the virtual world has its advantages, there may be no equivalent to beer and a lingering philosophical dispute in a university town.

We spent a good deal of time earlier chronicling the history of the university. We did this for a very important reason. The evolution of the university has demonstrated that the university is not immune to change, but it was designed to think change through carefully before that change is instituted. In our discussions of academic freedom from Lysenkoism in Soviet Russia to the events at Fairmont State College under McCarthyism, we saw what can happen when the power of the faculty is reduced or qualified.

Although the professoriate has resisted changes that would revolutionize their roles, the digital revolution has arrived, albeit a bit later than the banking industry's adoption of new technologies. The question is how can the university adopt digital technologies without losing its essence as a university. Can it change its mind without losing its heart?

FROM PAPER TO DIGITAL RECORDS

As we noted earlier, the whole of higher education was at one time bound up with the medium of paper. Books, notebooks, transcripts, blue exam books, grade sheets, attendance records and diplomas were, at one time, all held on paper. These documents literally bound the university together. The move from paper records to digital, from physical classroom to online course, from a physical library full of books to online texts has changed the nature and feel of the modern university.

To understand how universities are changing and the depth of this revolution, we only need to look at the worldwide production of paper. Paper mills are closing all over the globe as the demand for paper has been steadily dropping. As more information gets sent to digital devices, the reliance on paper decreases. "The sector is bracing itself for a crisis," said Dr. Wolfgang Palm, President of the German Paper and Pulp Association (Verband Deutscher Papierfabriken), in 2009 (Interpack 2009).

The medium of communication and its transmission has obviously changed. By going back to the work of the Toronto School that tied social change to changes in the medium of communication, we can easily see that we must expect changes in content as well as context (Innis 2007). As McLuhan said, "the medium IS the message" (McLuhan 2005).

Paper was not only involved with the daily business of a university but how other universities regarded it. A university's reputation was often associated with the number of paper books and journals inside its library. The professors were reputable because they produced paper books and scholarly manuscripts in large numbers.

From the student perspective, paper is still very much involved from the day one applies up through graduation day. It is interesting to note that early on paper was too expensive and rare to be used for college diplomas, so the degree was handwritten on an animal hide. Hence, the term "sheepskin" or "parchment" are still listed as synonyms for a college degree.

In the non-electronic, paper-based world, students applying for acceptance into college submitted a folder filled with papers. These applicants needed to collect and send in SAT scores, high school transcripts, letters of recommendation and often an essay on a particular subject. Eventually the applicant was informed through a snail-mailed paper acceptance letter. Today, the paper-based application process has been replaced by a wide variety of online college application processes. Acceptance letters, however, are typically still sent on paper via snail-mail, but electronic versions are also emailed to applicants.

Let us follow our freshman applicant living in the non-electronic, paper-based world. She was accepted into the college of her choice with an official enrollment date in the fall semester. She arrived on campus ready to register for classes. This was accomplished through a paper system in which someone was responsible for keeping track of the number of open seats available as well as for closing classes to new students when the maximum number of seats were filled. If the freshman student was lucky, she could get on a waiting list, which required filling out one more piece of paper.

Registering for classes typically entailed charging into a field house or gym where students would queue up in long lines, hoping to get into anthropology to zoology courses that were listed and identified on computer punch cards. These paper cards produced a scarcity of seats in key classes, which inevitably caused many students to come up with all sorts of creative solutions in order to get into the classes they wanted. Once successfully registered for class, our freshman went to the bookstore and loaded up on expensive text books that were "required reading." If she was ambitious, she would add a few texts that were labeled "recommended" or "supplemental." She ultimately came out of the bookstore, after waiting in another long line, loaded down with pounds and pounds of expensive paper. This was paid for by paper money or a check that will be filed somewhere in the bookstore. School was about to start!

During the registration period, registrar's offices and financial aid offices had lines that wrapped around the halls of the building, and they moved at a glacial pace because every piece of paper exchanged had to be logged in and accounted for. If a student record was filed in the wrong place, chaos could ensue.

Once actually in the classroom and the semester began, there were tests on paper. Students took written tests in blue books and often wrote research papers following some citation format or other specified by the instructor. The professor would then grade the test (using some magic formula often mysterious to the students) and return the paper to the students with a grade on it. That grade was also entered in a grade book by the professor who used the same book to keep track of other events such as participation, lateness or attendance in class. At the end of the semester, the professor would add up the grades and produce a final grade for each student. This grade book was then walked to the registrar's office and copied into a record where each student's whole grade point average or GPA could be manually calculated to see if they remained in good standing, kept their scholarship, earned honors and so on.

But it was not just students and faculty members living in the universe of paper. For the staff at the university, their world revolved around paper as well. Tracking and evaluating this paper was the bulk of the work of college admissions departments. There were other paper forms to be filled out for financial aid, which may include income and debt data from the student's parents. There were loan forms with promiory notes and small print about interest rates and time to repayment. If the student was going to live on campus, there were housing forms, food plans and so on. There were whole offices, such as advising, financial aid and the registrar filled with clerical workers whose sole function was to collect and process paper from the students.

When the student's education was completed, they received an official transcript, which is a special piece of paper designed not be counterfeited or copied. It often has a watermark stamped on it with the raised college seal. The registrar was the keeper the college seal. There was no appeal above the registrar.

The digital revolution is currently changing every single transaction we have described in this chapter. Some institutions have embraced the digital revolution early and are ahead of the curve. Others have resisted the digital revolution, for reasons both political and philosophical. What is the biggest difference between a bit of information on a piece of paper and that same information being digital? In our opinion, the greatest differences are related to access and transparency. One person can only view one paper at a time. It is physical and must reside in a place that, if it is an important piece of information, must be secure. Once a record is digitized, it can be easily shared, analyzed and combined with other information to identify trends or find areas of efficiency.

We noted earlier how the digital revolution had a devastating impact on employment in the banking industry when it migrated away from paper and essentially eliminated and changed millions of jobs in the banking industry. Employees were not the only people affected. It impacted the customers as well and how they thought about banking. Years ago, if you did not get to your bank during "banking hours," you could not cash a check or withdraw money (Kozak 2005). The customer was powerless after the bank closed. Technology has changed all of that.

In the same way that banks controlled the time when most business could be transacted, universities also controlled the time of its business practices. A professor's office hours, for instance, were often a student's only chance to get a clarification or a question answered. These office hours were listed on the paper class syllabus or posted on a piece of paper on the door of the professor's office.

Because there was only paper, it was difficult to track processes or understand which offices were efficient or inefficient. Transitions and transactions between different parts of the university could not be analyzed effectively, making it difficult to see where anything could be improved. This was exacerbated because faculty members felt they were different from the rest of the university staff. Additionally, some faculty departments felt they should be distinct from other faculty departments. Arts and sciences faculty saw themselves as different from business faculty. Faculty who taught more theoretical subjects saw themselves as distinct from those who taught more practical subjects, and so on.

With a paper-based system, it was hard to compare offices or departments, and the university became a collection of small fiefdoms that often had difficulty communicating with or appreciating each other (Birnbaum 1988). The introduction of digital technology centralized data and gave us transparency and the power to see across the oceans that had for centuries separated departments and offices inside of the university.

FROM PHYSICAL CLASSES
TO ONLINE COURSES

There are questions today about how digital the college classroom has become. Even as late as June 2012, Bill Gates, the former Chairman of Microsoft, noted that the Internet has had a negligible effect on college campuses (Coldeway 2012). In the same week in 2012, the president of the University of Virginia was removed from her position by the Board of Trustees for moving too slowly in adding online classes. A few days later, the Board of Trustees reversed itself, buckling under pressure from both inside and outside of the university, and reinstated the president (Perez-Pena 2012). The emotions around the online course run high because this represents a fundamental change in the nature of teaching and redefines the role of the professor. The arrival of the online course in the university has been a difficult birth to say the least.

As we explained earlier, before the advent of the digital revolution, a good deal of teaching took the form of the lecture, which is a kind of performance that is often repeated year after year (Brown and Lauder 2010). While a very few faculty in good grad schools vary their teaching load greatly, the vast majority of faculty repeat the same courses year after year. Like an old-fashioned craftsman, the faculty member became skilled at repeating the same tasks over and over, sometimes over their whole career.

For example, imagine a professor of philosophy who spends his career at a small private college. Our fictional professor teaches three sections of Introduction to Philosophy in the general education curriculum and one other section of something more advanced. Because there were few philosophy majors in this small college, the professor teaches the Introduction to Philosophy course over and over again for years. In this fictional example, every student in this college must take 60 credits of liberal arts in what is commonly called a "general education curriculum" and is sometimes called the "core." Most of the students in our fictitious college are majoring in business, computers, health care or education and have to get through the general education courses to fulfill their requirements for graduation. Our professor is not so far from reality. Many professors spend the bulk of their lives teaching the same course over and over, often at an elementary level. But the challenge to the professor does not end there. Because there were multiple sections of large general education courses, the books are frequently standardized so that the students do not buy the wrong books for the wrong section. So, our professor does not have the luxury of even choosing his own texts.

Our fictional professor of philosophy spends most of his three contact hours per week lecturing. Year in and year out, our professor lectures on the same books in the same class. The tendency over time has typically been to recycle the lectures notes and, in many cases, even the jokes. Before the digital age, there was no way to capture the event of teaching. It takes work to keep the same material fresh. But when the digital revolution arrived, forward-thinking professors started to realize that their lectures could be captured online, which, in turn, gave them more time to more productively interact with students.

Suddenly our fictional professor of philosophy saw a shift in his work, time and value. Part of his contract with the university called for a certain number of contact hours. Each of his four courses met for a little less than three hours each per week in a 15-week semester, equaling about 45 hours of face-to-face contact between our professor and his students. Lecturing often fulfills these contact hours or Carnegie units. If this lecture is captured once in a digital form, what does that mean for the value of the professor's labor and his contract for contact hours? If a student watches a lecture in her dorm room, what does that do to the contact hour?

We have noted that when the Higher Learning Commission of the North Central Association of Colleges and Universities attempted to give a simplistic definition of a credit hour in the controversial accreditation visit to AIU, they did not take into account the complexity of counting the contact hour. The upshot of the AIU visit was that the United States Department of Education threatened to strip North Central of its power to accredit colleges and have the federal government take over the process, a change that would overturn 150 years of academic tradition. Once the Department of Education believed that contact hours had not been accounted for correctly, they wanted to step in and do it right. But what was lost in this historic confrontation between the federal government and academia was that the credit hour is not what it was a quarter century ago. The introduction of digital technology that stores, transmits and shares information differently forces us to rethink the whole concept of contact hours as a physical sharing of space and time by the professor and students.

Our fictitious professor of philosophy now is living in a new world with new rules. He is a sharp young man who records his lectures, puts all of his notes online and now spends his time coaching students, leading discussion groups and mentoring rather than lecturing. Instead of giving the same lecture three times a week year after year on Plato's Cave, he can work with students one on one and use the Socratic method to draw out the ideas of others. Something has been lost, but something has been gained.

BEYOND THE ONLINE COURSE: THE ONLINE UNIVERSITY

The changes did not stop with the online course. That was only the beginning. Online learning has become a great catalyst for change in American higher education, and, for the most part, it has happened piecemeal. In the late 1980s and early 1990s, experiments with online learning began to accelerate in various pockets of innovation. At various universities, once there was a single online course, other elements of the college needed to go online. It became an obvious evolution. One online course led to a call for more online courses. Once a group of courses came online, there was the desire for whole degrees to be offered online. This meant the whole of the academic side of the college had to be on board (grudgingly, in some cases). Once the major courses in a degree were online, there was pressure to put the general education and liberals arts courses online so that a student at a distance could take a whole degree without setting foot on campus. In the early days, this wreaked havoc on curriculum committees. In some colleges, there were competences, such as public speaking or oratory skills, that were difficult to teach online. Other colleges had art history or music as part of their general education requirements. Putting a philosophy course or a writing course online is one thing, but try it with biology or music appreciation. With crude tools and unreliable methodologies in the early days, the move onto the Internet was chaotic and slow at first, but once the first prospectors staked their claim, the gold rush was on.

In 1849, John Sutter discovered gold in California. His find opened the floodgates for the migration out West. John Sutter never got rich himself, a metaphor not lost on those who we today might call "Internet pioneers." While the large online for-profit universities took the ball and ran with it, dedicated faculty often at small schools had discovered and deployed online learning early on. These faculty saw the chance to do something new and interesting in the classroom. But because of how universities are governed, it was hard for many colleges to take advantage of the digital revolution. The for-profits took what already was done and simply applied it to a new population.

The revolution that started with a single course going online did not stop at the door of a single physical classroom. Once a degree was online, it was natural for colleges and universities to reach new and different classes of students they had previously never had the opportunity to reach. Prior to the information age, colleges and universities held geographic monopolies on their prospective students. College X was the only Catholic college in a 100 mile radius. College Y had the only MBA in town. College Z was the only college with a major in cyber security. Suddenly, colleges from out of state and even out of the country could offer online degrees at lower prices or in accelerated format to a global audience. For the first time, it was possible to have multiple institutions compete for students in the same geographic area.

Elite colleges have always been able to attract a nationally diverse student body. But state and private colleges and universities in Ohio, for example, typically attracted Ohioans, and students from California typically enrolled in state schools. The growth of online education changed all that.

The Internet also allowed colleges to attract those students who could not attend physical classes during normal business hours. This allowed non-traditional students to fit higher education into their schedules more easily. In the early 1990s, Mercy College in New York had an advertising campaign with a simple slogan: "If you can't come to college, we will bring college to you." Smart marketing campaigns like this changed how institutions could reach a new, larger and geographically diverse audience of prospective students. Competition for students became fierce, and forward-thinking college administrators jumped on the bandwagon of a new future rapidly unfolding.

But this was only the beginning. Once students could take courses online, they wanted to do more of their business online. They wanted to register online. The students wanted to get their advising online. They wanted to view all their student information online, and finally they wanted to register and pay tuition online. At the outset of the digital revolution, these services were wedded to paper and the necessity to physically appear in certain college offices at certain designated times. But all that changed, and the pressure for student services to follow academics online took hold quickly. In progressive schools, the new and powerful ERPs that were running the computer systems in the 1990s were forcing the digitization of student services ahead of online class deployment. So, college by college, region by region, the evolution to a digital university created a new and scattered landscape.

FACULTY VERSUS ADMINISTRATION

There are many ways in which digital technologies arrived on college campuses. Two of the most common ways the university became digital was from the faculty or from the executive team. First, innovative faculty wanted to explore new pedagogies utilizing digital technologies. Often, the faculty who were involved in many early experiments at countless colleges and universities all over America were young and untenured. There was, and still is, excitement about the innovative possibilities and solutions that come with incorporating digital technologies into the traditional college classroom.

Second, top-down executive decrees also pushed forward the arrival of digital technologies at colleges and universities. Early on, few administrators and entrepreneurs recognized that digital learning was a game changer in higher education. That change sometimes came in the form of the adoption of an ERP system that would force digitalization across the campus. The motive of many of these presidents, boards or provosts was a simple one for those who had eyes to see that their draw for new students would no longer be limited by geography. With the advent of online learning, geographic monopolies were threatened. Those colleges who were on the forefront of this revolution could "invade the territory" of colleges that could not compete outside of their region.

These two ways that were bringing the online revolution to higher education had dissimilar aims. Faculty were experimenting online for the love of pedagogy and the creation of new learning opportunities. Administrators were going online to either improve their numbers, or, in some cases, make a name for the president or provost bringing the college into the digital age. In the old days, building a library or science building with her name on it insured a college leader's legacy. Today, an administrator's legacy may be the building of a digital backbone that brought the college into the digital age.

Both library buildings and digital networks are expensive and difficult to build. But there is a difference. A library will not challenge the age-old practices of a university, but a digital network will challenge those age-old practices.

Going digital from the top down has its dangers and its advantages. There have been famous examples of the dangers of top-down deployment of online learning led by the administration. Columbia University, NYU and the University of Illinois Worldwide all had spectacular failures when the administration tried to launch large online programs without the consent or cooperation of the faculty (Carlson 2003; Lederman 2009). Programs launched for the love of teaching and learning or pedagogical curiosity had a much better chance of maturing than those born in the heat of a marketing campaign to reach new audiences. In traditional colleges, it has often been difficult to launch a major overhaul of the university against the will of the faculty by the very nature of shared governance.

DIGITAL DISRUPTION AND THE FUTURE OF THE FACULTY

While it is not easy to make a causal argument about the impact of digital technology, we can notice correlations. As the digital revolution has impacted higher education, the role and power of the faculty have declined (Sweeny 2011). When the contact hour was more closely aligned with the physical proximity of the faculty to the students, the campus was a place where faculty ruled. Decisions could be made thoughtfully and slowly, and faculty senates were the seat of power that could only be circumvented by the most skilled college presidents and provosts. But all of this was about to change.

With the introduction of digital technologies, the university began to move at a quicker pace with decisions needed earlier and schedules that could not be delayed by dialogue or debate. This helped the rise of a professional class of managers and at the same time saw a decline in the power and reach of the faculty (Ginsberg 2011). The pace of decision making in faculty senates, curriculum committees and other traditional decision-making bodies could not keep up with the rapid processing of data that arrived with the digital revolution.

With the introduction of digital technologies, a whole new sector of higher education was able to expand its influence: the for-profit university. The idea of a privately owned university was not a new one. There have been private colleges often owned by a single individual, family or group of investors for hundreds of years. What changed the game was the embrace of technology by the new for-profits that allowed them to offer courses across wider geographic areas.

There was often, and still is, reluctance in traditional universities to embrace digital technologies. This has not been the case with the for-profit universities (Ruch and Keller 2003). Because their management structure is top-down, they are able to proceed at a pace that many traditional colleges cannot keep up with. While traditional colleges debated the new nature of higher education, the pros and cons of online learning and the dangers of going digital, the for-profit universities were embracing all of its elements.

The managers and owners of for-profit universities in the 1990s did not invest money in basketball gyms, football stadiums or expensive dorms or student centers. Instead, they invested in a digital backbone for their universities that could extend their reach first nationwide and eventually worldwide. With their penchant for hiring managers with experience in other businesses and industries, the for-profit universities brought in professional managers and experienced IT professionals who understood how businesses had already deployed digital technologies across an enterprise. These institutions often did not invest in faculty or scholarship and instead looked for speed and efficiency.

At the same time, because for-profit universities have been built more like businesses than traditional universities, they did not establish tenure or many other protections for faculty. Because many of the leaders of for-profit universities came from business and did not come from the ranks of tenured faculty, there was often little understanding concerning the central role of faculty and the importance of academic freedom in the life of the university (Bousquet 2008). As we repeatedly noted, one of the fundamental elements of a university is shared governance that is held up by academic freedom. For-profits simply are not built and managed this way.

The electronic classroom and online college does not necessarily entail the end of faculty power. There is no necessary or sufficient connection that the growth of one means the decline of the other. It is our contention that the digital university can be an efficient business where the word "customer" is not a dirty word, while at the same time have a strong faculty with power to stand up for academic issues against simple business decisions.

We understand that by going digital the university has changed how decisions are made and how power is shared. But if faculty are seen as a disposable commodity, then we are no longer talking about a university but something quite different. How can the university go digital and still preserve the voice of the faculty that would keep it from slipping into being simply another business?

The university is a very unique kind of "business." It is unique because its customers and its product are identical. It is unique because it is an ancient institution that has relied more on tradition than on embracing innovations and technology to move processes along. We believe that the disruptions caused by the digital revolution must settle along with the continuity at the heart of the university. This means that the voice of the faculty must not be muted by the din of enthusiasm for the coming digital utopia.

PART V

A NEW HIGHER EDUCATION ROOTED IN TRADITION AND SUPPORTED BY MODERN DIGITAL TECHNOLOGIES

Here, we start out the process of formulating our conclusions and summations with a description of for-profit higher education institutions and non-profit higher education institutions. We reveal the historic hostilities between the two, as well as the elements that both can take from each other in order for both to improve student learning.

We then segue into how today's digital revolution can and should help in educating our students. We then introduce four core competencies: critical thinking, ethical reasoning, aesthetic appreciation and STEM literacy.

In Chapter Seventeen, we offer some observations that bring to light what higher education has become today. We question the practice of "legacy" admission practices. We talk about the student loan debt problem. We show some cost-saving measures for both students and institutions that look very promising. We also ask if a college education is really worth it, and we return to our main question: What is the essence of the university?

In the final chapter, we lay out our vision of the digital university, wrapping everything up with our notions about what is needed for the student, the faculty, the staff and all the external constituents that form the universe of a university. We also present a kind of laundry list of "must dos."

And we reemphasize how higher education is extraordinarily diverse – a world that does not take standardization across the board.

In the end, we present the "idea," which essentially is that the digital university will not replace the traditional classroom, but it will certainly enhance it.

CHAPTER FIFTEEN
HOW TRADITIONAL NON-PROFITS
AND MODERN, ONLINE
FOR-PROFITS CAN FIND A BALANCE
THAT SATISFIES ADMINISTRATORS,
FACULTY AND STUDENTS

*When you wish to instruct be brief ... Every word that is
unnecessary only pours over the brimming mind.*
— Marcus Tuillus Cicero

A new kind of university is emerging. It has elements of a traditional brick-and-mortar university combined with a digitally
sophisticated online for-profit institution. They can both learn from
each other, yet oftentimes each thinks the other has nothing to offer.

To begin, we caution the reader on the concepts "for-profit"
and "non-profit." There are more than 4,000 for-profit higher education institutions in the United States of America ranging from
truck repair schools to doctoral institutions. They come in all shapes
and sizes and often have little in common. The thousands of non-
profits include Bible colleges in the Ozarks with a faculty of six to
the nation's most elite universities. Non-profits include community
colleges with a graduation rate of less than 6% to the most presti-
gious medical schools. It is important to keep this diversity in mind
when discussing both terms. Often, people use these terms as if
they describe one thing. But we are more often the six blind men in
the Indian fable grabbing a different part of the elephant.

THE HOSTILITY BETWEEN NON-PROFITS AND FOR PROFITS

Unfortunately, there has been hostility between non-profits and for-profits. Civil debate between the two has frequently been all but impossible. Emotion about the word "profit" has often obscured the conversation. The authors have each spent a total of 35 years in the non-profit sector before moving into the for-profit sector. There are things that each sector does well. There are things we learned in each sector. There are things each has to contribute to the future of higher education in America.

The for-profits pushed into digital technology quicker than many of the non-profits. Their streamlined administrative structures allowed for the rapid deployment of digital technologies. This allowed them to adapt to a rapidly changing information environment.

In recent years, there has been a spate of negative press about the for-profit world, with numerous articles focused on their unethical behavior, lack of quality, antagonism toward true academics and brutal desire for cash and profit at the expense of their students and the taxpayers who are underwriting their loans.

The for-profits have also criticized non-profit colleges. Some in the for-profit world see the non-profits as dinosaurs that are slow to change, as well as backward, anti-technological and inefficient organizations where the comfort of the faculty and resistance to change trumps the needs of the learner. Deans, department chairs and senior faculty at many non-profits have the ability to stall initiatives, and faculty senates have the ability to stop changes they do not agree with.

In many non-profits, the CIO does not report to the provost, leaving IT with the power to veto or slow down any changes in academic technology. CFOs, CIOs, COOs and Chief Academic Officers (CAOs) often have different aims and power structures in non-profits that make swift adaption to change difficult. In many institutions, IT possesses academic data, and it resides outside of any academic power. This means that the use of data to influence change is not a simple process. The tug of war between IT and faculty in non-profits does not need to be footnoted. Most faculty members in America can tell you of their frustration with IT and the inability to get what they need from it.

In non-profits, complex administrative structures often allow tenured faculty to obstruct change (Riley 2011). Powerful elements in faculty senates of many non-profits can use Robert's Rules of Order to slow things down to a crawl. This kind of resistance to change in traditional higher education is so well known that it has been the subject of countless satires and comic novels (Kramer and Hamm 2003).

When we arrived in the for-profit world, we found a disdain for the non-profits. Many of the executives in the for-profit world come from the world of business. They know about accountability, computer systems and budgets. They do not speak "academic," and there is some suspicion about academics, in general. The atmosphere in many for-profits is often more like an insurance company than a college. They dress more traditionally and do things more conventionally. Their politics are also different from traditional colleges.

Studies show that most traditional college professors not only vote Democratic but call themselves "liberal" (Brooks 2012). On the other hand, for-profit leadership has been aligned with the Republican Party, which has often argued for their role in the ecology of American higher education (Fain 2011). These are two very different mindsets that it is often hard to reconcile.

Many in the for-profit sector feel under siege from the non-profit sector. For the past two decades, the for-profit sector has often been excluded, ignored or attacked by the traditional college sector. In short, there is a lack of trust on both sides.

HOW NON-PROFITS AND FOR-PROFITS CAN LEARN FROM EACH OTHER

Nonetheless, there are simple things that the for-profits and non-profits can learn from each other. For example, for-profits have to pay much closer attention to academic quality than they have in the past. Traditional colleges have to realize that the world has changed and become more digital and efficient. In short, a new university is emerging that can combine the best of both worlds.

There have been privately owned colleges, technical schools and trade schools in America for centuries. These are not new phenomena. But in the last two decades, a new kind of institution has evolved that is substantially different from anything that came before it. This new institution is the online for-profit higher education university. What made this possible? The answer is simple. These institutions are creatures of the digital revolution, which is the result of inexpensive smart chips that automate what was formally done by human labor. Just as the robots of Toyota and Honda destroyed the unionized assembly lines of Detroit, the digital revolution has arrived in higher education.

The digital revolution has impacted many different industries at different times and in different ways. When online learning was in its infancy, many in higher education could already see the impact it would have on the classroom. Colleges were labor-intensive places. Professors gave the same lecture over and over; the registrar's assistants calculated GPAs by hand; librarians patiently helped students find resources; and an army of workers moved and stored paper, keeping grade records as the primary method for evaluating student learning.

Early on, the for-profits realized the value of technology and its impact on both cost and the student experience. By automating those things that used to be done by hand, they could improve both the efficiency and costs of the university. Efficiencies in operations generated additional cash to fund more automation. Many of the online for-profits can now operate far more efficiently than any of our former non-profit colleagues could envision.

The question that must be asked now is how much can be automated before we lose the essence of the university? What must remain for a university to retain its soul?

For-profits differ from non-profits. For-profits, for instance, have a single mission or direction that all aspects of the organization support. While this mission or direction differs from institution to institution, it is organized to ensure goals are met and objectives achieved. For-profit institutions measure how they are meeting these goals on a daily, weekly, monthly and quarterly basis, and they make changes on the fly when objectives are not being met. They make changes much quicker than non-profits. This has good and bad consequences.

Much has been said about "profit" in the for-profit model. We would argue that if the non-profit sector had a clearer idea about profit and return on investment college costs would not have sky-rocketed out of control as they have. One of the good things about the concept of profit is that it focuses the organization on metrics that drive profit. For example, recruiting students is expensive. If academic quality is poor and students drop out and tell other students of their poor experience, this is a bad outcome for a for-profit institution. It is therefore in the best interest of the for-profit university to have existing students and graduates become advocates for the quality of its academics instead of critics. The metrics and data analysis used in many of the for-profits has application to a wider higher education audience. But this must be done in the context of shared governance and an understanding of faculty control over academics. This has not always been the case in the for-profit sector.

Many non-profits, on the other hand, are not as mission driven. The marketing department may have one set of goals, the provost a second and the faculty senate may work to obstruct both plans or perhaps try to promote one of their own. We know of non-profit institutions where the provost and the president are pursuing different agendas. Unfortunately, the terms "faculty governance" or "shared governance" ensure there will be conflicts and resistance to change because of the very nature of its faculty. In a T-governed Teacher Centered model, all decisions must be reached by gaining the consensus of a large number of professors who are trained in the arts of argument and debate. This kind of consensus has its advantages and disadvantages.

Many for-profit colleges and universities are not very aware of the history of higher education. Many of the managers of for-profit institutions were not schooled in Aristotle or Matthew Arnold but in corporate ideas about Deming, TQM, Six Sigma, The One Minute Manager and so on. MBAs and JDs are as plentiful among the managers of these new universities as PhDs.

Most academics have little regard for these management theories. In the older traditional university, a professor of Dante could rise to become a dean and then eventually a college president. This is not as easy in the for-profit world, where efficiency and learning outcomes are goals, and the "customer" experience is just as important, or more important, than faculty rights. The student is a customer, and the for-profit institution wants to make sure that each student graduates and tells others about the positive experience they have had. However, in the older, traditional university, referring to the student as a customer still gets met with hostility today.

Many of the for-profits are not easy places to work for someone from a non-profit institution. The profit motive is geared toward keeping costs down, and one of the best ways to do this is to digitize manual tasks. The workforce at a for-profit is smaller and driven harder than in many traditional colleges. For example, one non-profit we worked at was closed from December 15 through sometime during the first week of January every year. Staff could take off and relax. At one online for-profit university, a new freshman class of more than 3,000 students starts on the first Monday of every single month. If that Monday happens to fall on New Year's Day, the staff must go to work anyway. If it falls on the Fourth of July, it has to be staffed and running. There is no spring break or summer in Tuscany for the workers in the for-profit world. It is all business.

Many non-profits have a work force that has been in place for decades. These workers have a loyalty toward the institution. We have a friend, for instance, who works in an advising office at a small liberal arts non-profit college. The employees at this small college call in sick often; the pace is leisurely, and a number of them play instruments in the university orchestra, are actors in local plays or have fish to fry other than their jobs at the advising office. The pay is low, but they have been there a long time, they know the job and they are there for life. There are a lot of personal relations and institutional knowledge in that office. There is not much chance for advancement and not much of chance of getting fired. The status quo is moving paper and keeping the lines of students moving. These folks have a job for life, and there is little incentive to change or improve their processes. Any rapid change could threaten their lifestyle and their world. These are folks who would resist a change in their office and pace. They are not digital natives.

Actually, there is much to enjoy about the world of the slow-moving traditional colleges. Like the difference between home cooking and fast food, this slow pace can allow for real attention to detail. You can work in a traditional college and be a human being. There is often time for the arts and conversations about great books. There is a caring and a safe environment for students. It is handcrafted, like a quilt made by a favorite aunt. But just as hand weaving gave way to the looms of the Industrial Revolution, changes are happening with college records and administration. These changes have brought ill feelings concerning how non-profit faculty feel toward the for-profits that are similar to the Dickens' view of what the machine had done to the poor of London or to Blake's revulsion of the "Dark Satanic Mills."

EXAMPLES OF THE REAL DIFFERENCES THAT EXIST BETWEEN NON-PROFITS AND FOR-PROFITS

Following are some examples of how for-profits differ from non-profits, along with some of the typical bottom-line results that occur at both types of institutions. For example, at large for-profit institutions, the admissions process is fully automated, with the applicant able to complete everything online without any human intervention. The registration process is automated, so students cannot take the wrong course by accident. A computer program attached to their degree plan locks them in. The admissions staff, while small, can handle a large volume of incoming students very quickly and efficiently.

But at the old, non-automated non-profit institution, if a student wanted to take a course outside their degree plan, they had to speak with someone and make sure that they fully understood what courses may or may not have contributed toward their degree. The unfortunate result of this kind of system was at graduation time, a good number of students were typically both surprised and dismayed because they had missing credits or were lacking a course they should have already completed.

Today, enrolling at many of the large for-profit online universities is as easy as buying a book at Amazon. But at many non-profits today, students are amazingly still standing in long lines at the registrar's office before they can even be notified that they must first go to the bursar's office across campus. These frustrating experiences students encounter at traditional colleges have helped make online for-profit universities successful. At the same time, however, the for-profit institution may not provide the one-on-one professional guidance and attention that students typically receive at a traditional college. Something is gained and something is lost.

What has been the payoff for converting over to automation, less human touch and the digitization of data once held on sheets of paper? Here is an example from the American Public University System, one of the larger for-profits. The American Public University System did not raise its undergraduate tuition one cent from 2001 to 2012. While other colleges were raising tuition by double digits every single year, the American Public University System held its costs down and made college affordable. They accomplished this by heavily reliance on digital technologies that did the work faster and cheaper than human beings. What armies of clerical workers typically did at traditional colleges was fully automated at the American Public University System. The end result was that students realized the benefit of lower tuition costs.

Another advantage that the for-profits have is the data they have and use freely. The attention the for-profit world pays to data and analytics is truly amazing. Most traditional colleges have end-of-course student evaluations that are sent to the dean of that school. In some schools, the data in these evaluations is never heard of again. Deans and provosts at the large for-profits, on the other hand, have been empowered to see how each class, program professor, and school stacks up in terms of drops, withdrawals and failures. Data is now widely shared and not hidden to protect the faculty. At many for-profits, for example, totally transparent data provided by its institutional research department can show where students are succeeding and where they are being shipwrecked.

Here is another example how the transparency of data and the ability to act on it improved learning: At another large for-profit, the administration found that in one of their largest majors a professor was teaching a large number of students in an upper division course that had a combined drop, withdrawal and failure rate of 94%. This meant that only 6% of the students who signed up for the class actually passed. The college administrators then looked at the end-of-course surveys and discovered how the students claimed that the professor was opaque and did not interact with them. When the dean made an inquiry, the professor defended the teaching methods he utilized in the class and, in the end, accused the dean of attempting to "dumb down" the course. In the old non-profit world, if this professor had tenure, it would have been all but impossible to curb his egregious behavior.

In the for-profit realm, accountability is a key term. Colleges should add value; colleges should educate the students, but they should not let the actions of a single professor make it all but impossible to pass. When many of us were undergraduates, there were students who knew which professors had been there forever and had typically flunked almost everyone. At one private college, the same kind of professor had been doing the same thing for two decades inside a fairly empty classroom. Students avoided this professor like the plague, but he still collected his paycheck and continued to be a terrible teacher immune from any improvement. While there must be room for strong, academically demanding courses, it is wrong to wait until a student's senior year and have them face a course that nobody can pass. To any school where this kind of behavior is tolerated, we say "shame on you." That is right, shame on you.

Every year at another for-profit university, the provost sends a data sheet on each full-time faculty member to the department chairs and deans. The data shows all of their stats and student evaluations, and the data is then matched against the course, program, school and university averages. While this university has multi-year contracts for professors with a solid track record, there is no tenure. As we have noted before, in the non-profit world, this data was often protected, so one faculty member could not see the data on another, or a dean from one school could not see the data from another school. There are no such silos in most for-profit universities today. In short, we demand transparency in banking and government, so why not in academia?

Nevertheless, what we have been advocating with regard to transparency and data analysis is not a simple calculation. Good teaching is not something that can be determined by quantitative measures alone. But this is not just raw data. That can be misleading.

There are things, magic things that can happen in a classroom that will never be captured in a spreadsheet. At the same time, we have to account for learning and student success and both of these are measurable. There are differences in teaching music, algebra and physics. It takes technical expertise and some wisdom and age to know the subjects in which students stumble.

At another for-profit university, there is a metric to show the level of difficulty of instruction in various majors. For example, teaching English composition, where there are numerous rewrites of student papers, may take more work than teaching an Introduction to Philosophy class. The metrics in such courses are where the conversation can begin. All colleges have teachers with high dropout and withdrawal rates who were supported for reasons beyond simple metrics. But the rest of the management has to be educated about what it means to be a university. One for-profit provost said, "we are a university that happens to be a business, not a business that happens to be a university." That simple distinction is the difference between a good for-profit university and a bad one. While there has been a lot of bad press about the for-profit universities, they realized early how students wanted to go to school and how information was being learned and shared. These are lessons that will persist long after the for-profit debate has ended.

In addition to this kind of internal data, some for-profits also use external, nationally benchmarked measures. These measures indicate student outcomes that tell us how prepared graduates are when they leave college. By using the Proficiency Profile and the Major Field Tests, both by Princeton's ETS, for example, many for-profit institutions measure their students' knowledge of their major course of study, and by their literacy, analytic and quantitative skills against national and sector averages. In addition, many for-profits use the National Survey of Student Engagement (NSSE) from the University of Indiana as another form of measurement against a national average.

For end-of-course surveys, many colleges first used their own in-house-created surveys. Many online colleges have migrated to a scientifically validated instrument called the Community of Inquiry (COI) Survey. This is a survey that more than one million online students have completed. When you combine internal metrics, nationally benchmarked tests and progression and graduation rates, an institution can get a good picture of where it is successful and where it needs to improve.

In the non-profit world, the classroom was a private and sacred space belonging to the professor. A dean could only come in once a year, and this was only allowed with a 30-day written notification that they were coming. This ensured faculty freedom. Data was not shared, and there were black holes that nobody could view. One dean of online learning at a non-profit college we are familiar with was forbidden by the faculty senate rules to observe classes. He was told this would violate the academic freedom of the faculty. If this dean received student complaints, he would have had to forward them on to the school dean for that faculty member, in which case action may or may not be taken to correct the situation. Remember that departments often elect their chairs and this means that faculty often has a say in those who have a say over them. In some political environments, this can impact the correction of poor pedagogy.

In the L-governed or Learning Centered Model institution, ideally, all should be transparent and on the table. The learning experience is transparent to all and is subject to a group analysis. It is no longer the private property of a single professor. It is part of the data that the institution learns from. This is a fundamental change in the university.

LESSONS TO BE LEARNED

We have now seen some of the things for-profits have accomplished well, along with what can be considered their inadequate practices. For example, all of these metrics and systems have weakened the faculty at these institutions. For-profits often get by with a large number of adjuncts, and any full-time faculty they hire do not usually have a strong voice. In a number of the larger online for-profits, there is little or no faculty input. This means that the business could be running the curriculum as well as the balance sheet – clearly a bad idea that has given for-profits a poor reputation.

So, there is obviously a lesson in all this that the for-profits need to take from the traditional colleges. For-profits need to empower faculty more without giving them veto power over things that could hurt the university or the students. Faculty must be paid a living wage, so that they do not have to work at multiple part-time jobs (called being an "adjunct," a term which fits the role) to pay the rent. Student complaints must be looked at in a careful and factual way before deciding on either the side of the faculty or the student in the dispute. Overall, the lesson for-profits need to learn is to make sure the academics run academics. At the same time, the college must run efficiently and on schedule. To do this, they must create a Chinese Wall between the business side and the academic side of the college, where both can do what they do best.

What is in store for the future of the university? It should be a combination of the best of the digital revolution without losing the heart of what it means to be a university. Traditional colleges have to embrace technology, and this means they must break down the silos that have characterized the university since its founding. Online for-profits have to pay much more attention to academic quality. Only by giving faculty a voice within their expertise and lanes can this be done.

The rubber band has to snap back to the center. For-profits need to make sure academics have a strong voice that ensures academic quality and a solid learning environment. They must protect the academic side of the house from the pressures of profit, quarterly reports and micromanaging. However, this is easier said than done. The non-profits need to come into the digital age, get rid of silos, get rid of fiefdoms that do not communicate with each other and begin to see the student experience as a whole.

The two forms of higher education must be able to learn from each other. The practical lessons forged by the for-profits can be combined with the academic strength of many non-profits. The university must be both a humming digital business and place where faculty can do what they do best at their own pace. Cardinal Newman saw that the university was not simply a place to prepare one for a job. It was a place to prepare students for life. He thought the edification of a true university education would prepare someone to become a moral and analytical human being who could cope with change. In his own day, the management theories were not Six Sigma, but Bentham and Mill's Utilitarianism, which equated what was good with what was useful. We have not progressed too far from that debate.

CHAPTER SIXTEEN
A CORE CURRICULUM IN TODAY'S DIGITAL AGE BASED ON TRADITIONAL PHILOSOPHIES

Every maker of video games knows something the makers of curriculum don't seem to understand. You'll never see a video game being advertised as being easy. Kids who do not like school will tell you it's not because it's too hard. It's because it's ... boring.

— Seymour Papert

In this chapter, we will lay out four competencies we think every college student should possess upon graduation. We do not advocate for adoption of texts, authors or subject areas, but we do think there are a number of competencies that college graduates should possess. In short, every college student should be able to think critically, understand ethics, appreciate good work in their area of expertise and understand the STEM disciplines that are so critical in our digital age. Digital technology has given us tools to improve the teaching of these and the measuring of their success. We need only to employ these technologies in the service of these aims to achieve these modest goals. In coming up with these competencies, we have looked to educate the student as a citizen of our democracy as well as giving her the skills she will need to be successful.

Despite sweeping political efforts to "solve the crisis" in higher education, there is no one-size-fits-all solution for higher education in the United States (Searle 1993). Calls for a common curriculum or

cultural literacy fail to understand the vast diversity of all higher education institutions (Hirsch 1988). Our system of higher education takes in
students whose preparation for college varies from institution to institution. Unlike many nations in the world, there is no national ministry of
education that sets national standards and benchmarks that all students
and schools must follow. It is amazing to some writers how little attention American thinkers have paid to the Bologna Process that is seeking
unified standards across Europe (Gaston 2010).

In the administration of President George W. Bush, a national
standard was applied to grammar and high schools with the No
Child Left Behind Act. This act caused a firestorm of controversy
because from the beginning it did not take into account the diversity of the educational experience (Meir and Wood 2004). In recent
years, most calls for "accountability" coming from Washington D.C.
rest on some notion of a rubric or standard that can be applied to
all colleges and all college students.

We think that the founding fathers had it right when they left
the word "education" out of both the Declaration of Independence
and the Constitution. Coupled with the Tenth Amendment to the
Constitution that reserves all powers not expressly granted to the
federal government to the states, it becomes clear that we should be
careful when talking about national standards enforced by federal law.

The freshman at an elite Ivy League should be more prepared
for college than a single mother of 35 coming to college for the first
time as a night student at a community college. One may have just
completed French II and have calculus and chemistry fresh in their
mind. The other may have been out of school and out of practice
for a decade or more. Should we hold them both to the same en-
trance and exit exam? America has some of the best universities in
the world. Do we really want an Ivy League student taking the same
test that a part-time student at a technical college or community college would take? The same logic applies to federal mandates about
course content andtextbooks or. It may be that tribal colleges may
teach American history differently than bible colleges. The literature
selections taught at a rabbinic school might be different from those
offered to students at a state college.

If the federal government starts to dictate national standards, the next icy patch on the slippery slope down to oblivion could be enforcing agreement on texts, textbooks and "appropriate materials." Most professors can quickly detect what these code words really mean. Professors have battled for decades to present alternative points of view. We need only to remember what McCarthyism did to higher education to realize what a federal law could mean for the teaching of alternative points of view. It may be that Democrats could be in power and want education to do one job, while a new Republican administration would want to reverse engines at ninety miles an hour.

With the diversity of American higher education firmly in mind, we do not advocate standardizing academic content, but we do believe we can set out some guidelines. We may not want all students to read the same texts, but there may be some skills and competencies a college graduate will need to be successful, living in a modern capitalist democracy.

One of the main hallmarks of the capitalist system is that there is no central planning where economic decisions are made by the government or some central agency. This means that individuals are responsible for their own economic decisions. With this freedom comes the responsibility to make intelligent choices. There have been economic systems throughout history that made all of the decisions from above. There was no need for an economic education or an understanding of all of the disciplines that make up economics. This means that citizens in our nation need to be educated about the fundamentals of economics and have the skills to be economically successful. In our capitalist system, the individuals are responsible for their own wealth or poverty. This means that the citizens must be educated enough to be economically successful. This has been a criticism of college for decades. It is thought that a college education, the way it is understood today, does not present students with the tools for success. While this point of view gets a lot of ink in the popular press, we believe that the diversity of institutions makes it hard to sustain such generalizations.

Because we live in a democracy we need to have an educated citizenry. A strong relationship exists between education and democracy (Dewey 1997). In Plato's *Republic*, a work on the best state, he spent most of the dialogue on education and how it produces good citizens. In the early days of our republic, only landed gentry could vote. They argued that only they had the education and the wisdom to elect our officials. Over time, more and more people were enfranchised. Civil rights legislation, the suffragette movement, which gave women the right to vote, and countless other efforts have been made to include more citizens in the voting process. For a long time in some states, there were "literacy tests" meant to exclude African American voters. They were done away with, allowing African Americans access to the polls.

There should be some basic competencies that we can ask from all college degrees that would lift up the most remedial students while ensuring that excellence and genius were not capped on the top end. So, we can begin with rethinking the curriculum. The world has changed, and college students have changed just as much. So, our first question is who are today's college students?

HAMPERED BY LIMITED DATA

Much of the data about higher education in America that is used by news outlets comes from the Federal Government database that measures first-time, full-time students. Many metrics for graduation, grade inflation and student behavior are drawn from this limited database. It is limited because first-time, full-time students accounted for only 14% of higher education enrollments in the United States in 2010. The other 86% of college students are not included in this most essential of government metrics. In talking about curriculum, we want to make sure it is fit for today's students. In 1776, when our nation was founded, less than 1% of our population was college educated. We cannot let our nostalgia for that narrow time obscure our understanding of higher education today (Hass and Fishman 2010). As we become more inclusive, we become messier and the conversation becomes both richer and more chaotic.

Data for the most common database that the press and politicians see are drawn from the Integrated Postsecondary Education Data System, abbreviated as IPEDS. This information is maintained by the National Center for Education Statistics (NCES) that operates within the United States Department of Education. The collection and submission of IPEDS data is mandatory for all institutions participating in Title IV programs. So, to participate in the student loan program, institutions must supply the information the government requires. This data has been collected by NCES since 1993 and is frequently cited by many surveys, as well as journal, magazine, and newspaper articles. When IPEDS computes institutional graduation rates, only the completion of first-time, full-time students are used as the basis of the calculation.

Under the IPEDS definition, a student must complete a degree within 150% of the normal time to completion while maintaining a certain GPA. For example, a typical full-time student would have to complete their degree within six years of beginning classes. Part-time degree-seeking students are not included in this calculation. IPEDS defines an undergraduate, part-time student as one who is enrolled in either less than 12 semester hours or quarter hours or less than 24 contact hours a week each term. For graduate students, part time is defined as less than 9 semester or quarter hours. In 2011, a federal panel titled Committee on the Measures of Student Success (CMSS) submitted a report to the Department of Education that recommended including part-time, degree-seeking students in the federal IPEDS completion calculations, in addition to the full-time students.

To recognize how this way of collecting and calculating data shortchanges our understanding of student behavior, let us take one subgroup of college students. Every year, several hundred thousand active-duty military personnel attend higher education institutions. It is rare for a service member to be both active-duty military and a first-time, full-time student. Data from some of the largest providers of higher education to the military indicate that the average military student currently takes less than three courses a year. These military students are not included in the IPEDS first-time, full-time completion calculation because they do not typically complete their degrees within the 150% timeline (normally six years from beginning to completion of a BA or BS degree).

The active-duty military force is increasingly mobile and prefers the flexibility and portability of online courses. Years ago when military members were transferred to a new base, they had to apply to a new college. Oftentimes, however, the new college would not accept all the credits that these students successfully completed at their previously attended institution(s). Because of the difficulty of transferring credits between physical campuses and maintaining the same course of study for earning a specific degree, the flexibility of anytime/anywhere online degree programs have grown in popularity, especially among mobile students such as those who are in the military.

The Department of Defense (DoD) Voluntary Education Fact Sheet reported that 73% of all service members participating in the military tuition assistance program in financial year 2011 enrolled in online classes (McCluskey 2012b). Military personnel today can take advantage of the most lucrative GI Bill program in history, featuring 100% tuition-assistance reimbursement (with limitations), along with the development of service-specific virtual education portals. Educational achievement remains relatively low but stable among the active-duty force. Data from the FY 2011 DoD Voluntary Education Levels Report indicates that approximately 85% of the enlisted force do not possess at least an associate's degree; nearly 95% of the enlisted force do not possess a bachelor's degree or higher; and approximately 58% of the officer corps do not possess a master's degree (McCluskey 2012d).

Military students behave differently than other non-traditional adult populations. Because of deployments and the rapid pace in theater in recent years, it is often difficult for these students to predict when it is a good time to start a course or if they will be able to complete it on time. Recent examples include the rapid and unanticipated deployment required for the Hurricane Katrina rescue and cleanup operation. For this reason, institutions that serve the military must have very liberal withdrawal and leave-of-absence policies that will not punish service members for things that are beyond their control. This is just one of many subgroups that do not appear in the graduation data of the United States Government. We must keep this diversity in mind when considering any global fixes we might want to make in higher education.

A MODEST PROPOSAL

Requiring certain authors and texts for a college curriculum has always been more controversial than requiring certain competencies. Colleges such as Western Governors University, Excelsior College and Thomas Edison University have adopted some variation of the competency model (Voorhees 2001). The competency model is one in which we do not count Carnegie Units or seat time hours for graduation but test students to see if they are competent in a particular area. These competencies denote broad sketches about what is essential and what is accidental in our college curriculum.

College should prepare its students for economic success but it should aim to do much more. In the curriculums of grammar schools and high schools over the past decade, art and music courses have been squeezed out. We believe in the classical ideal that an educated person can think but also must be able to value and appreciate. We believe the digital university now has the power to do it all. But first we must ask what basic competencies we need.

We live in a nation that is both democratic and capitalist. Our citizens have to be educated to make choices in both the political and economic spheres. In addition, we live in a connected world with a global economy (Friedman 2007). Our graduates should have a grasp of the world they live in and some understanding of the parts that make up the whole. Additionally, life is not just politics, work and consumption; it is being a successful and happy human being. We all wish success and even happiness for our children, and college should aid them in this important part of their development.

AN EDUCATED PERSON IN THE DIGITAL AGE

College students need to think critically in evaluating choices presented to them. College students should have enough acquaintance with ethics to help them understand the impact of their decisions on themselves and others. Finally, while this next area has gotten short shrift in recent debates, college students should understand aesthetics to help them appreciate the beauty in life that can widen their horizons. All of these have traditionally been discussed as college faculties have rethought their curriculum, liberal arts and sciences and general education requirements.

But the title of this book contains the word "digital," and that is now an essential part for any education. A minister, art historian, stockbroker, grade school teacher and emergency services worker must understand the role digital technologies play in their world. A basic education in the STEM disciplines is also essential for economic success for most college graduates in today's world. While there will be those who live on the other side of the digital divide, an educated person in the digital world should not be ignorant of those technologies.

Finally, we must remember what the philosopher Hannah Arendt wrote in her seminal work *The Life of the Mind,* as she rephrased the Biblical quote: "We are not beings in the world but we are of the world." Arendt saw life in a condition of plurality, which means we live in a world with different people, different ideas and different values. It is essential that a human being understands this plurality and their ethical duty to preserve these differences. A whole human being appreciates differences, questions assumptions, is open to new ways of thinking and can change his mind. No matter what kind of education we talk about, it should preserve these values that are essential to the American experience.

If today you were to move to Japan and spend the next 30 years being a good member of that community, doing everything you can to fit in, you will still never be Japanese. There are even debates about whether Japanese born in Hawaii or Guam are really and purely "Japanese." Some believe that you are not pure Japanese if you were born in Japan but one of your parents is not Japanese. The same can be said with less clarity about many other nations in the world. There are nostalgic ideas of what it means to be French or Italian or British that may have little to do with the multi-ethnic societies that exist today, but still these ideas persist. America, like Australia and few other countries, are invented nations populated by waves of immigration. The only real Americans are the Native Americans, and they came here over the Bering Straits. To exist in an increasingly diverse society, one needs to understand that there are many ways to approach issues and live harmoniously in our global society.

Not only is our society diverse, the reasons why students want to attend college are just as varied. Taking our differences in mind, we cannot talk about the goals of a university education unless we remember the variety of motives that students have when they enroll in college. Technical colleges, community colleges and agricultural and mechanical colleges are filled with students whose primary goal is to improve their economic condition by mastering a skill or series of skills. These students want to become nurses, firefighters, police officers or auto mechanics. However, colleges can give them much more than a credential to obtain a decent job.

The authors of this text took most of their courses in philosophy, the classics, history, literature and psychology. That, in and of itself, might indicate to some a lack of awareness about our future job prospects. But we were not enrolled in college for a degree as much as for the pleasures of the texts and the subject matter. Most of our classmates in the same building were there to get a job and make a certain salary. In rethinking the curriculum, we must keep in mind both those who want an education and those who need a degree.

In thinking about college curriculum, we contend that there can no longer be any content that is universally relevant to all college students. There may have been a time when music appreciation exposed all students in a college to the works of Bach, Mozart and Beethoven. In today's world, no argument about the universality of any content can be made. However, we can argue that students can be taught to articulate their own ideas, positions and aesthetics with the use of tools that colleges have always had at their disposal.

A democratic and capitalist economy requires an educated citizenry that can intelligently elect politicians who set the course for the nation and make intelligent economic decisions. They must be educated so that they can follow the issues on which elections are won and lost. They also have to make intelligent decisions about purchases, going into debt, managing their finances, buying a car, entering into a 30-year mortgage, picking long-term stocks for an IRA, etc. College should help the citizenry make such choices intelligently by including elements of critical thinking, practical ethics and the expansion of our horizons in their curriculum. These abilities can be taught just as easily in a course on auto mechanics or drafting as they can in a course on philosophy or Victorian poetry.

There is no need to make a decision between the Utilitarian aims of John Stuart Mill and the more elevated aims of Cardinal Newman. In the digital age, we can accommodate both points of view. Critical thinking, ethics and aesthetics were often taught historically in the general education curriculum or what many colleges call, quite rightly, the "core." Today, as digital tools become available, individualized learning becomes more of a distinct possibility. It allows for more gaming, more self-testing and different ways to make the same point. Just as there are different learning styles, it is possible to customize a personal learning environment, or PLE, to fit each student.

Dr. Nish Sonwalkar of MIT did pioneering work on these ideas in the 1990s that is only beginning to be understood today (Sonwalkar 2012). One student may be a visual learner, while another requires a more tactile approach. The same content can be presented to both in the digital classroom via two different pathways. This is much harder to do in the traditional physical classroom and is yet another instance of how digital technologies can enhance traditional methods of instruction.

Finally, the digital course is a team effort. It is not the invention of a single professor who has been teaching the same course for years. It is the result of subject matter experts, instructional designers, educational psychologists, assessment professionals and so on. Some know how to add video content, others may know how a good discussion board is created, someone else may understand learning styles and Bloom's taxonomy and so on. In this way, the course can be designed to teach both content and competencies. A digital course can teach the content while at the same time producing an educated citizen and consumer. This goes for a technical college as well as the most elite institutions. The content can be more challenging, but both the technical college student and the Ivy Leaguer must be encouraged to think, decide and judge. The future of our Republic depends upon this.

THINKING, JUDGING AND VALUING

We will take a short detour and look at the works of the German Idealist philosopher Immanuel Kant as a model for our curricular design. Beginning in 1781, Kant wrote three critiques in which he set out to limit and define spheres of reason, action and judgment. Our model is going to follow his and talk about the competencies of critical thinking, ethical reasoning and appreciating. We begin with these critiques as our guide to the curriculum of the twenty-first century, but we add a fourth competency, digital literacy. We proceed in order, beginning with critical thinking.

COMPETENCY ONE: CRITICAL THINKING

In his *Critique of Pure Reason*, written in 1781, Immanuel Kant sought to set limits and definition to reason. In our own time, the term "critical thinking" has often been used in discussions of college curriculum. A college degree is not the end, but the beginning of a student's critical thinking.

In the digital age where change is more rapid, we need to think with agility and creativity. Today, the odds are that most recent college graduates will not retire in the first job of their career (Rhoads and Torres 2005). Just a few generations ago, a college degree was a sign the person was educated or smart. But today there are myriad ways to achieve this goal. What does it mean to be educated today? It might be argued that the digital revolution has made definitions formed in 1781 obsolete. It might be argued that the new world does not obey the rules of the old. The digital age has shown us that machines can do many tasks that human beings once did.

The time has long passed when you could assume you had a job for life. Workers today change their jobs and careers more frequently than in the past. Successful people have to learn more quickly and be able to think more creatively and critically than did their grandparents. But what exactly is critical thinking? Critical thinking begins by asking the right questions. To ask the right questions, we need the right tools. To obtain these tools, we need to look no further than the origins of Western logic employed by Kant but invented by the philosopher Aristotle.

Aristotle was the first philosopher to write a systematic treatise on logic. It is far outside our scope here to do an exhaustive study of his system, but we can take a look at some of Aristotle's concepts that students should be aware of today. In this way, we separate what is true from what is not true. This surely must be one mark of an educated person.

The concept of truth has a long philosophical history (McCluskey 1977). One of the key concepts in theories about truth is appreciating the difference between a theory and fact. While this distinction may seem obvious, it is often ignored in modern conversation and investigations. In even discussing what is a fact and what is theory, we can open a student's mind to thinking in new ways about their world. What do they know for sure? What can they prove? What is assumed and what is known? In making the determination about both facts and theories, an educated person will question assumptions, look for evidence and provide proof for their conclusions.

The logic used by Kant and Aristotle showed us the difference between truth and validity. Something can be true without being valid or valid without being true. Here is an example in which we begin with the terms "cat" and "paws." The terms (cat and paws) in themselves are neither true nor false; only their combination makes them true or false. For instance, we can put those terms to work in propositions such as the "the cat has paws." A proposition consists of two of these terms, in which one term (the "predicate") is "affirmed" or "denied" of the other (the "subject"), which is capable of being either true or false. Propositions can then be linked together to make arguments such as "Fluffy is a cat; all cats have paws; therefore, Fluffy has paws." Propositions are true and the arguments that connect them are valid. The two premises that precede it entail the conclusion "Fluffy has paws."

Philosophers such as Kant and Aristotle sought to put arguments into logical forms called syllogisms to better organize them. They understood that the argument could be valid even if the propositions were not true. Let us take for example a syllogism involving a black cat named Fluffy. For example, the argument "Fluffy is a cat;

all cats are black; therefore, Fluffy is black" is valid, although the second proposition is not, in fact, true. Something can be true but not valid or valid without being true.

So, having students understand and recognize the distinction between truth and validity is key. Once this difference is recognized, they can begin to understand the concept of inference or how one idea can lead to another. Many political arguments about our most fundamental rights and responsibilities are framed using terms and propositions with conclusions such as "You should vote for X" or "Vote YES for Proposition X." Advertising, marketing and commercials are, in fact, arguments whose conclusion is always "You should buy Brand X." World financial markets rise and fall based on inferences from propositions. Understanding how good these inferences are is a prerequisite for understanding our world.

Once the concepts of inference and argument are grasped, students should learn the four basic forms of propositions traditionally used in logic. The four forms are Universal Affirmative (all men are mortal), Particular Affirmative (some men are tall), Universal Negative (no man is over twenty feet tall) and Particular Negative (some men are not tall). These propositions entail one another. For example, if we were to assert "all men are mortal" is true, then, by deduction, we can say that "some men are mortal" is true while the propositions "no man is mortal" and "some men are not mortal" would be false. Understanding these forms helps us to think clearly about issues in all areas.

Philosophers also distinguish two kinds of arguments: induction and deduction. Induction takes a particular proposition and attempts to find a universal principle in it. This is what science does. But it is tricky to take one example and find a scientific law. Here, we give an example of the difficulties with inductive reasoning.

How an idea that was once considered true can be shown to be false is contained in the concept of "falsifiability." The most famous example of this is when Aristotle used the expression "all swans are white" as an example of a Universal Affirmative statement. When he wrote this, it seemed true because no one had ever seen a swan that was not white. It turns out that as explorers set sail for new worlds, they came across black swans. How many black swans did it take to disprove the theory? The answer is just one single swan. A British philosopher of science, Karl Popper, popularized this idea in saying that science moves ahead by this kind of testing of hypothesis, propositions and arguments. The ability to let go of false beliefs and rethink the evidence is an essential part of critical thinking.

In addition, colleges should help students become intelligent observers. Students should understand the basics of induction and deduction. If you have ever spent any time with Arthur Conan Doyle's remarkable fictional detective Sherlock Holmes, you can see the power of logic and observation. Holmes shows us how a thinking aware person lives and observes the world around him. There is one passage from the short story *A Scandal in Bohemia* where we find Dr. Watson admiring Holmes's power of observation:

> I could not help laughing at the ease with which he explained his process of deduction. "When I hear you give your reasons," I remarked, "the thing always appears to me to be so ridiculously simple that I could easily do it myself, though at each successive instance of your reasoning I am baffled until you explain your process. And yet I believe that my eyes are as good as yours."
>
> "Quite so," he answered, lighting a cigarette, and throwing himself down into an armchair. "You see, but you do not observe. The distinction is clear. For example, you have frequently seen the steps which lead up from the hall to this room."
>
> "Frequently."
>
> "How often?"
>
> "Well, some hundreds of times."
>
> "Then how many are there?"
>
> "How many? I don't know."
>
> "Quite so! You have not observed."
>
> "And yet you have seen. That is just my point. Now, I know that there are seventeen steps, because I have both seen and observed."

College needs to help students be as observant and logical as Holmes. Colleges need to help our students both "see and observe."

This is the beginning of critical thinking. While there is much more that can be learned and gleaned from logic, these elements must be considered the essential building blocks for educated analysis.

Our brief tour through the elements of logic and argument shows the tools that can help students make political decisions, understand data, question assumptions and think above their pay grade. These tools can help our students make intelligent decisions, make them critical viewers, readers and listeners. The digital age gives us tools to help students be more logical. Video clips from political ads can be used to see what is assumed and what is proved. A commercial might be viewed and broken down in terms of evidence and the validity of the argument. There are software programs that teach logic and give students the chance to explore logic in an entertaining way. The new digital tools can be used to shed new light on ancient texts and classical ideas. In bringing together the logic of Aristotle with the dazzle of software, we can begin to see what the digital university can do.

COMPETENCY TWO: ETHICAL REASONING

Kant's second major work, *The Critique of Practical Reason*, was published in 1788. This work dealt primarily with ethics. In the age of cultural relativism, ethics has had a tough time in the university curriculum (Bloom 1988). It would be wrong to suggest that all colleges should teach some form of an ethical system, but it is important that colleges educate students in the language and concepts of ethics.

As far back as the dialogues of Plato, we can find suspicion that what is good can be either taught or learned. But what is more doable is to expound on the questions of ethics and the tools students need to think about them. Here, we can talk about the contrast between happiness and duty, which is at the core of many moral dilemmas. The Greeks developed a *eudiamonistic* ethics whose core concept was happiness. What does it take to say a person is happy? Now, this is not simply a hedonistic concept of what makes us happy at the moment, but rather it is what makes for a happy life.

In the modern times, two competing theories have arisen. The Utilitarian model advocated by Bentham and Mill can be formulated in its simplest form in the principle of utility. When asking if an act is good or not, we ask what will produce the greatest good for the greatest number. Goodness is utility.

Opposed to this is the system of Kant with its Categorical Imperative. The Categorical Imperative is a rule by which we act in a way that we would wish any other actor to act in similar circumstances. But Kant does not want to attach what is good to a good outcome. He wants to say that the act is good in and of itself. This means, for example, that lying is never good even if it leads to someone's happiness or pleasure. It is not good even if the lie leads to some greater good or avoids harm. The Categorical Imperative is not dependent on happiness, or even bringing good, but on what is unconditionally and morally right. Kant argued that we should act in way that we would wish all men at all times to act in the same way, regardless of the consequences.

While there are numerous ethical systems we could use to make our point, these two ethical systems take quite different views of ethical action. One, the Utilitarian, looks for the greatest good for the greatest number. The other, the Kantian, believes that ethical acts are good in and of themselves no matter what their outcome. For one the goodness is found in the result; for the other the goodness is found in the intention that is behind the act.

An understanding of ethical reasoning would give college graduates the tools to think ethically. Whether they use them or not is their choice but the tools should be there for the global good.

Wall Street employs the smartest graduates from the best colleges. Yet, in 2008, they oversaw an economic meltdown that destroyed the life savings of many people and damaged our nation. Asking not what will make me happy but what is good should be part of the college experience. There are digital tools that can help us do this. For example, there are ethical situations that can be presented digitally and how the decision is made will influence the result. Would you lie to save a life? Would you lie to make someone happy on his or her deathbed. Would you go back in time and shoot a terrible dictator in their crib even though they had not yet done anything wrong? We can now play and replay ethical scenarios and see how one outcome is better or worse than another. Ethical elements can be placed in the curriculum of any major or area of study. While the most well known are business ethics and medical ethics, there are ethics for software developers and even for those involved in sport. For the Greeks, the aim of all education was to live the good life. Knowing what is good is essential for us to get there.

COMPETENCY THREE: AESTHETIC APPRECIATION

In Kant's *Third Critique*, published in 1790, he focused on aesthetics. The Greeks believed that a happy life involves the ability to appreciate the beautiful. Socrates tells us in *The Apology* that the "unexamined life is not worth living" (Plato 1928). Part of being fully human is appreciating beauty. To appreciate beauty is to be able to articulate the principles that make something beautiful. The knowledge of what is beautiful can give our students an enhanced appreciation of the work. Here we use an example of enjoying a glass of wine. For most people, the appreciation of a glass of wine is in the tongue and nose. If one reads about wine tasting, a person can get a vocabulary to say a wine is vanilla or tastes like black cherry or liquorish. This can enhance the experience. Better still, reading about the region or vineyard that produced the wine helps to get the mind more involved, resulting in a better appreciation of the experience. In the same way, understanding the principles of classic literature can help students appreciate the principles in current television, film or other forms of media.

But we do not need so elevated an example as wine tasting to show the importance of aesthetics. What made Apple and Steven Jobs so successful was not just how the products they made worked but the aesthetics of those products. When the iPod first came out, there were dozens of MP3 players on the market that did the same job, some of them quite well. But the design and functionality of the iPod was so superior that it absolutely dominated the market. Aesthetics are important in our choice of automobiles, phones, computers and even drinking glasses. The ability to articulate why we like something and what those principles are that make it appealing make our life richer and more fun. Auto mechanics, designers, developers, software engineers and chefs all need an understanding of the elements of design and what appeals to people. It helps us in our economic life and in our personal life to appreciate beauty.

COMPETENCY FOUR: STEM (SCIENCE, TECHNOLOGY, ENGINEERING AND MATHEMATICS) LITERACY FOR THE DIGITAL AGE

Lastly, students must be digitally literate. This cannot be done in one single course, but in a school that understands McLuhan's dictum that the medium is the message. In other words, while obtaining their education, students are already employing the technologies that are changing society. The digital age empowers users, but the better a college graduate's technology skills, the more opportunities they will have in the digital economy. This means that mathematics and science have to be more central to the curriculum, as unpalatable as that may seem for many American students. The immediate future is digital, and the digital world rests on the STEM backbone. To be digitally literate is to have a firm grounding in STEM disciplines. There is no way around that. One of the great things about the digital revolution is that the teaching of STEM skills can be done more attractively and entertainingly than in the past. Often in the college curriculum of the past, there was little coherence in the curriculum. A student went from English literature to algebra to history without seeing any connection between the three. With digital tools, it is possible to link disciplines, embed videos and unify classes. Once the physical class is online, there can be digital student commons, team teaching and all sorts of collaborations that were not possible before. Algebra now has many software programs that teach it simply and coach students one on one. We no longer have to rely on a math teacher to break down the concepts. Students can have as much tutoring and coaching as they need with no added expense to the university. Making sure our students are prepared for their lives and not just their first job is what a modern university education can do. This is not possible without an understanding of the principles and skills that underlie the digital world.

AN EDUCATED CITIZENRY

The university should be a place where reason is developed, values are made clear, aesthetics can be improved and students receive the tools needed to be successful in the modern world. Each college must find a coherent package for these four competencies and present them in a way that is relevant and interesting to the student.

We know that the educational theories of Rousseau and Dewey show that imagination should lead the way in any educational venture (Rousseau 2003). When the imagination is fired up, students become engaged in their own education. When a student wants to learn, the path ahead is easier. When a student is convinced of the value of the education, their motivation will be different. There are several current developments that are combining the theories of Rousseau and Dewey with new digital technologies, such as personal learning environments (PLEs) (Chang, Hwang, Chen, and Mueller 2011). Effective PLEs are comprised of automated software, semantic networks and artificial intelligence that fit the educational content to the student and not the other way around. During the Industrial Revolution, people had to be subjected in large groups to the pace of a mechanical machine. In the digital revolution, the software adapts to us. The Google ads we see are tailored to us specifically. When we shop on Amazon or Netflix, computer-generated purchase suggestions are delivered to us based on our past choices and preferences.

It is a new world, and universities can prepare students not only in new ways but also in better ways. The web and other digital tools give us the power to educate more citizens in a more economical way. What has been seen as a crisis in higher education can well be looked at as the golden dawn of a new era. We just need the courage and wisdom to see it.

CHAPTER SEVENTEEN
THE ECONOMICS OF HIGHER EDUCATION

What we're learning in our schools is not the wisdom of life. We're learning technologies and we're getting information. There is a curious reluctance on the part of faculties to indicate the life of values in their subjects.

— Joseph Campbell

Should a university education guarantee its graduates a job? If it does not, what is the use of a college degree? These are not new questions. These were questions that were not unfamiliar to Cardinal Newman when he wrote *The Idea of the University* in the early 1850s. Today, as it was back then, we continue to ask what the relationship is between acquiring knowledge and its practical application.

College professors have long been portrayed in literature and film as being out of touch with the practical realities of everyday life (Kramer and Hamm 2003). From the 1930 German film *Der blaue Engel* (the Blue Angel) where an out-of-touch professor falls in love with a cabaret singer to the character of Dean Wormer in *Animal House*, professors have had a difficult time in the popular media. Many theorists who are the leading voices in higher education have spent their entire adult lives inside the so-called "Ivory Tower." This term has its origins in the *Song of Solomon*, chapter 7, verse 4, where it was written, "your neck is like an ivory tower." It was also used in the Middle Ages as a description of Mary the mother of Jesus and a metaphor for purity. But for the last two centuries, the word has had a negative connotation that refers to out-of-touch intellectuals and has become a synonym for academics, especially those teaching the humanities.

The Ivory Tower is the nickname for Hawksmoor Towers at All Souls College, the only pure research college at Oxford University (Tolles 2011). Going back to *The Ivory Tower*, a novel by Henry James, published in 1917, we can find literally hundreds of college novels critical of academics disconnecting from the lives of students and lacking an understanding of what happens to them after graduation (Kramer and Hamm 2003).

It is common for college students to refer to the universe outside of the college quad as the "real world" (Schwartz 2011). Many professors of the previous generation have spent their entire lives inside this insulated world of the college campus. Many went to graduate school with a teaching assistantship directly after getting their bachelor's degree. When they get their PhD, they may get a position on the faculty, and if they are lucky, they will achieve tenure and be guaranteed a job for life. Many college professors, and a large number of its more prominent scholars and authors, have never spent a day working outside of the college walls. This had led to the perception by some that college professors are out of touch with the real world and living in a kind of dream world.

Cardinal Newman is part and parcel of the tradition of the Ivory Tower. He was a man who spent most of his life inside of the walls of the university. While he spent some time preaching, early on he was connected to Oriel College, Oxford and never really left the influence of university life (Dawson 2001). Similar to many theorists of higher education since the writings of Plato, Cardinal Newman saw the university falling from a golden age where it once flourished.

We have noted how the role of nostalgia has distorted our thinking on the current state of higher education (Hass and Fishman 2010). Newman longed for the university that he knew as a young student. He criticized the current state of higher education in the British Isles. He thought that graduates had their heads filled with facts but did not have the critical thinking skills to conceptualize problems. He worried that students were being trained too narrowly for a profession. He wrote that graduates often lacked the broader education that would have prepared them to switch careers if they grew and changed as human beings do. He noticed that literature, philosophy, theology and the classics were being neglected for more career-oriented studies. He was suspicious that the goal of education had devolved into the quest for a paycheck. He believed that a university should give its graduates something more. His greatest worry was that the education they were receiving was not what it once was (Newman 2002).

WHAT IS COLLEGE GOOD FOR?

Fast forward to the twenty-first century. The debates that Newman engaged in have not subsided. The tension between education for education's sake and the practical economic needs of graduates to find meaningful work still animates our conversation. The role of higher education in society has become more confused and less clear. In the last half century, the role of the liberal arts has undergone a siege in an attempt to bring more diversity into the curriculum, but the issues here again are by no means settled (Nussbaum 2012). To confuse matters more, the profile of the average college student has been changing steadily since Newman's time. As this has happened, the definition and goals of higher education have changed, and society has not yet processed these changes.

Assumptions that might be made about a small elite portion of the population may not apply to a more diverse student body that we find today in our colleges and universities (Birnbaum 1988). As de Tocqueville noted, the conflict between equality and excellence is at the heart of the American experiment, and these contradictions animate many modern political debates. To put it in its most simplistic form, liberals have emphasized the value of equality while conservatives have focused more on individual excellence, freedom and responsibility. The debates about higher education, its purpose and future, reflect these philosophical differences. One group wants more inclusion while the other does not want to dilute what are seen as the world's best universities.

But the most profound change that has impacted higher education fits right into the same concern that Newman had with higher education as a pragmatic way to find a job and be employable. The fact that college tuition has risen faster than the rate of inflation, while at the same time middle-classes wages have stagnated, has put a spotlight on the value and cost of a college education (Brown and Lauder 2010). As youth unemployment has risen along with the percentage of student loan debt, questions have begun to be asked about the very nature and purpose of the university (Wolfgang 2011). In the nineteenth century, the Industrial Revolution called for less agricultural workers and more workers with different skill sets. The increasing need for bankers and accountants, for instance, was rapidly changing the workforce of Europe and America (Hepplewhite 2009). The digital revolution has accelerated similar kinds of mass trends, challenging colleges and universities in ways they have not been challenged before.

WHO GOES TO WHAT COLLEGE?

The economics of a college education have a lot of do with the social class of the student who attends college. As we noted earlier, when our nation was founded, less than 1% of the population attended universities (Brubacher and Rudy 1997). With the exceptions of the University of Virginia and the University of Pennsylvania that had the guiding wisdom of Thomas Jefferson and Benjamin Franklin, religious groups sponsored our earliest universities. These institutions were originally set up for the dual purpose of producing ministers and to edify the children of the wealthy ruling class. University education was a gift for the few, focused on the Greek and Latin classics with a religious emphasis (Graff 1989).

Today, more than 66% of high school graduates go on to some form of higher education. The old models of college and learning have to change just as the student population has changed. Because there is no central ministry of education in the United States, the market has compensated for these changes in population and the evolution of technology.

A class system has evolved in American higher education that is based on "tiers." At the top tier you have Harvard, Princeton, Yale and the others whose names all of us in higher education know well. It is hard to think of another industry in America where the top companies today were exactly the same top companies 200 years ago. But that is the case in higher education. With huge endowments and political connections that have allowed them to resist the digital revolution for the longest time, there has been little incentive for them to conform to the market, because the market has conformed to them. It is a simple case of supply and demand. When these old and elite institutions have 20 applicants for every freshman spot, they can pick and choose what kind of freshman class they will accept. However, this process is not so much about merit as it about class and economics (Golden 2007). While some percentage of the freshman class of the best university is based on brains and grades, there are other elements that influence the makeup of the freshman class. Those applicants whose parents, and, more importantly, grandparents and great-grandparents, attended the same college are termed "legacies" in the admissions process. Their stories tell us a great deal about the class structure in American higher education.

Daniel Golden of *Bloomberg News* provided a lot of numbers about the real nature and social impact of legacy admission practices in his 2005 book *The Price of Admission*. A more recent work edited by Richard Kahlenberg and published by the Brookings Institute in 2012, titled *Affirmative Action for the Rich: Legacy Preferences in College Admissions*, gives us more up-to-date statistics.

In 2009, Princeton University admitted 41.7% of legacy students, which was 4.5 times the rate for non-legacies (Kahlenberg 2010). There is evidence that Harvard admits mediocre students who have the "legacy" designations (Kahlenberg 2010). Kahlenerg's book also claims one elite institution admits 70% of its legacies and has a 21% rate of admissions for everyone else. The research also shows that legacy students who are given the advantage over more academically prepared and talented applicants often underperform and are academically average at best.

We have repeatedly noted that at the founding of our republic 1% of the population attended college. In our current political climate, there has been a polarized discourse about the difference in wealth between the 1% and the 99%. While 1% of our population have the bulk of wealth in America and may not be exactly the same 1% that was here at our founding, there is more continuity than one might think (Golden 2007). Just as the elite were the only ones being educated at the founding of our nation, the elite still populated our most elite colleges and universities.

College was once thought of as a way to advance one's social and economic standing. While this assumption has come to be questioned by the tens of thousands of college graduates who have a degree but no job, the sons and daughters of the elite often have no such worries.

A LEGACY OF PRIVILEGE

The job prospects of a third- or fourth-generation legacy student attending Yale are likely to be very different than a graduate of a community college or for-profit trade school who is the first in her family to attend college. Let us look at two famous legacy students to show what job prospects one might expect with the right connections. They both ran for president in the year 2000 and their names are George Bush and Al Gore.

George W. Bush, the 43rd President of the United States, was born in Connecticut where his grandfather, Prescott Bush, was a United States Senator.George W. Bush's father held several posts, including ambassador to China, head of the C.I.A., Vice President and eventually President of the United States. George W. Bush attended Andover Academy, which is a recognized "feeder school" for legacy students bound for the Ivy League. Sure enough, George W. Bush was smart enough to get into Yale, graduate with a 77% average and then be accepted to the Harvard Business School, which has one of the most elite admissions standards of any graduate school in the nation. His working resume was not bad after graduate school. He made an unsuccessful bid for Congress, ran several oil companies, one of which went bankrupt and eventually became part owner of the Texas Rangers baseball team. Not a bad resume for an average college student. This is but one well-known example of the advantage that money, power and connections have in American higher education. The top-tier colleges are not just for educating students. They have another purpose that they do not trumpet but is very well known. Students go to these schools to make connections and meet other sons and daughters of the powerful who may help their careers in the future.

To be even-handed, let us look at George W. Bush's opponent in the 2000 election. Al Gore, who also had a father who was a United

States Senator, went to Saint Alban's Prep, another "feeder school" for the Ivy League. When not living on Embassy Row in Washington D.C. with his parents, young Al Gore spent time on their Tennessee plantation where they raised tobacco and cotton. He was admitted to Harvard where his freshman roommate was the future movie star Tommy Lee Jones. He eventually got his father's job as Senator from Tennessee. George Bush also got his father's job, President of the United States. These are not coincidences. This is how the top tier works, and this is what it does for the right people who have the money and influence so that their family power can be extended.

In our thinking about the digital future of the university, we believe that the top-tier colleges are serving other sociological, economic and political purposes that have made them immune from a lot of the questions about the quality of higher education in America. You rarely read accounts of a legacy student from Yale who is in a dead-end job with a mountain of student debt. But the same cannot be said for a first-generation college student in a trade school or online university.

The cost of a top-tier university includes connections that can help you for the rest of your life. The right institution, linked perhaps with the right fraternity, sorority or secret society gives their members a head start on life and economic security. If you wonder if college is worth the cost, the answer is yes if you have enough money.

THE DIGITAL REVOLUTION IS NOT ONE SIZE FITS ALL

The elite, top-tier colleges can continue to operate as they have because in many ways they are beyond criticism. There may not be an effective way to measure what Ivy League students have learned, but their political and economic connections give them a leg up on many other college graduates. The pressure to improve curriculum, give students better job skills and make college more affordable will not be applied equally to all colleges. But for those colleges and universities not in the top tier, the pressure to become more digital, is an imperative.

As colleges digitize, they can save costs. We have noted the importance of cost in discussions about college education. But we must emphasize that college is not only about cost. One of the complaints about for-profit institutions is that they put profit ahead of education (Nusssbaum 2012). Just because a university is for-profit does not mean that it cannot be a good university. It is the same way with the term "non-profit," which ultimately tells absolutely nothing about a university's true academic quality.

Nonetheless, all costs savings are not equal. We believe that the trend toward more and more adjunct professors in higher education, in both for-profit and non-profit institutions, has been destructive to the quality of education. This has been done under the guise of "cost savings." It is our belief that there are other areas where costs can be more effectively curtailed than by eliminating full-time faculty positions. The use of digital technologies is a more effective way to do this.

It has been said that any business should concentrate on its core competencies and outsource everything else (Drejer 2002). Many universities spend their energies building new buildings, running food services, supporting athletic teams and countless other activities that are not central to academic learning. All of these activities add to the cost of a college education. To keep costs down and improve the educational experience, we need to differentiate between those things that are essential and those that are not.

GLOBALIZATION AND STUDENT DEBT

As resentment grows over rising tuition prices nationwide, costs must be contained. In addition, globalization and the digitization of work have put a spotlight on the question of student debt. In 2012, economist Richard Vedder of Ohio University wrote a series of editorials about the severity of student debt, and he offered some radical solutions. He realized that the country was turning out more college graduates for jobs that no longer existed because they had been transformed by the deployment of digital technologies. In one article, he quoted that the Bureau of Labor Statistics reported there were 115,000 janitors, 83,000 bartenders, 323,000 restaurant servers and 80,000 heavy-duty truck drivers with bachelor's degrees – a number exceeding the uniformed personnel of the U.S. Army (Vedder 2012b).

Many of these janitors and bartenders were also saddled with a mountain of student debt. They started their working lives in very different places than the legacy graduates of one of the old universities.

Here is another fact that many people do not know. Student loan debt cannot be discharged in a bankruptcy. A student loan debt must be honored before one passes away, no matter what job an individual obtains, no matter how an individual's economic life turns out. It is not uncommon today to talk with young people who are earning low wages while paying $600 a month toward their student debt. Moreover, with the way interest is calculated, they may pay this for much of their working lives. This kind of expense sometimes puts home ownership out of reach for people with substantial college loans.

Amazingly, it is not just the student who has to repay these debts. Loans are frequently co-signed by a parent or other party when a student applies for financial aid. For example, there was a story reported in the *Wall Street Journal* of a 25-year-old New Jersey student who died owing $44,000, which his parents must now repay (Pilon 2010). So, the loan can live on even after the person who was supposed to earn enough to pay it back is dead.

There has been a lot of ink written about the impending bubble of student loans and how they may keep the holders of those loans from consuming the other goods that keep a capitalist economy going. Debt is a problem in many countries but the student debt in the United States is so large and unique that it is attracting political attention. The amount of student debt owed to banks now exceeds one trillion dollars. During the Occupy Wall Street movement that occurred in the wake of the 2008 financial collapse triggered by the housing crisis, derivatives packaging and failures of AIG and Lehman Brothers, the issue of student debt became linked to the question of economic justice.

WHAT IS A COLLEGE EDUCATION WORTH?

What is a college degree worth? Most professors have a different point of view about this than students and parents. There have always been a small number of students who are in college for an education in literature or archaeology or philosophy for the sheer love of the subject. But for the vast majority of college students, they want a degree that will help them become an economic success. The difference between getting an education and getting a degree can be seen at the heart of many of the current debates about higher education. Both citizens and politicians question the value of a liberal arts degree that does not lead to a job. The worth of a college degree could be calculated by seeing how much more in a lifetime a college degree would be worth to the graduate after subtracting the cost of college, including the interest on college loans. Because the increase in tuition has constantly outrun both inflation and even health care costs, the value of a college degree has been called into question.

Reactions to the high price of college have created a movement to offer new forms of higher education that are much less expensive and geared very specifically toward helping people to quickly earn credentials that have labor value. The concept of earning a "badge," for instance, is one of these new trends that is entering the marketplace and starting to garner attention. While large companies such as Mozilla and Google are exploring how to give badges, many colleges oppose this trend. These colleges have made it their business to authenticate or certify learning. If students can obtain credentials outside of college, this would be seismic for the industry.

We know that most college students today attend more than one college (McCormick 2003). When a student transfers between colleges, credits may not get accepted. English 101 at school A may have a totally and completely different syllabus and learning objectives than English 101 at school B. The transfer student often gets caught in the middle of an inadequate transfer system that causes them to take more credits than the customary 60 credits for an associate degree and 120 credits for a bachelor's degree. The situation gets cloudier when advanced-level courses and the prerequisites to such courses are required in the various majors.

The concept of badges, however, measures competencies, not transfer credits (Carey 2012). There are a number of institutions of higher education that are competency based, such as Western Governors University. In addition, other institutions, such as Empire State College of the State University of New York System, Thomas Edison State College, Excelsior College and Charter Oak

College of the State University of Connecticut System are liberal in their assembly of prior learning and transfer of skills and competencies into college credit. In short, the increasing call for competency-based, accelerated degrees (be it badges, prior-learning or skills-based credit) has been gaining momentum across the country.

MOOCS AND THE QUESTION OF COST

Another reaction to the increased cost of college has been the introduction of Massively Open Online Classes (MOOCs). Here, online teaching and learning technologies are utilized to teach hundreds of thousands of students in a single course that so happens to be designed by a world-class professor, with the backing of an elite university. This makes it possible to offer Ivy League courses without the Ivy League price tag (McKenna 2012). EdX, a joint education venture run by MIT and Harvard, for example, will begin offering online classes in Fall 2012. About 120,000 students signed up for the first MITx course, "Circuits and Electronics," in March 2012. In a video on their website, their President, Anant Agarwal, explained that similar to Coursera, the Stanford version of a MOOC, EdX courses will also be open to anyone and everyone (McKenna 2012).

These types of initiatives take us back to the notion of technology, automating those tasks previously provided by humans who would deliver content and grade papers. Professor Laura McKenna described the phenomenon of MOOCs in an *Atlantic Monthly* article published on May 11, 2012, titled "The Big Idea That Can Revolutionize Higher Education: MOOC":

> Using new technology and crowd sourcing innovations, both programs hope to bypass the problem of needing human beings to moderate discussions and grade assignments.
>
> Multiple choice tests can be easily graded using technology, but essays, the most accepted form of assessment for the humanities and the social sciences, have proven to be trickier. It would be impossible to hire enough people to grade the essays for a class that served 20,000. At Coursera, three engineers worked for two months on

creating a system similar to Amazon Mechanical Turk for peer evaluation. This program will launch in about a week. EdX will use essay-grading software.

Peers "vote" on which discussion board comments are good. Voters also push bad comments and spam to the bottom of the discussion threads. The class uses technology to steer itself and save money. The class in effect almost teaches itself. After the videos are created, the assignments are written, and the initial kinks are ironed out, Koller expects that these courses should be self sustaining and run on auto-pilot.

EdX and Coursera are funded differently. EdX is overseen by a not-for-profit organization, which is owned and governed by both universities. MIT and Harvard have committed to a combined $60 million ($30 million each) in institutional support, grants and philanthropy to launch the collaboration (McKenna 2012).

If one were to read the comments from traditional professors in reaction to positive articles about MOOCs, there is a sharp negative reaction within the academy to MOOCs. One reason is that it automates many of the tasks traditionally done by professors. The model of the professor as craftsman has given way to technology, just as the world of work was dramatically altered during the first Industrial Revolution. The cliché in higher education has been that the sage on the stage has been replaced with the guide on the side. While this was popular with theorists of active learning and constructivism, online learning made it happen. The new classroom was a new medium with a new message.

DIGITAL DESTRUCTION AND DIGITAL RESURRECTION

Universities have been devastated by the digital revolution. Online learning lured students out of the physical classrooms and created whole new institutions where nothing existed before. Virtual libraries made the libraries of the great universities almost empty. Online systems reduced the need for the armies of clerical workers who were the mainstay of the university's labor force. These and other changes occurred at the same time as tenure lines were shrinking and the number of adjuncts or piece workers was mushrooming. To keep up with growing student numbers, universities spent a fortune on building dorms, exercise facilities, gyms and student centers and that drove their tuition to expand faster than the pace of inflation.

Because tuition outpaced inflation every year for decades, eventually the cost of a college education could not be paid for in cash. Instead, students were forced to go heavily into debt with the hope that the degree they were earning would pay them enough to repay the debt and more. At the same time, globalization was having a negative impact upon the United States economy. Jobs were being lost as first manufacturing and then white-collar jobs were outsourced to other countries. The pace of globalization has outstripped any attempts to stop it or, perhaps, even understand it. In the last decades of the twentieth century, there was concern that America was losing jobs to Japan and Japan would be the world's new superpower. This concern was so pervasive that America modeled many business and educational practices on Japanese businesses and schools that they saw as more successful.

But it turns out our worries were misplaced. Japan has been in recession now for more than a decade, and their currency has lost much of its value. In addition, now Japan is seeing its manufacturing base weakened as globalization pushes manufacturing jobs to other parts of Southeast Asia where labor is cheaper (Economist 2012). Still, our workforce is left with high unemployment and stagnant wages for the foreseeable future. The digital revolution has injected a speedball into the global economy and accelerated these seismic economic shifts.

While the digital revolution has devastated the university, at the same time, it has opened up new possibilities that we could only dream of. Should universities resist the digital revolution? Should they embrace it? Before we can answer these questions, we must return to the question we began this book with: What is the essence of the university?

CHAPTER EIGHTEEN
THE MAJOR ELEMENTS AND ESSENCE
OF THE DIGITAL UNIVERSITY

The philosophy of the schoolroom in one generation is the philosophy of government in the next.

— Abraham Lincoln

As we noted earlier, Clark Kerr, the president of the University of California, coined the term "multiversity" to make sense of all of the various activities going on in and around the modern university. Schools are in the business of fund-raising, athletics, entertainment, research and so on. We also want to point out that many of the goals pursued by modern universities conflict with each other. A successful football program must generate money for the new dorm. This can be a cause of friction. This has created confusion and muddied the conversation about higher education.

In this final chapter, we lay out our vision of what higher education could be in the digital age. We note that different constituencies have often looked to the university for very different results. For this reason, we look first at the university as a whole. We then at the university from the student's point of view. Finally, we also look at the future of the faculty and university staff. And we provide a brief overview concerning the external stakeholders, such as parents, alumni, citizens and the taxpayers, who support our institutions directly or indirectly.

HIGHER EDUCATION CONSTITUENTS

All the players can and should benefit from the use of digital technologies to import knowledge, keep costs down, improve campus communication and assess learning. This goes from the most elite colleges to the most hard-pressed urban community college. The use of predictive analytics, Big Data and digital technologies may never replace the classroom, but they can enhance the classroom. These improvements can help make us competitive in the age of globalization (Brown and Lauder 2010). Transparency will improve the function of the university by making clear what was in the past only vaguely understood (Fain 2012). The use of rubrics makes clear the expectations of the class and the skills and competencies needed for success (Burke 2010). With the aid of digital technologies, rubrics can be charted and followed to map a student's progress. This would allow for early interventions and better advising. This, in turn, should lead to better graduation and retention rates.

However, while there is plenty to share in the digital age, there are also areas for each constituency in which interests may not align. Following is an overview of each of the higher education constituents that coalesce into the major elements and basic essence of the digital university.

THE MARKET-SMART, MISSION-DRIVEN UNIVERSITY

Bob Zemsky of the University of Pennsylvania coined the term "Market Smart, Mission Driven" (Zemsky 2005). This means that while all universities do not need to be doing the same thing, they all must understand their market, prepare their students for it and stay close to their mission. A tribal college has a very different market and mission from an Ivy League school, and a tribal college must stay true to its mission, which is a needed one. Have you ever heard the term "creeping Harvardism"? It means that many colleges stray from their market, their mission or both when they try to imitate the most traditional of schools. A small private college may go deep into debt to build an edifice they do not really need. Another school may start a program that has little financial gain but may have the promise of great prestige. Schools often lose their focus by straying from the core of what they should be: learning institutions that serve a particular constituency.

The great research institutions like MIT and Stanford are an important part of the fabric of American higher education. But not all colleges need to emulate them. There are colleges where the teaching of skills and competencies are the most important thing they do. This does not mean that research is not accomplished at these schools, but that research should take a backseat to teaching. There has even been recent interest in the scholarship of teaching where the college's research focuses on how to better serve its students and fulfill its mission.

STUDENTS OF THE DIGITAL AGE

Students are already living in a digital world. Colleges must prepare them to be successful in that world. Being a critical thinker is important in the modern world. It is key to staying up on the latest developments. To be successful in almost any job, evenbeing a rock star, they will have to master a number of the STEM disciplines (science, technology, engineering and mathematics). Students must also have values that can help them as citizens in a democracy. Finally, students must be digitally literate to use the tools of the digital age. By thinking of things in these ways, we do not need to decide between education for its own sake or a more pragmatic approach to career preparation. We can do both at the same time. It is not the texts or authors that make for an educated citizen. An educated citizen today has an understanding of clear thinking, values, the scientific method and the tools needed to succeed in the digital age.

FACULTY IN THE DIGITAL AGE

The university began with the establishment of a faculty guild. The future of the university is dependent on a faculty that is free to speak, empowered and financially secure. Research is important as it both moves along with industry and society and insures that professors are keeping up with their discipline. While we have worked in schools with large adjunct populations, we have come to the conclusion that full-time faculty with protections and a living wage are at the heart of a good university. At the same time, we recognize the frustrations that entrenched faculty have caused by holding back change at their universities (Reily 2011). We suggest a "Chinese Wall" be built between the faculty and the administration. In short, faculty should not be deciding policy about the efficiency of the college or the implementation of new technologies. At the same time, administrators should not be deciding academic issues that require the expertise of professors. Professors must allow data about student success to guide their thinking about pedagogy and curriculum. Administrators must respect those faculty activities that may be beyond measurement. It is possible to be a transparent and productive university while maintaining the independence of the faculty.

HIGHER EDUCATION STAFF OF THE DIGITAL AGE

In the learning organization, the learning is not confined to the classroom. Every interaction a student has on campus should be a learning experience for both the student and the institution. A learning organization improves via these interactions. This means that the traditional hierarchy that has existed with the faculty on top and staff on the bottom must be reexamined. Registrars have often not been senior decision makers in colleges, but they are ones who best understand issues with grading, reporting, schedules and other key events in college life. In a true learning organization, those with the most knowledge and stake in the outcome should have a seat at the table. This also means that senior staff and boards must rethink their mass importation of business types without any prior experience in the university. The learning curve is steep and too often these new managers are pressured to create efficiencies before they understand the unintended consequences of their actions.

EXTERNAL UNIVERSITY CONSTITUENTS IN THE DIGITAL AGE

There are many who have a stake in the future of the university. Parents want to make sure their children will have a degree that is useful to them. Taxpayers want to make sure they are getting their money's worth. Alumni want to make sure that the value of their degree is not diminished by actions taken in the short run. The collection and transparency of data will help answer all of these questions. But this data must be placed in context. For instance, community colleges have a lower graduation rate and retention rate than elite colleges. But this does not mean they are not doing their job. An algorithm must be developed that will place these variables in context. The federal government should not demand that all colleges be held to the same standard as they so disastrously tried to do during the administration of George W. Bush with the No Child Left Behind Act for K-12. The richness of our higher education landscape would be horrifically damaged by any attempt to have a single curriculum or criteria applied. The top 50 colleges in the United States have very little incentive to change. But even though this is true, we have seen such bastions of tradition as Harvard, MIT and Stanford on the cutting edge of the many new developments in digital higher education.

UNIVERSITY AS A UNIVERSE

We will now look at these constituents individually, beginning with the university as a whole. To see it as whole is to see a whole universe of goals, needs and players. We have made the point previously that higher education is not a monolithic enterprise. With rabbinical schools, tribal colleges, research universities and online graduate schools, there is very little we can say about these institutions as a whole. What we can say, however, is that they do what they claim to do. For example, if a research school trains someone for graduate school, they have a record of placement that is available to those applying for that level of education. If a career college claims to prepare a student for a career as a chef or technician, there must be data to show what percentage of students make it to graduation and what their placement rate is in the field they studied. A community college might show its rank with similar community colleges to demonstrate to students that its retention rate is in line with the particular population it is recruiting. A research university might be measured by it grant or the number of patents it holds.

American higher education is wonderfully diverse. Any one-size-fits-all solution will hurt it. A college should be true to its mission and serve its students who are also there in harmony with that mission. What is the goal and heart of a particular university and how can it best achieve that goal?

COLLECTING DATA FOR ADMISSIONS TRANSPARENCY

Graduates of both traditional private colleges and newly founded online for-profits often voice their anger, claiming that they were "deceived" or not given correct information when they first applied and were accepted. A transparent series of metrics universally agreed upon would address this issue. In short, colleges have to start measuring what they think they are trying to accomplish. It may be that the most elite colleges will not need to do this, but most other colleges will definitely require it. The elite colleges do not have to prove their academic quality or promise because their value is already well known. This shows the power that tradition and nostalgia has in our discussion (Hass and Fishman 2010). For the rest, the transparency of data will have to do.

Currently, much of the data collected by the Department of Education comes from its IPEDS (Integrated Postsecondary Education Data System) survey. The IPEDS measures first-time, full-time college students. The government, accrediting agencies and publications that rate colleges use this formula. But first-time, full-time students only account for 14% of the college population. Therefore, 86% of the students in college today are absent from many discussions about data, graduation or retention. A more inclusive metric is needed, and this metric must be connected to an algorithm that takes into account factors that influence attrition. If a student works more than 35 hours a week, this variable can help predict retention. If a student lives in poverty, this can help predict their retention. If a student is a parent or a single parent, this can help predict their retention in college. Ethnicity is a predictor of college retention. Career colleges, community colleges and for-profit colleges have large numbers of these types of students impacting their retention and graduation rates.

TEACHING TWENTY-FIRST CENTURY SKILLS

It is obvious that transparency of data and performance is important. Next is the question of what should be taught. We have learned from the quarrel between the ancients and moderns in France and the "Battle of the Books" in England that it is difficult to make a decision about authors and texts that will have universal agreement. We fall out on both sides of the controversy. Co-author Dr. Frank McCluskey is a philosopher who loves the classical texts and great books along with a strong dose of logic and science. Co-author Melanie Winter has argued for a more relevant and inclusive curriculum that is a better fit for the modern age. This debate will not go away. However, there are a number of skills that are needed for the twenty-first century that can be taught and learned regardless of which texts are used.

Critical thinking is one of those skills. Students must learn to question assumptions and understand how arguments are constructed. Students must get into the habit of questioning received wisdom and accepted practices. Students must understand how an argument is constructed from premises and conclusions, and they must understand how to infer a conclusion from premises. Such critical thinking skills help students because, as their tools and work environment evolve, they can think through what will happen next and how they should ultimately approach life. Understanding and using the scientific method, where a hypothesis is tested for proof, is part of this education.

Students must also understand the language of ethical arguments. We do not advocate the teaching of a value system per se. It may be that a bible college or tribal college or historically black college or university may find that certain values are part and parcel of its educational curriculum. It is also the case that religious schools, such as the many Catholic colleges and universities, have the teaching of values at the core of their curriculum. This is a matter for individual colleges to decide. We believe, however, that if critical thinking is taught across the curriculum, the students will learn how to identify fallacies, poor thinking and bad arguments in a way that will make them better citizens and more capable of making intelligent value judgments. A citizen must be able to reason through propaganda and arrive at the right conclusion even when using a faulty argument.

We also believe that a college education should include an exposure to the language of appreciation. Aesthetics may not be limited to the Louvre or the Villa Borghese. It can be the appreciation of the kind of design that Steve Jobs or Frank Lloyd Wright envisioned. It is an understanding of the role form plays in our world and how we should relate to it. Education should help us get a job, but it can and should be so much more.

Additionally, students need to understand the underpinning of the digital world we live in. Quantitative reasoning is an important skill in the digital age. It has been argued that the United States lags behind many other countries in STEM education. Science, technology, engineering and mathematics are crucial to the processes of the digital age. The number of degrees in STEM majors must increase if we are to remain competitive in the world economy. Our students must learn the tools that other nations have used to overtake us in manufacturing for export. An increased emphasis on STEM elements in the curriculum will make for a workforce able to cope with the skills of the information age.

Digital literacy is a necessity for our age. Students must understand the basics of digital devices, how they work, what they can do and what their limitations are. From a cashier at Walmart to a designer at Apple, digital tools are part of the job today. The more understanding of digital technologies a person possesses, the more adaptable he may be in finding new employment if the market shifts. Schools must make a commitment to making sure their students have these tools that will help them succeed after graduation.

MORE TRANSPARENCY ON LEARNING OUTCOMES

Students have a right to know what they can get out of their college education. In his poem "Metaphors of a Magnifico," the American poet Wallace Stevens writes "twenty men crossing a bridge into a village are twenty men crossing twenty bridges into twenty villages." This is the same with college. There are a million reasons why students come to college and a million reasons why they leave. In the same classroom, there are students who are learning and students who are frustrated. The data on what the college is and how it operates must be more transparent, and prospective students must be able to compare that data to other schools. At the same time, students are responsible for their own education. It is not the "college that makes the man" but rather the person who comes to a college with the desire to learn and be a lifelong learner that makes for a successful educational experience.

Faculty are the heart and soul of a college. They are the coaches and interpreters of knowledge. But the digital revolution has rocked their world. By giving students access to more information more rapidly, the concept of learning has changed. Digital devices have shortened the attention span (Carr 2011). "Multi-tasking" can be seen as somebody simply doing two things at once and paying full attention to neither. But the reality is that students are no longer the passive vessels they were 50 years ago. The world has changed, and they have changed. Just two decades ago, the word "Edutainment" was created, combining education and entertainment together. Professors did not have an expectation to entertain their students in 1950, but there is that expectation today. There are some very intelligent teachers who do not possess entertainment skills. This is an issue in the digital age to rethink, and it goes beyond these pages.

MAINTAINING THE POWER OF FACULTY

Faculty must be paid a living wage so they do not need other employment to survive. If a faculty member is an adjunct professor at five colleges teaching seven courses a semester and driving a hundred miles in between, the students are the losers. More colleges are using adjuncts in lieu of full-time faculty, and this has led to changes in the quality of instruction (Bousquet 2008). There are ways to control costs in college. The growth in spending and the rise of tuition beyond the rate of inflation has not been because of an increase in faculty costs, but it has been caused by an inability to control administrative costs (Ginsberg 2011). We can cut costs dramatically once we have made the big leap and adapted to digital technologies (Finkelstein 2000). This can lead to a rethinking of the faculty role and maybe even a rebirth of the profession (Schuster and Finkelstein 2008).

We also need to empower the faculty in academic matters. In the past, in T-governed universities, faculty members were able to dictate policies for their benefit that were sometimes to the detriment of both the students and the institution (Gumport 2008). In addition to preventing inadequate faculty governance, higher education administrators must move back from a generation of professional managers with little academic experience and rely more on those who have cut their teeth in financial aid, admissions, advising and the registrar's office. In many B-governed universities, there are VPs of HR, Marketing or Ops professionals who have more power than registrars, directors of financial aid or directors of admissions. It makes more sense that those who are responsible for processes and their policies have more input into their structures.

DASHBOARDS AND DATA WAREHOUSES

The digital college must embrace those technologies that can do the work that was once done by human beings. While it is true that the digital revolution has disrupted the university, if we embrace that same technology, it can see us through this crisis to the other side.

Here is another example: Many colleges rely on a data person to give them reports. If this person gets sick or is busy, the report will not get out. More sophisticated colleges have gone to data warehouses where the college staff and faculty can run their own reports. Those who are more digitally savvy have developed dashboards where the data from the reports can be graphically displayed, color coded, or both, so that successes and failures can be more easily interpreted. This allows those who may not be close to the data, such as presidents and provosts, to have a better handle on the day-to-day data. Dashboards and data warehouses make data available across the institution and make what was once secret or siloed now common knowledge. Knowledge is power and not just because Francis Bacon said so. With the proliferation of data tools and digital representations, more members of the community can see the successes, failures and concerns of of a given institution.

The growth of online registration systems, student portals and self-service websites for student services are coming into the modern age. Colleges and universities should do all they can to expedite the move to these digital technologies. These should not be matters of academic debate or concerns about saving clerical jobs. Registering for a college class should be as easy as buying a book on Amazon.com. While this approach can be debated, this would put more burden on the student and at the same time free staff and faculty for more creative coaching and student assistance. For this to work, faculty must allow administrators to move in more creative digital directions.

INSTITUTIONAL DIGITAL REPORT CARDS

The external constituents have the right to ask if the university is being true to its mission. We have made the point that community colleges have a different mission than elite private colleges. Tribal colleges are doing something different than musical conservatories or schools of dance. In the modern higher education landscape, there must be room for all of these and more. There has to be a digital report card that will let prospective students know their chances of success and the success of previous graduates. This kind of data will quickly show which institutions are doing a good job and which are not. At the current time, many schools do not publish enough data. A prospective parent or student can be lured by sexy ads or high-pressure sales techniques. A national database that is easily accessible would eliminate these unreliable practices. In addition to College Navigator there are new proposals by the Department of Education that will make the value of an education clearer. It is not a question of for-profit or non-profit, but we should know about institutions that are educating their students in accordance with their mission and those that are not. With the rise of the digital revolution, the ability to run through masses of data and come up with conclusions that almost anyone can understand makes it possible for us to measure what was previously invisible.

The digital revolution has wreaked havoc on the university. The university made its business on the storage, transmission and creation of information. The digital revolution changed how information is stored, transmitted and created. In some ways, it cheapened what was once mysterious. In another way, it democratized the ability to access information. The digital revolution has thrown people out of work, displaced families and made whole neighborhoods in cities like Detroit into ghost towns. It has also given us new tools to measure what was once mysterious.

THE IDEA OF THE DIGITAL UNIVERSITY

What is the idea of the digital university? The digital university should retain the heart of a traditional university. The great texts are still great. Proust, Tolstoy and Joyce have not lost their relevance. Neither have Sophocles, Socrates or Herodotus. The changing population of our colleges have also brought with them new tastes, new literature and new values. There is room for both in the digital university. Because learning can be individualized via new technologies, it may provide more choices for the student who in the past could choose only one from column A and one from column B. In the digital university, it is not texts that are being taught but critical thinking, argument analysis, fallacy identification and the questioning of assumptions. Students preparing for the digital age must have an understanding of the basic tools of STEM. Finally, students must have more than a passing acquaintance with digital technologies that are at the heart of our new world.

The digital university will not replace the traditional classroom but enhance it. It will not put an end to the library. Instead, it will add to the library with the resources of the planet. The new classroom will realize the student is not a passive receptacle but an active learner. While talk of active learning has been around for a long time, digital technology allows students to search on their own, find new resources and check out what is being said in the lecture.

In his work *The Idea of the University*, Cardinal Newman showed us that the university is a place where knowledge is promoted for its own sake. In the modern world, we have found that those whose skills are limited to a single job are at risk in this changing world of work. The digital revolution has taught us that education is a buffer against changing times. We need to promote an education that teaches students to reason, value, analyze and even invent. New companies like Apple and Google require their workers to be flexible, inventive and creative and be able to work in teams. These are the skills that are at the heart of the digital revolution. Young people collaborate via social media and vote for the best restaurants and best movies. Social media can make or break a new actor on the scene. Digital natives are used to democratic voting on what is good or bad. In the past, there were those who worried that what is popular will swallow what is excellent. But the battle between excellence and egalitarianism in higher education is nothing new (Trow and Burrage 2010).

We also need a strong and secure faculty. We need an administration committed to using technology to enhance all systems. We need students who understand they are in college to get a job and also to get those skills and competencies that will make them good citizens and desirable workers. We need boards and citizens and politicians to stop living in the past and start embracing the future.

Transparent data and a commitment to the value and importance of education in a global world can secure the future of the university. Cardinal Newman wrote in a time of stress when some questioned whether the university would become irrelevant. It survived then, and it will survive now. It will combine the wisdom of the past and the technologies of the future.

Imagine being on the deck of a virtual Pequod where we can sail with Ahab and Ishmael and hunt Moby Dick. Imagine being able to walk through virtual Athens and sit at a symposium with Socrates and his young pupil Plato. We can refight D-Day and see what would have happened if Hitler would have released his armor in a counter-attack. We will be able to walk through the cities of the world and speak to students at Ulan Bator University in Mongolia or the University of Central Lancaster in England. Every day students and faculty from all over the world are collaborating in ways that would have been all but impossible just a few decades ago. The future is limitless, but to get there we must rethink the concepts of education, learning and teaching. The digital revolution will sweep away many institutions and many institutional practices. We cannot fight it, but we can adapt to it and preserve what is noble and good in our colleges and universities. It is a new age, and it is time we think about the idea of the digital university.

AUTHORS' BIOGRAPHIES

Dr. Frank Bryce McCluskey has spent 35 years in higher education. He received his Ph.D. in Philosophy from the New School for Social Research with an award-winning dissertation on Hegel and his B.A. from Bloomfield College. He has been involved in online learning for decades and the programs that he has overseen have won numerous awards. He was a tenured professor at Mercy College in New York where he founded their program of online learning in 1990. He has also taught at Marymount College and Western Connecticut State College. From 2005 to 2011, he was provost of the American Public University System, overseeing a staff of more than 50, with 1,800 faculty and 80,000 students. Dr. McCluskey guided the university through its initial accreditation. The university won the Sloan C Foundation's Ralph E. Gomery Award for Quality Online Education. The university had a lead role in a Bill and Melinda Gates grant for the use of data to improve higher education in 2011. Dr. McCluskey has published on philosophy, semiotics, artificial intelligence and higher education theory. Dr. McCluskey also served as a volunteer firefighter and fire chief in New York and follows issues in emergency services.

Ms. Melanie Lynn Winter has had an extensive career in both non-profit and for-profit higher education. She has worked in both campus-based and online schools and has worked with student populations ranging from 3,000 to 60,000. She took her undergraduate degree from the University of Minnesota in human relations. She has a master's degree from Saint Mary's University of Minnesota in counseling and psychological services. She has worked in libraries as well as the areas of admissions, marketing, advising, departmental operations and institutional research, with the bulk of her work being in the office of the registrar and student services. Some of her positions have included work in the library at the University of Minnesota and director of operations for the Center for Law & Financial Markets at the Illinois Institute of Technology. She was registrar and then director of the office of the provost at the American Public University System, where she first met Dr. McCluskey. She was registrar at Walden University where she oversaw more than 50,000 students who studied worldwide. She most recently served as the registrar and director of institutional research at Shenandoah University in Virginia where she implemented the digitization of student records and a degree audit system. Ms. Winter's interests include women's studies, environmental causes, alternative medicine and media theory.

The authors can be contacted at thedigitaluniversity@gmail.com.

BIBLIOGRAPHY

Allen, C. (2008). *Why Do Textbooks Cost So Much, Minding the Campus*, Reforming Our Universities Blog. Accessed August 15, 2012.

Allen, M. (1984). *The Platonism of Marsilio Ficino: A Study of His Phaedrus Commentary, Its Sources and Genesis*, University of California Press, Berkeley, CA.

Altbach, P., Gumport, P. (2011). *American Higher Education in the Twenty-First Century*, Johns Hopkins Press, Baltimore, MD.

Applegate, R. (2007). Whose decline? Which academic libraries are "deserted" in terms of reference transactions?, *Reference and User Services Quarterly*, Vol. 48, No. 2, p 176–194.

Aquinas, T. (2010). *Summa Theologica*, Coyote Canyon Press, Claremont, CA.

Arendt, H. (1957). *The Human Condition, Hannah Arendt*, University of Chicago, Chicago, IL.

Arendt, H., McCarthy, M. (1981). *The Life of the Mind*, Mariner Books, Boston, MA.

Arendt, H., Scott. J. (1996). *Love and Saint Augustine*, University of Chicago Press, Chicago, IL.

Aristotle (1984). *Complete Works*, Princeton University Press, Princeton, NJ.

Arum, R., Roksa, J. (2011). *Academically Adrift: Limited Learning on College Campuses*, University of Chicago Press, Chicago, IL.

Aschheim, S. (2001). *Hannah Arendt in Jerusalem*, University of California, Berkeley CA.

Augustine (2011). *The Confessions of Saint Augustine*, Random House, New York, NY.

Austin, A. (1991). *Assessment for Excellence*, McMillan Publishers, New York, NY.

Austin, A. (1993). *What Matters in College?*, Jossey Bass, Hoboken, NJ.

Bacon, F. (2010). *New Atlantis*, Kessinger Publishers Whitefish, MT.

Barendt, E. (2010). *Academic Freedom and the Law*, Hart Publishing, Oxford, UK.

Barr, R., Tagg, J. (1995). From teaching to learning: A new paradigm for undergraduate education, *Change Magazine*, Vol. 27, No. 6, p 48–62.

Basit, T. (2012). *Social Inclusion and Higher Education*, Policy Press, Bristol, UK.

Battles, M. (2004). *Library: An Unquiet History*, W.W. Norton, New York, NY.

Bauerlein, M. (2008). *The Dumbest Generation: How the Digital Age Stupefies Young Americans and Jeopardizes Our Future*, Tarcher Press, New York, NY.

Beach, J., Grubb, W. (2011). *Gateway to Opportunity: A History of the Community College in the United States*, Stylus Publishing, Sterling, VA.

Berry, J. (2005). *Reclaiming the Ivory Tower: Organizing Adjuncts to Change Higher Education*, Monthly Review Press, New York, NY.

Berube, M., Berube, C. (2010). *The Moral University*, Rowen and Littlefield Publishing Group, Lamham, MD.

Betsey, C. (2008). *Historically Black Colleges and Universities*, Transaction Publishers, Piscataway, NJ.

Berger, J. (1998). Revising Tinto's interactionist theory of student departure through theory elaboration, *Research in Higher Education*, Vol. 39, No. 2, p 103–119.

Bidgoli, H. (2004). *The Internet Encyclopedia*, Volume 1, John Wiley & Sons, Hoboken, NJ.

Birnbaum, R. (1988). *How Colleges Work: The Cybernetics of Academic Organizations and Leadership*, Jossey Bass Publishers, Hoboken, NJ.

Black, D.L. (1990). *Logic and Aristotle's Rhetoric and Poetics in Medieval Arabic Philosophy*, Brill Publishers, Leiden, NL.

Bloom, A. (1979). *Emile: Or; On Education*, Basic Books, New York, NY.

Bloom, A. (1988). *The Closing of the American Mind*, Simon and Schuster, New York, NY.

Bloom, A. (1991). *The Republic of Plato*, Basic Books, New York, NY.

Bok, D. (2004). *Universities in the Marketplace: The Commercialization of Higher Education*, Princeton University Press, Princeton, NJ.

Bok, D. (2007). *Our Underachieving Colleges: A Candid Look at How Much Students Learn and Why They Should Be Learning More*, Princeton University Press, Princeton, NJ.

Bolton, R. (1992). *Culture Wars: Documents from the Recent Controversies in the Arts*, Longman Press, Hoboken, NJ.

Boorstin, D. (1985). *The Discoverers*, Random House, New York, NY.

Borglum, K., Kubala, T. (2000). Academic and social integration of community college students, *Community College Journal of Research and Practice*, Vol. 24, No. 7, p 567–476.

Boston, W., Diaz, S., Ice, P., Gibson, A., Richardson, J., Swan, K.(2010). An exploration of the relationship between indicator of the community of inquiry framework and retention in online programs, *Journal of Asynchronous Learning Networks*, Vol. 13, No. 3, p 67–83.

Bousquet, M. (2008). *How the University Works: Higher Education and the Low Wage Nation*, New York University Press, New York, NY.

Bowman, J. (1998). *America's Black and Tribal Colleges*, Sandcastle Publishing, San Diego, CA.

Boyer, E. (1987). *The Undergraduate Experience in America*, Harper Collins, New York, NY.

Boyer, E. (1997). *Scholarship Reconsidered: Priorities of the Professoriate*, Jossey Bass, Hokoken, NJ.

Bradley University (2006). The History of Bradley University, http://www.bradley.edu/campuslife/studenthandbook/history/ Accessed August 20, 2012.

Bradley, M. (2011). *Saving Higher Education: The Integrated, Competency-Based Three-Year Bachelor's Degree Program*, Jossey Bass Publishers, Hoboken, NJ.

Braskamp, L., Ory, J. (1994). *Assessing Faculty Work: Enhancing Individual and Institutional Performance*, Jossey Bass Publishers, Hoboken, NJ.

Braxton, J. (2000). *Reworking the Student Departure Puzzle*, Vanderbilt University Press, Nashville, TN.

Breneman, D., Nelson, S. (1981). *Financing Community Colleges: An Economic Perspective. Studies in Higher Education Policy*, Brookings Institute, Washington, DC.

Bretz, R. (1989). College grade point average as a predictor of adult success, *Public Personnel Management*, Vol.18, No. 1, p 11–22.

Brint, S., Karabel, J. (1989). *The Diverted Dream: Community Colleges and the Promise of Educational Opportunity in America, 1900–1985*, Oxford University Press, Oxford, UK.

Brook, L., Webb, R. (1999). *Daily Life in Ancient and Modern Timbuktu (Cities through Time Series)*, Runestone Press, Minneapolis, MN.

Brooks, D. (2012). Where are the liberals?, *The New York Times*, New York, NY, 9 January.

Brown, S., Rice, P. (2008). *Lecturing: A Practical Guide*, Kogan Page Limited, London, UK.

Brown, P., Lauder, H. (2010). *The Global Auction: The Broken Promises of Education, Jobs and Incomes*, Oxford University Press, Oxford, UK.

Brubacher, J.S., Rudy, W. (1976). *Higher Education in Transition: A History of American Colleges and Universities; 1636–1976*, Harper & Row, New York, NY.

Buckler, S. (2011). *Hannah Arendt and Political Theory*, Edinburgh University Press, Edinburgh, UK.

Bundy, M., Stielow, F. (1987). *Activism in American Librarianship 1962–1973*, Greenwood Press, Westport, CT.

Burke, E. (2009). *Reflections on the Revolution in France*, Dover Books, Mineola, NY.

Burke, K. (2010). *From Standards to Rubrics in Six Steps: Tools for Assessing Student Learning*, Corwin Press, Thousand Oaks, CA.

Callan, P. (1997). *Stewards of Opportunity, America's Public Community Colleges*, Daedalus Press, Los Angeles, CA.

Campbell, H. (2012). *Digital Religion: Understanding Religious Practice in New Media Worlds*, Rutledge Publications, London, UK.

Campbell, R.F., Boyd, W.L. (1970). Federal support of higher education: Elitism versus Egalitarianism. *Governance in Higher Education Journal*, Vol. 9, No. 4, p 232–238.

Campbell, T., Campbell, D. (1997). Faculty-student mentorship program: Effects on academic performance and retention, *Research in Higher Education*, Vol. 38, No. 6, p 727–742.

Campbell-Kelly, M. (2004). *Computer: A History of the Information Machine, Second Edition*, Westview Press, Boulder, CO.

Canfora, L. (1990). *A Wonder of the Ancient World*, University of California Press, Berkeley, CA.

Carey, K. (2012). A future full of badges, *Chronicle of Higher Education*, Washington, DC, 8 April.

Carlson, S. (2003). After losing millions, Columbia U. will close online-learning venture, *Chronicle of Higher Education*, Washington, DC, 7 January.

Carr, N. (2008). Is Google making us stupid?, *The Atlantic*, Washington, DC, July.

Carr, N. (2011). *The Shallows: What the Internet Is Doing to Our Brains*, W. W. Norton, New York, NY.

Carter, V. (1996). Do media influence learning? Revisiting the debate in the context of distance learning, *Open Learning*, Vol. 11, No. 1, p 31–40.

Chait, R., Altbach, R., Chronister, J. (2005). *The Questions of Tenure*, Harvard University Press, Cambridge, MA.

Chang, M., Hwang, W., Chen, M., Mueller, W. (2011). Edutainment technologies, *Educational Games and Virtual Reality/Augmented Reality Applications: 6th International Conference on E-Learning and Games*, Springer Verlag, Berlin, Germany.

Christensen, C. (1997). *The Innovator's Dilemma: When New Technologies Cause Great Firms to Fail*, Harvard Business School Press, Cambridge, MA.

Christensen, C., Eyring, H. (2011). *The Innovative University: Changing the DNA of Higher Education from the Inside Out*, Jossey Bass Publishers, Hoboken, NJ.

Christensen, C., Johnson, C., Horn, M. (2008). *Disrupting Class: How Disruptive Innovation Will Change the Way the World Learns*, McGraw Hill, New York, NY.

Cohen, P. (1980). Effectiveness of student rating feedback for improving college instruction, *Research in Higher Education*, Vol. 13, No. 4, p 321–341.

Cohen, E., Hughes, W. (1994). A benefit-cost analysis of investment in college education in the United States 1969–1985, *Economics of Education Review*, Vol.13, No. 1, p 109–123.

Colby, A., Erlich, T. (2002). Moral and civic development during college, *Peer Review*, Vol. 4, No. 4, p 23–27.

Coldeway, D. (2012). *Gates: Higher Education Has Not Been Substantially Changed by the Internet*, msnbc.com. Accessed August 20, 2012.

Cook, C. (1998). *How Colleges and Universities Influence Federal Policy*, Vanderbilt University Press, Nashville, TN.

Cook, C.E. (1998). *How Colleges and Universities Influence Federal Policy*, Vanderbilt University Press, Nashville, TN.

Coleman, P. (1984). *Rousseau's Political Imagination: Rule and Representation in the Lettre a d'Alembert*, LibrarieDroz, Geneva, Switzerland.

Collins, A. (2009). *Rethinking Education in the Age of Technology: The Digital Revolution and Schooling in America*, Teachers College Press, New York, NY.

Coplestone, F. (2003). *A History of Philosophy*, Doubleday Image Books, New York, NY.

Cosgrove, R. (2009). *Critical Thinking in the Oxford Tutorial*, M.Sc. Thesis submitted to the University of Oxford, Oxford, UK.

Cowen, T. (2006). *What Are Independent Bookstores Really Good For?* Slate, Washington, DC.

Cremin, L. (1970). *American Education: The Colonial Experience 1607–1783*, Harper and Row, New York, NY.

Davenport, T. (1997). *Information Ecology: Mastering the Information and Knowledge Environment*, Oxford University Press, Oxford, UK.

Dawson, C. (2001). *The Spirit of the Oxford Movement and Newman's Place in History*, The Saint Austin Press, Ave Maria, FL.

Deem, R. (2008). *Knowledge, Higher Education and the New Managerialism: The Changing Management of UK Universities*, Oxford University Press, Oxford, UK.

DeMillo, R. (2011). *Abelard to Apple: The Fate of American Colleges and Universities*, MIT Press, Cambridge, MA.

Derrida, J. (1998). *On Grammatology*, Johns Hopkins University Press, Baltimore, MD.

Descartes, R. (2007). *Discourse on Method and Meditations on First Philosophy*, Barnes and Noble, New York, NY.

Dewey, J. (1997). *Democracy and Education*, Basic Books, New York, NY.

Dickens, C. (2004). *The Annotated Christmas Carol*, W.W. Norton, New York, NY.

Dobson, M. (1992). *Fairly Brave New World: Shakespeare, the American Colonies, and the American Revolution*, Renaissance Drama, New Series 23, p 189–207.

242

Dolnick, E. (2012). *The Clockwork Universe, Isaac Newton, The Royal Society and the Birth of the Modern World*, Harper Perennial Series, New York, NY.

Donoghue, F. (2008). *The Last Professors: The Corporate University and the Fate of the Humanities*, Fordham University Press, New York, NY.

Drejer, A. (2002). *Strategic Management and Core Competencies: Theory and Application*, Praeger Press, Westport, CT.

Duhig, C. (2012). How companies learn your secrets, *The New York Times*, New York, NY. 16 February.

Duryea, E. (1973). *Faculty Unions and Collective Bargaining*, ProQuest Publications, Ann Arbor, MI.

Economist (2012). The Hollow men: The deindustrialization of Japan may be neither as complete or damaging as feared, *The Economist*, London, UK, 9 June.

Fain, P. (2012). Big data's arrival, *Inside Higher Ed*, Washington, DC, 1 February.

Fain, P. (2011). Congresswoman says for-profit colleges more efficient, *Inside Higher Ed*, Washington, DC, 6 December.

Fassinger, P. (1995). Understanding classroom interaction, *Journal of Higher Education*, Vol. 66, No. 1, p 83–96.

Feldman, K. (1972). Some theoretical approaches to the study of change and stability of college students, *Review of Educational Research*, Vol. 42, No.1, p 1–26.

Feldman, K., Newcomb, T. (1969). *The Impact of College on Students*, Jossey Bass, Hoboken, NJ.

Finkelstein, M. (2000). *Dollars, Distance and Online Education: The New Economics of College Teaching and Learning*, Oryx Press, Phoenix, AZ.

Finkelstein, M., Schuster, J. (2011). *A New Model, the Next Higher Education Takes Shape, Advancing Higher Education*, TIAA CREF Report, New York, NY.

Foucault, M. (2007). *The Order of Things: An Archaeology of the Human Sciences*, Routledge Publishing, London, UK.

Fountain, W. (2005). *Academic Sharecroppers: Exploitation of Adjunct Faculty and the Higher Education System*, Authorhouse Publishers, Bloomington, IA.

Franklin, F. (2010). *The Life of Daniel Coit Gilman*, General Books, Memphis, TN.

Freedland, R. (1992). *Academia's Golden Age: Universities in Massachusetts, 1945–1970*, Oxford University Press, Oxford, UK.

Friedman, T. (2007). *The World Is Flat 3.0: A Brief History of the Twenty-First Century*, Picador Books, New York, NY.

Fryshman, B. (2010). The Carnegie unit: Articulate and expressive, *Inside Higher Ed*, Washington, DC, 27 January.

Gappa, J., Leslie, D. (1993). *The Invisible Faculty: Improving the Status of Part-Timers in Higher Education*, Jossey Bass, Hoboken, NJ.

Garben, S. (2011). *EU Higher Education Law: The Bologna Process and Harmonization by Stealth (European Monographs)*, Kluwer Law Publications, Berlin, Germany.

Gaston, P., Schneider, C. (2010). *The Challenge of Bologna: What United States Higher Education Has to Learn from Europe, and Why It Matters That We Learn It*, Stylus Publications, Sterling, VA.

Gerber, M. (2005). *E Myth Mastery*, Harper Business Books, New York, NY.

Ginsberg, B. (2011). *The Fall of the Faculty: The Rise of the All Administrative University and Why It Matters*, Oxford University Press, Oxford, UK.

Golden, D. (2007). *The Price of Admission: How America's Ruling Class Buys Its Way into Elite Colleges and Who Gets Left Outside the Gates*, Three Rivers Press, New York, NY.

Graff, G. (1989). *Professing Literature and Institutional History*, University of Chicago, Chicago, IL.

Gramling, T. (2011). *All-Out War: A Case Study of Media Coverage of For Profit Higher Education*, Sage Open Press.

Greenberg, M. (1997). *The GI Bill: The Law That Changed America*, Lickle Publishing, West Palm Beach, FL.

Gumport, P. (2008). *The Sociology of Higher Education*, Johns Hopkins University Press, Baltimore, MD.

Habermas, J. (1971). *Toward a Rational Society: Student Protest, Science and Politics*, Beacon Press, Boston, MA.

Habermas, J. (1975). *Legitimation Crisis*, Beacon Press, Boston, MA.

Hacker, A. (2010). *Higher Education? How Colleges Are Wasting Our Money, Failing Our Kids and What We Can Do about It*, Times Books, New York, NY.

Hall, M. (1988). *The Last American Puritan: The Life of Increase Mather, 1639–1723*, Wesleyan University Press, Middletown, CT.

Harvard School of Education (2009). *Pathways to Prosperity: Meeting the Challenge of Preparing Americans for the 21st Century*, Harvard University Press, Cambridge, MA.

Hass, E., Fishman, G. (2010). Nostalgia, entrepreneurship and redemption: Understanding prototypes in higher education, *American Education Research Journal*, Vol. 47, No. 3, p 532–562.

Hawkins, H. (2002). *Pioneer: A History of Johns Hopkins University*, Johns Hopkins University Press, Baltimore, MD.

Hazen, D., Fernbach, D. (2011). *The Invention of Paris: A History in Footsteps*, Verzo Press, London, UK.

Hegel, G. (1981). *Lectures on the Philosophy of World History*, Cambridge University Press, Cambridge, UK.

Hegel, G. (1991) Elements of the Philosophy of Right, Cambridge University Press, Cambridge, UK.

Heidegger, M. (1982). *The Question Concerning Technology and Other Essays*, Harper Torchbooks, New York, NY.

Hemel, D. (2005). *Summers' Comments on Women and Science Draw Ire*, The Harvard Crimson, Cambridge, MA.

Hentschke, G., Lechuga, V., Tierney, W. (2010). *For-Profit Colleges and Universities: Their Markets, Regulations, Performance and Place in Higher Education*, Stylus Publications, Sterling, VA.

Hepplewhite, P. (2009). *Victorian Education*, Franklin Watts.

Hess, F. (2008). *When Research Matters: How Scholarship Influences Education Policy*, Harvard University Press, Cambridge, MA.

Hirsch, E. (1988). *Cultural Literacy, What Every American Needs to Know*, Vintage Press, New York, NY.

Hitchcock, S. (2012). *The University of Virginia: A Pictorial History*, The University of Virginia Press, Charlottesvill, VA.

Hodgson, G. (2010). *The Myth of American Exceptionalism*, Yale University Press, New Haven, CT.

Hofstadler, R. (1963). *Anti-Intellectualism in American Life*, Alfred P. Knopf, New York, NY.

Huba, M., Freed, J. (2000). *Learner-Centered Assessment on College Campuses: Shifting the Focus from Teaching to Learning*, Allyn and Bacon, Boston, MA.

Huffington Post (2010). Countries with the most college graduates. Accessed September 10, 2012.

Hunt, J. (2008). *The University in Medieval Life, 1179–1499*, McFarland Publications, Jefferson, NC.

Hutcheson, P. (2002). The 1947 President's Commission on Higher Education and the national rhetoric on higher education policy, *History of Higher Education Annual*, Vol. 22, Fall issue, p 107–114.

Hutcheson, P. (2007a). The Truman commission's vision of the future, *Thought and Action*, Fall issue, p 107–114.

Hutcheson, P. (2007b). Setting the nations agenda for higher education: A review of selected national commission reports 1947–2006, *History of Education Quarterly*, Vol. 47, No. 3, p 359–367.

Illeris, H. (2009). *Contemporary Theories of Learning: Learning Theorists in Their Own Words*, Rutledge Publishers, London, UK.

Innis, H. (2008). *The Bias of Communication: Second Edition*, University of Toronto Press, Toronto, CA.

Innis, H. (1952). *Changing Concepts of Time*, University of Toronto Press, Toronto, CA.

Innis, H. (2007). *Empire and Communication*, Rowan and Littlefield Publishing, Lanham, MD.

Interpack (2009). Turbulent times in the worldwide paper industry, *Interpack Magazine*, Dusseldorf, Germany, 3 October.

James, M. (1903). *The Ancient Libraries of Canterbury and Dover*, Cambridge University Press, Cambridge, UK.

Jay, M. (1996). *The Dialectical Imagination: A History of the Frankfurt School and the Institute for Social Research*, University of California Press, Berkeley, CA.

Jeffers, M. (2010). *LA Times Article Sparks Differing Views of Libraries' Role*, American Library Association, Chicago, IL.

Johnson, P. (2009). *Fundamentals of Collection Development and Mangement 2nd Ed.*, American Library Association.

Kahlenberg, R., editor (2010). *Affirmative Action for the Rich: Legacy Preferences in College Admissions*, Brookings Institute Press, Washington, DC.

Kamenetz, A. (2010). *DIY U: Edupunks, Edupreneurs and the Coming Transformation of Higher Education*, Chelsea Green Publishing, White River Junction, VT.

Kant, I. (2011). *Anthropology, History and Education*, Cambridge University Press, Cambridge, UK.

Kant, I. (1999a). *Critique of Pure Reason*, Cambridge University Press, Cambridge, UK.

Kant, I. (1999b). *Critique of Practical Reason*, Cambridge University Press, Cambridge, UK.

Kant, I. (2001). *Critique of the Power of Judgment*, Cambridge University Press, Cambridge, UK.

Karabel, J. (2005). *The Chosen: The Hidden History of Admission and Exclusion at Harvard, Yale and Princeton*, Houghton Mifflin, Boston, MA.

Karen, D. (2002). Changes in access to higher education in the United States 1980–1992, *Sociology of Education*, Vol. 75, No. 1, p 191–210.

Keen, A. (2007). *The Cult of the Amateur: How Blogs, Myspace, Youtube and the Rest of Today's User-Generated Media Are Destroying Our Economy, Our Culture and Our Values*, Doubleday, New York, NY.

Kennedy, G. (1952). *Education for Democracy*, Heath and Company. Lexington, MA.

Kerr, C. (1963). *The Uses of the University*, Harvard University Press, Cambridge, MA.

Kerr, C. (1973). Four decades of education commissions, *Change*, Vol. 5, No. 9, p 4–7.

Kerr-Tener, J. (1987). Eisenhower and federal aid to higher education, *Presidential Studies Quarterly*, Vol.17, No. 3, p 113–156.

Kezar, A. (2012). *Embracing Non-Tenure Track Faculty: Changing Campuses For the New Faculty Majority*, Routledge Publishers, London, UK.

Killian, J. (1957). William Barton Rogers, *Technology Review*, Vol. 60, December issue, p 113–156.

Kinser, K. (2003). *From Main Street to Wall Street: The Transformation of For-Profit Higher Education*, Jossey Bass Publishers, Hoboken, NJ.

Kirp, D. (2003). *Shakespeare, Einstein and the Bottom Line: The Marketing of Higher Education*, Harvard University Press, Cambridge, MA.

Knox,W., Lindsey, P. (1993). *Does College Make a Difference?*, Greenwood Press, Westport, CT.

Kozak, S. (2005). The role of information technology in the profit and cost efficiency improvements of the banking sector, *Journal of Academy of Business and Economics*, Vol. 5, No. 2, p 1–19.

Kozma, R. (1994). Will media influence learning? reframing the debate, *Educational Technology Research and Development*, Vol. 42, No. 2, p 7–19.

Kramer, J., Hamm, R. (2003). *The American College Novel, An Annotated Bibliography*, Scarecrow Press, Lanham, MD.

Kraus, J. (1961). The development of a curriculum in the early American colleges, *History of Education Quarterly*, Vol. 1, No. 2, p 64–76.

Kuh, G., Schuh, J. (1991). *Involving Colleges: Successful Approaches to Fostering Student Learning*, Jossey Bass Publishers, Hoboken, NJ.

Kuhn, T. (1996). *The Structure of Scientific Revolutions*, University of Chicago Press, Chicago, IL.

Kumashiro, K. (2008). *The Seduction of "Common Sense": How the Right has Framed the Debate on America's Schools*, Teachers College Press, New York, NY.

Lakoff, G. (1987). *Women, Fire, and Dangerous Things: What Categories Reveal about the Mind*, University of Chicago Press, Chicago, IL.

Lakoff, G. (2002). *Moral Politics: How Liberals and Conservatives Think*, 2nd Ed., University of Chicago Press, Chicago, IL.

Lakoff, G. (2008). *The Political Mind: Why You Can't Understand 21st-Century American Politics with an 18th-Century Brain*, Viking Press, New York, NY.

Lagemann, E., Lewis, H. (2012). *What Is College For? The Public Purpose of Higher Education*, Teachers College Press, New York, NY.

Lauren, B. (2006). *The Registrar's Guide: Evolving Best Practices in Records and Registration*, American Association of College Registrars, Washington, DC.

Lederman, D. (2009). Layoffs mark the end of controversial U of Illinois online effort, *Inside Higher Ed*, Washington, DC, 31 August.

Lederman, D. (2011). More on trial than just Bridgepoint, *Inside Higher Ed*, Washington, DC, March 11.

Levine, J. (1999). *Between the Ancients and Moderns: Baroque Culture in Restoration England*, Yale University Press, New Haven, CT.

Lewin, T. (2010). Once a leader, U.S. lags in college degrees, *The New York Times*, New York, NY, 11 July.

Lim, S., Simon, C. (2011). Credibility judgment and verification behavior of student concerning Wikipedia, *First Monday*, Vol. 18, No. 4, p 1–11.

Locke, J. (1996). *Some Thoughts Concerning Education and the Conduct of the Understanding*, Hackett Publications, Indianapolis, IN.

Lomas, R. (2002). *The Invisible College: The Royal Society, Freemasonry and the Birth of Modern Science*, Headline Books, Terra Alta, WV.

Lowry, M. (1979). *The World of Aldus Manutius: Business and Scholarship in Renaissance Venice*, Blackwell, Hoboken, NJ.

Lyons, R. (2007). *Best Practices for Supporting Adjunct Faculty*, Jossey Bass Publishers, Hoboken, NJ.

Lyons, W., Drew, J. (2006). *Punishing Schools: Fear and Citizenship in American Public Education*, University of Michigan Press, Ann Arbor, MI.

Maker, W. (1987). *Hegel on Economics and Freedom*, Mercer University Press, Macon, GA.

Maker, W. (1994). *Philosophy without Foundations: Rethinking Hegel*, State University of New York University Press, Albany, NY.

Maki, P., Borkowski, N. (2006). *The Assessment of Doctoral Education: Emerging Criteria and New Models Improving Outcomes*, Stylus Publishing, Sterling, VA.

Manyika, J., Chui, M. (2011). *Big Data: The Next Frontier for Innovation, Competition and Productivity*, Global Institute, Chicago, IL.

Marx, K., Engles, F. (1978). *The Marx-Engles Reader*, 2nd Ed., W.W. Norton, New York, NY.

Maskell, D. (2002). *The New Idea of a University*, Imprint Academic Publishers, Exeter, UK.

McCluskey, F. (1977). *The Concept of Truth in the Phenomenological Theories of Hegel and Husserl*, Doctoral dissertation, Graduate Faculty of the New School for Social Research, New York, NY.

McCluskey, F. (1978). Book review of Richard Rorty's philosophy and the mirror of nature, *Graduate Faculty Philosophy Journal*, Vol. 5, No. 1, p 160–162.

McCluskey, F. (1989). From classroom to computer: Rethinking the history of philosophy in the age of Semiotics, *Proceedings of the Eastern Small College Computer Consortium*, p 65–74.

McCluskey, F. (2012a). The professor as craftsman: Pedagogy in the digital age, *Internet Learning*, Vol.1, No. 1, p 1–16.

McCluskey, F. (2012b). What traditional colleges and online for-profit universities can learn from each other, *E-Mentor Journal*, Vol. 5, No. 4, p 13–24.

McCluskey, F. (2012c). Teaching philosophy online, American Philosophical Assocation, *Philosophy and Computers*, Vol. 16, No. 1, p 12–20.

McCluskey, F., D'Huerle, A. (1980). *Power, Prediction and Control: Simulation Techniques and Game Theory in the Social Sciences*, Institute for Humanistic Studies, State University of New York at Albany, Albany, NY.

McCormick, A. (2003). *Swirling and Double Dipping: New Patterns of Student Attendance and Their Implications for Higher Education, New Directions in Higher Education*, Vol. 2003, No. 121, p 13–24.

McCormick, C. (1989). *The Nest of Vipers: McCarthyism and Higher Education in the Mundel Affair, 1951–1952*, University of Illinois Press, Champaign, IL.

McJohn, S. (2009). *Copyright: Examples & Explanations*, 2nd Ed., Aspen Publishers, Aspen, CO.

McKenna, L. (2012). The big idea that can revolutionize higher education: MOOC, *The Atlantic*, Washington, DC, 11 March.

McLemmee, S. (2005). Academic freedom, then and now, *Inside Higher Ed*, Washington, DC, 17 February.

McLuhan, M. (2011). *The Gutenberg Galaxy*, University of Toronto Press, Toronto, Canada.

McLuhan, M. (2005). *The Medium Is the Message*, Ginko Press, Berkeley, CA.

Meiners, R. (2004). *Fawlty Towers: Tenure and the Structure of Higher Education*, Independent Institute Press, Oakland, CA.

Meir, D., Wood, G. (2004). *Many Children Left Behind: How the No Child Left Behind Act Is Damaging Our Children and Our Schools*, Beacon Press, Boston, MA.

Miller, B. (2010). What got the Ed Department so mad about American Inter-Continental University and its accreditor? *The Quick and the Ed Newsletter and Blog*.

Miller, L. (2007). *Reluctant Capitalists: Bookselling and the Culture of Consumption*, University of Chicago Press, Chicago, IL.

Milner, G. (2009). *Perfecting Sound Forever: An Aural History of Recorded Music*, Faber and Faber, London, UK.

Mitchell, H. (2004). *America after Tocqueville: Democracy against Difference*, Cambridge University Press, Cambridge, UK.

Mumpher, M. (1996). *Removing College Price Barriers: What Government Has Done and Why It Hasn't Worked*, State University of New York Press, New York, NY.

Murray, C. (2008). *Are Too Many People Going to College?* The American Enterprise Institute, Washington, DC.

Murray, S. (2009). *Libraries: An Illustrated History*, Skyhorse Publishing, New York, NY.

Nakanishi, A. (1990). *Writing Systems of the World: Alphabets, Syllabaries and Pictograms*, Charles Tuttle, Clarendon, VT.

Nash, G., Crabtree, C., Dunn, R. (2000). *History on Trial: Cultural Wars and the Teaching of the Past*, Vintage Press, New York, NY.

Nelson, C. (1997). *Will Teach for Food: Academic Labor in Crisis*, University of Minnesota Press, Minneapolis, MN.

Newfield, C. (2008). *The Unmaking of the Public University: The Forty Year Assault on the Middle Class*, Harvard University Press, Cambridge, MA.

Newman, J. (2002). *The Idea of the University*, University of Notre Dame Press, South Bend, IN.

Nussbaum, M. (2012). *Not for Profit: Why Democracy Needs the Humanities*, Princeton University Press, Princeton, NJ.

Nussbaum, M. (1998). *Cultivating Humanity: A Classical Defense of Reform in Liberal Education*, Harvard University Press, Cambridge, MA.

Nutton., V. (2005). *Ancient Medicine*, Routledge Publishers, London, UK.

Ong, W. (2002). *Orality and Literacy*, Routledge Publishers, London, UK.

Parker, K., Lenhart, A., Moore., K. (2011). *The Digital Revolution and Higher Education: College President, Public Differ on Value of Online Learning*, Pew Foundation, Philadelphia, PA.

Pascarella, E., Terenzini, P. (2005). *How College Affects Students, Volume 2, A Third Decade of Research*, Jossey Bass Publishers, Hoboken, NJ.

Pelikan, J. (1992). *The Idea of the University: A Reexamination*, Yale University Press, New Haven, CT.

Perez-Pena, R. (2012). Ousted head of university is reinstated in Virginia, *The New York Times*, New York, NY, 26 June.

Picciano, A. (2005). *Data-Driven Decision Making for Effective School Leadership*, Prentice Hall, Upper Saddle River, NJ.

Pichnarcik, L. (1996). On the threshold of improvement: Women's education at the Litchfield and Morris Academies, *Connecticut History*, Vol. 27, No.1, p 129–158.

Pilon, M. (2010). When student loans live on after death, *Wall Street Journal*, New York, NY, 7 August.

Plato (1928). *The Works of Plato (Jowlett translation)*, Modern Library, New York, NY.

Pope, L. (2006). *Colleges That Change Lives: 40 Schools That Will Change the Way You Think about Colleges*, Penguin Publishers, London, UK.

Postman, N. (1987). *Teaching as a Conserving Activity*, Laural Publications, Miller Place, NY.

Postman, N. (1995). *Amusing Ourselves to Death*, Penguin Publishers, London, UK.

Postman, N., Weingartner, C. (1969). *Teaching as a Subversive Activity*, Delacorte Press, New York, NY.

Preinkert, A. (2004). *The Work of the Registrar*, American Association of College Registrars, Washington, DC.

Rait, R. (2010). *Life in the Medieval University*, Nabu Press, Charleston, SC.

Rashdall, H. (2010). *The Universities in Europe in the Middle Ages: Volume 1*, Salerno, Bologna, Paris, Cambridge University Press, Cambridge, UK.Ratner, B. (2011). *Statistical and Machine-Learning Data Mining: Techniques for Better Predictive Modeling and Analysis of Big Data*, 2nd Ed., CRC Press, London, UK.

Rauch, A. (2001). *Useful Knowledge: The Victorians, Morality, and the March of Intellect*, Duke University Press, Durham, NC.

Rhoads, R., Szelenyi, K. (2011). *Global Citizenship and the University: Advancing Social Life and Relations in an Interdependent World*, Stanford University Press, Palo Alto, CA.

Rhoads, R.,Torres, C. (2005). *The University, State and Market: The Political Economy of Globalization the Americas*, Stanford University Press, Palo Alto, CA.

Ridder-Symoens, H. (2003). *A History of the University in Europe: Volume 1, Universities in the Middle Ages*, Cambridge University Press, Cambridge, UK.

Riley, N. (2011). *The Faculty Lounges: And Other Reasons Why You Won't Get the Education You Pay For*, Ivan R. Dee Publishers, Lanham, MD.

Riley, N. (2012). Why tenure should be abolished: It is bad for students, *Wall Street Journal*, New York, NY, 24 June.

Riordan, M., Hoddeson, L. (1998). *Crystal Fire: The Invention of the Transistor and the Birth of the Information Age*, W.W. Norton, New York, NY.

Robinson, A. (2007). *The Story of Writing: Alphabets, Hieroglyphs & Pictograms*, 2nd Ed., Thames and Hudson, London, UK.

Rojcewicz, R. (2006). *The Gods and Technology: A Reading of Heidegger*, State University of New York Press, Albany, NY.

Roll-Hansen, N. (2004). *The Lysenko Effect: The Politics of Science*, Humanities Press, Atlantic Highlands, NJ.

Rosch, E. (1977). Human categorization. In Warren, N. (Ed.), *Advances in Cross-Cultural Psychology Vol. 1*, Academic Press, Waltham, MA.

Rosch, E. (1978). Principles of categorization. In Rosch, E., Lloyd, B.B. (Eds.), *Cognition and Categorization* (pp. 27–71). Erlbaum Press, Mahwah, NJ.

Rosch, E. (1999). Reclaiming cognition: The primacy of action, intention and emotion, *Journal of Consciousness Studies*, Vol. 6, No. 11–12, p 41–60.

Rosen, A. (2011). *Change.edu: Rebooting for the New Talent Economy*, Kaplan University Press, Davenport, IA.

Rousseau, J. (2003). *Emile or Treatise on Education*, Prometheus Books, Amherst, NY.

Ruben, B. (2008). *Assessing the Impact of the Spellings Commission: The Message, the Messenger, and the Dynamics of Change in Higher Education*, National Association of College and University Business Officers, Washington, DC.

Ruch, R., Keller, G. (2003). *Higher Ed, Inc: The Rise of the for Profit University*, Johns Hopkins University Press, Baltimore, MD.

Rudolph, F., Thelin, J. (1991). *The American College and University: A History*, University of Georgia Press, Athens, GA.

Sabloff, P. (1998). *Higher Education in the Post-Communist World: Case Studies of Eight Universities*, Rutledge Publishers, London, UK.

Sampson, Z. (2012). College trustees press for business-style approaches to face fiscal and other challenges, *The Washington Post*, Washington, DC, 23 June.

Scheper-Hughes, N. (2011). The crisis of the public university, *Chronicle of Higher Education*, Washington, DC, 19 December.

Schrader, R. (1969). The growth and pitfalls of federal support for higher education, *The Journal of Higher Education*, Vol. 40, No. 9, p 704–716.

Schrecker, E. (1986). *No Ivory Tower: McCarthyism and the Universities*, Oxford University Press, Oxford, UK.

Schrecker, E. (2010). *The Lost Soul of Higher Education: Corporatization, the Assault on Academic Freedom, and the End of the American University*, New Press, New York, NY.

Schulman, B. (2005). *The Betrayal of Work, How Low-Wage Jobs Fail 30 Million Americans*, The New Press, New York, NY.

Schuster, J., Finkelstein, M. (2008). *The American Faculty: The Restructuring of Academic Work and Careers*, Johns Hopkins University Press, Baltimore, MD.

Schwartz, M. (2011). *The University of Last Resort: The Story of a College That Has No Class*, I-Universe Press, Bloomington, IN.

Searle, J. (1993). Is there a crisis in American higher education? *Bulletin of the American Academy of the Arts*, Vol. 46, No. 1, p 24–38.

Seeger, M., Sellnow, T., Ulmer, R. (1998). Communication, organization and crisis, *Communication Yearbook*, Vol. 21, p 231–275.

Senge, P. (2000). *Schools That Learn*, Doubleday, New York, NY.

Slaughter, S., Rhoades, G. (2009). *Academic Capitalism and the New Economy: Markets State and Higher Education*, Johns Hopkins University Press, Baltimore, MD.

Sloan Consortium for Asynchronous Learning (2011). *Going the Distance: Online Education in the United States 2011*, Sloan Foundation, New York, NY.

Smith, P. (2010). *Harnessing America's Wasted Talent: A New Ecology of Learning*, Jossey Bass Publishers, Hoboken, NJ.

Sonwalkar, N. (2012). *Changing the Interface of Education with Revolutionary Learning Technology*, I-Universe Press, Bloomington, IN.

Stanford Encyclopedia of Philosophy. Accessed August 2012.

Stave, B., Burmeister, L. (2005). *Red Brick in the Land of Steady Habits: Creating the University of Connecticut, 1881–2006*, University of Connecticut Press, Storres, CT.

Stielow, F. (2003). *Building Digital Archives*, Neal Schuman Publishers, New York, NY.

Stielow, F. (2012). *The New Academic Library*, Unpublished manuscript.

Strauss, L. (1988). *Persecution and the Art of Writing*, University of Chicago, Chicago, IL.

Strauss, L., Cropsey, J. (1987). *History of Political Philosophy*, University of Chicago Press, Chicago, IL.

Swan, K. (2002). Building learning communities in online courses: The importance of interaction, *Education Communication and Information*, Vol. 2, No. 1, p 23–49.

Sweeny, I. (2011). *Students Losing Out: Four Essays on Adjunct Labor in Higher Education*, Amazon Digital Services, Seattle, WA.

Taylor, M. (2010). *Crisis on Campus: A Bold Plan for Reforming our Colleges and Universities*, Knopf, New York, NY.

Teschner, G., McCluskey, F. (1988) Reflections on the city in speech: Deconstructing the First Amendment. In Kevelson, R. (Ed.), *Law and Semiotics*, Plenum Press, Norwell, MA.

Teschner, G., McCluskey, F. (1990). *The Impact of Pictographic Reasoning on Contemporary Pedagogy*, Institute for Critical Thinking, Montclair State College Press, Montclair, NJ.

Tierney, W., Hentschke, G. (2007). *New Players, Different Game: Understanding the Rise of For Profit Colleges and Universities*, Johns Hopkins University Press, Baltimore, MD.

Tierney, W., Rhoads, R. (1993). *Enhancing Promotion, Tenure and Beyond: Faculty Socialization as a Cultural Process*, Jossey Bass Publishers, Hoboken, NJ.

Thelin, J. (2004). *A History of American Higher Education*, Johns Hopkins University Press, Baltimore, MD.

Thom, H. (2009). *Johns Hopkins*, Johns Hopkins Press, Baltimore, MD.

Thompson, B., Schneider, V. (2007). Team-based learning at ten medical schools: Two years later, Medical Education, Vol. 41, No. 3, p 250–257.

Tinto, V. (1994). *Leaving College: Rethinking the Causes and Cures of Student Attrition*, University of Chicago Press, Chicago, IL.

Tocqueville, A. (2003). *Democracy in America*, Penguin Classics, London, UK.

Tolles, B. (2011). *Architecture and Academe: College Buildings in New England before 1860*, University Press of New England, Lebanon, NH.

Trow, M., Burrage, M. (2010). *Twentieth Century Higher Education: Elite to Mass to Universal*, Johns Hopkins University Press, Baltimore, MD.

Tuchman, G. (2009). *Wannabe U: Inside the Corporate University*, University of Chicago Press, Chicago, IL.

Ulmer, R., Sellnow, T., Seeger, M. (2006). *Effective Crisis Communication: Moving from Crisis to Opportunity*, Sage Publications, Thousand Oaks, CA.

Urban, W. (2010). *More than Science and Sputnik: The National Defense Act of 1958*, University of Alabama Press, Tuscaloosa, AL.

Vedder, R. (2012a). Why did 17 million students go to college? *Chronicle of Higher Education*, Washington, DC, 20 October.

Vedder, R. (2012b). End student loans, don't make them cheaper, *Bloomberg View*, New York, NY, 17 June.

Von Bertalanffy, L. (1969). *General System Theory: Foundations, Development, Applications*, Revised edition, GeorgeBraziller Inc, New York, NY.

Voorhees, R. (2001). *Measuring What Matters: Competency-Based Learning Models in Higher Education: New Directions for Institutional Research*, Jossey Bass Publishers, Hoboken, NJ.

Wagner, C. (2008). *The New Invisible College, Science for Development*, Brookings Institute Press, Washington, DC.

Walker, G., Golde, C. Jones, L. (2008). *The Formation of Scholars: Rethinking Doctoral Education for the Twenty First Century*, Jossey Bass Publishers, Hoboken, NJ.

Warner, L., Gipp, G. (2009). *Tradition and Culture in the Millennium: Tribal Colleges and Universities in the 21st Century: Opportunities, Challenges and Solutions*, Information Age Press, Charlotte, NC.

Washburn, J. (2006). *University, Inc: The Corporate Corruption of Higher Education*, Basic Books, New York, NY.

Watson, B. (2005). *The Idea of the American University*, Lexington Publishers, Lanham, MD.

Watson, R., Blondheim, M. (2011). *The Toronto School of Communication Theory: Interpretations, Extensions, Applications*, University of Toronto, Toronto, CA.

Webb, D. (2005). *The History of American Education: A Great American Experiment*, Prentice Hall, Upper Saddle River, NJ.

Wellmer, A. (2001). Arendt on revolution. In Aschheim S (Ed.), *Hannah Arendt in Jerusalem*, University of California Press, Berkeley, CA.

West, T., West, S. (1998). *Four Texts on Socrates: Plato's Euthyphro, Apology and Crito and Aristophanes Clouds*, Cornell University Press, Ithaca, NY.

White, L. (2008). Case in point: Stronach v. Virginia State U.: Does academic freedom give a professor the final say on grades?, *Chronicle of Higher Education*, Washington, DC, 25 April.

Whitehead, A. (1970). *Process and Reality*, Free Press, New York, NY.

Wilson, J. (2008). *Patriotic Correctness: Academic Freedom and Its Enemies*, Paradigm Publishers, Boulder, CA.

Wittgenstein, L. (2009). *Philosophical Investigations*, Wiley-Blackwell, Hoboken, NJ.

Wolf, R. (1995). *The Ideal of the University*, Transaction Publishers, Piscataway, NJ.

Wolfgang, B. (2011). Colleges raise tuition as much as 22 percent: Students also hit with bigger classes, fewer opportunities, *The Washington Times*, Washington, DC, 11 July.

Yates, F. (1991). *Giordano Bruno and the Hermetic Tradition*, University of Chicago Press, Chicago, IL.

Yates, F. (2001). *The Occult Philosophy in the Elizabethan Age*, Routledge Classics, London, UK.

Zemsky, R. (2005). *Remaking the American University: Market Smart and Mission Centered*, Rutgers University Press, New Brunswick, NJ.

Zemsky, R. (2009). *Making Reform Work: The Case for Transforming American Higher Education*, Rutgers University Press, New Brunswick, NJ.

INDEX

Made in the USA
Lexington, KY
22 October 2013